The
Sharpeville
Six

The Sharpeville Six

PRAKASH DIAR

With contributions by Lloyd Vogelman

Toronto and London

Cataloguing in Publication Data
Diar, Prakash
    The Sharpeville Six

ISBN 0-7710-2717-6

1. Massacres – South Africa – Sharpeville.   2. South Africa – Race relations.
3. Trials (murder) – South Africa.   I. Title.

DT941.D53 1990   345.68'02523   C90-095274-1

McClelland & Stewart Inc.
The Canadian Publishers
481 University Avenue
Toronto, Ontario
M5G 2E9

Distributed in the United Kingdom by Sinclair-Stevenson Ltd.

Design: Avril Orloff

Printed and bound in Canada

This book is
dedicated to all the victims of Apartheid

and

for my wife, Manjoola,
and my children, Nishal and Nirosha

CONTENTS

ACKNOWLEDGMENTS

A very special and warm thanks to Verna Hunt for so much help in putting my book together. She unselfishly gave me much more of her time than I could have hoped for, and I am fortunate to have worked with her.

Lloyd Vogelman of the Department of Psychology, University of the Witwatersrand interviewed my clients and their families and created helpful psychological profiles.

I also wish to thank:

All those individuals, organizations, political parties and governments from all corners of the globe who helped save my clients from the gallows.

Jack Unterhalter, S.C., Edwin Cameron, and Ismail Hussain, who read my manuscript and offered helpful suggestions. I would also like to thank Edwin not only for his brilliant legal insights, analyses, and his strong concern for justice and the rule of law but also for having the courage to challenge the establishment in attempting to right the wrongs done to The Six.

The Embassy of Switzerland in Pretoria, especially George Martin, for making it possible for me to meet some of my initial disbursements.

The South Africa Education Trust Fund, for bringing me to Canada on their exchange program, thereby giving me the opportunity to finalize my book.

The Common Law Faculty and the Human Rights Research and Education Centre, University of Ottawa, for providing a fellowship that allowed me the time needed to complete my work on the book. I am especially grateful to Magda Seydegart, Executive

Director of the Centre, for her advice and for introducing me to my editor, Charis Wahl.

Graeme Simpson, for providing research and background material on the political, social and economic situation in the South Africa and Sharpeville of that time.

Gail Irwin, for providing the graphics.

Em Beale, who assisted Lloyd Vogelman with interviews of family members of The Six.

Father Patrick Noonan of Sharpeville, who allowed his church to be used on numerous occasions as a venue for me to consult with my clients' families. Father Patrick also interpreted for those family members who preferred to speak South Sotho. He also very kindly agreed to be part of the legal delegation that met with the ambassadors from the United States of America, the United Kingdom and West Germany to seek their support in the campaign to save my clients from the gallows.

The Pretoria News and the International Defence & Aid Fund for Southern Africa, London, for providing the photographs.

Nadine Gordimer, for her valuable time and helpful advice, especially at the very early stages of my manuscript.

Avie Bennett, Chairman and President of McClelland & Stewart, Inc. for his encouragement of my book and his support, past and present, to the struggle for justice in South Africa.

The
Sharpeville
Six

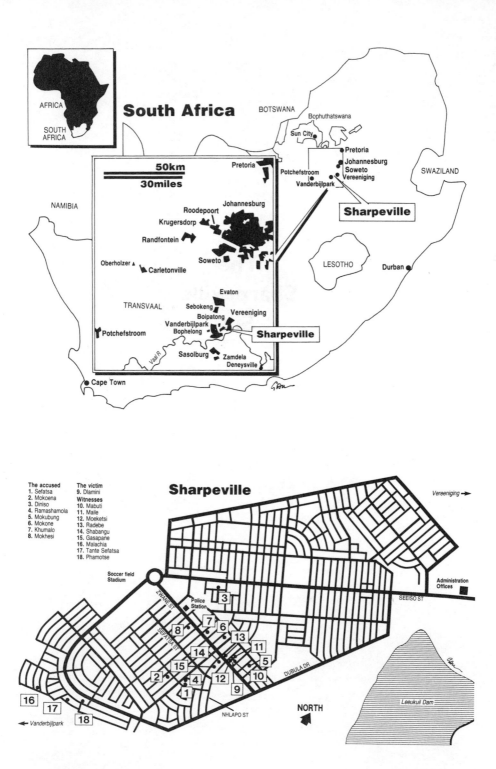

South Africa

AFRICA
SOUTH AFRICA

BOTSWANA

Bophuthatswana

Sun City

Pretoria

Johannesburg
Soweto
Vereeniging

SWAZILAND

Potchefstroom

Vanderbijlpark

Sharpeville

NAMIBIA

50km
30miles

Pretoria

Johannesburg

Roodepoort

Krugersdorp

Randfontein

Soweto

Oberholzer

Carletonville

LESOTHO

Durban

Evaton

Sebokeng

Boipatong

Vereeniging

TRANSVAAL

Vanderbijlpark

Bophelong

Sharpeville

Potchefstroom

Vaal R.

Sasolburg

Zamdela
Deneysville

Cape Town

Sharpeville

The accused
1. Sefatsa
2. Mokoena
3. Diniso
4. Ramashamola
5. Mokubung
6. Mokone
7. Khumalo
8. Mokhesi

The victim
9. Dlamini

Witnesses
10. Mabuti
11. Maile
12. Moeketsi
13. Radebe
14. Shabangu
15. Gasapane
16. Malachia
17. Tante Sefatsa
18. Phamotse

Vereeniging →

Administration Offices

SEEISO ST

Soccer field
Stadium

ZWANE ST

Police
Station

SEFATSA ST

DUBULA DR

NORTH

Leeukuil Dam

NHLAPO ST

← Vanderbijlpark

Sharpeville

"You can't pay such rent when your wages are also so small."
SHARPEVILLE RESIDENT

For many who have not seen it, Sharpeville is a date, rather than a place. It is March 21, 1960, the day on which a large crowd gathered at the local police station to protest against the pass laws that forced all black adults to carry an identity document at all times, everywhere. The "pass" showed date and place of birth, ethnic origin, employment history and, above all, whether its owner complied with the stringent requirements for permission to be in an urban area for more than 72 hours. The police lost their heads and fired into the crowd, killing 69 people and injuring 186. The world was outraged.

At once the South African government declared a state of emergency and banned the black people's principal organizations, the African National Congress (ANC) and the Pan Africanist Congress (PAC). In the months that followed, much capital and many whites left South Africa.

In time, confidence returned to the white community and the Johannesburg Stock Exchange. The state of emergency was lifted before the end of the year, but for nearly thirty years the banned organizations remained banned. Nothing was quite the same in South Africa after Sharpeville.

But what about the place? It returned to obscurity and, in the early 1980s, it was much the same nondescript, dusty, typical South African black township it had always been, a labour dormitory for the iron-and-steel industry based in Vereeniging and Vanderbijlpark, white towns some sixty kilometres south of

Johannesburg. (Those two towns, with Sasolburg, the centre of South Africa's oil-from-coal industry, across the Vaal River in the Orange Free State, form the "Vaal Triangle.")

Sharpeville was born during the Second World War, when black workers were drawn to the area by the boom in munitions production. When the township was opened in 1942, the mayor of Vereeniging was one John Sharpe. In those days, urban housing for blacks was a white municipal responsibility, and the Vereeniging town council was keen to move the inhabitants of its overcrowded and insalubrious "Top Location" farther out of town.

On about 350 hectares of vacant veld some five kilometres west of Vereeniging, the new "location" was laid out: 5,466 small brick houses were built in neat rows, back to back. Most consist of two bedrooms, a living room, and a kitchen, the whole covering perhaps forty-five square metres. Their roofs are curved caps of pale grey corrugated asbestos.[1] The houses have no ceilings and no bathrooms, though each has a toilet outside in the yard. There are also some two-roomed houses, with fronts similar to the four-roomed buildings but, from the side, looking as if the back portion has been broken off, leaving half a house.

By 1984, there were only 480 more houses than there were in the 1940s, and nothing else had changed much, except that most residents had enjoyed the use of electricity for three years or so, and water-borne sewerage had replaced the old bucket system. Each stand or lot had a tap with running water, and although there were no ordinary street lamps, high-mast Apollo lights, like those used in sports stadiums, cast their harsh glare over parts of the township at night.

Zwane Street, the main thoroughfare, was clearly laid out and surfaced at the outset to carry the cars of white officials, but most of the other streets are still dirt roads, badly rutted and pot-holed. Some have no name, but this is not important, for every address is simply a four-digit house-number.

Many residents have replaced the standard municipal number-plates with large ornamental numerals, displayed diagonally across the front façade. More expensive attempts to escape the crushing uniformity include decorative plastering, wooden front doors, bigger windows, and curly wrought-iron burglar-proofing, but not many houses have had much money lavished on them. The place is poor, and it shows.

Sharpeville has churches, a library, many schools, two community halls, and a soccer field and stadium. The registered population in 1984 was just over 40,000, but official figures are notoriously lower than actual ones, and the many backyard shacks tell a different story.

❖

In 1983, the central government drew "coloureds" – people of mixed blood – and South Africans of Indian origin into its tricameral parliamentary system, from which blacks continued to be excluded.

The United Democratic Front (UDF) was formed in 1983 expressly to oppose the new dispensation. It is a broad, nonracial grouping of between six hundred and seven hundred progressive extra-parliamentary organizations and trade unions, and enjoys wide popular support among those who share the ideals of the African National Congress. As a result, it was harassed from its inception, and operated, until the ANC and PAC bans were lifted on February 2, 1990, under all manner of restrictions and handicaps. The State held the UDF largely responsible for the protest that swept the country after September 3, 1984.

To compensate black South Africans for having no say in the government of the country, the government passed the Black Local Authorities Act in 1982. This act provided for elected black town councils, which would assume a whole string of administrative responsibilities formerly carried by government boards: electrification, road construction and maintenance, housing and prevention of illegal occupation, waste disposal, sewerage, control of health hazards, welfare, sport and recreation, and employment of staff. But a black population interested in real political power was not to be fobbed off with a vote for a toothless local council.

The government boards retained ownership of the land and of the "improvements" (houses), for which they continued to receive rent and which they were attempting to sell (on 99-year lease) to the tenants. In 1986, when the boards were completely disbanded, ownership of all these passed to the office of the administrator of each province.

The act brought Sharpeville and five other townships[2] – more than a quarter of a million people – under the administrative umbrella of the Lekoa (Sesotho) town council. Evaton, an old, partly freehold area that dates back to 1902, has its own council. It was in these seven "townships of the Vaal Triangle" that all the trouble began.

In November 1983, when the first Lekoa election took place, at least 160,000 adults resided in the area. Less than 100,000 of them registered to vote. Some of the abstainers did not fulfil various eligibility conditions, and some deliberately refrained from registering as an act of protest. In the end, when only 14,321 people voted, this represented an official poll of 14.7 per cent (official polls being a percentage of registered voters), although it was only 9 per cent of the adult population. The Evaton council was elected in an official poll of 3.5 per cent.

The councillors elected were seen as government stooges for consenting to participate, as the new councils had no political powers.

The National Party has ruled South Africa without interruption since 1948. It was not until the early 1980s that the permanent nature of the black urban population was officially recognized. Previously, ideology had considered the black townships to be temporary camps for labourers who really lived in some distant "homeland." As such, urban infrastructure had been grossly neglected, and what the newly elected "autonomous" black councils inherited was poor and costly to maintain, let alone upgrade.

Financial disaster stared the new councils in the face from the day they took office, because the central government decreed that they must be "self-financing." Their sources of revenue were site rents, service charges,[3] lodgers' fees,[4] fines for infringing by-laws, and trade and animal licences.

The councils lacked industrial and commercial enterprises, normally the backbone of municipal rates. They also lacked that traditional source of black township revenue: beer and liquor sales, which had given the government boards 70 per cent of their income. The boards retained the revenue from sorghum beer sales in the beerhalls, and most other liquor sales were privatized; thus, the new councils' income from them was restricted to liquor-store licences. The boards continued to receive house rents, for all houses remained their property until they managed to sell them off to the tenants.

Despite the broader revenue base the boards had enjoyed, they apparently passed on huge deficits to the new councils. As a result, these councils started off with severely impaired creditworthiness, and could not borrow in the market.

Inflation was running high: it was officially 13.25 per cent for 1984, and during the year the price of petrol had gone up twice. The councils were hard-pressed to continue to deliver such services as they provided, let alone improve conditions. Their only source of revenue was their residents.

What was the financial situation of the urban township inhabitants? Were they really, as a Minister of Co-operation and Development claimed during the planning stage of the new black local administration, "in a position to make substantially increased contributions towards service charges"?

In 1984, the minimum monthly sum on which a black family of six could survive was calculated[5] to be R330.25 in the Vaal Triangle, where their cost of living was the highest in the country and 13.4 per cent higher than the previous year.

R65 a week or R286 a month, was the approximate wage an unskilled black industrial worker could expect in the Vaal area. In its 1984 report, the National Manpower Commission gave R363 as the national average black monthly wage for all but domestic and farm workers, which was an increase of 17 per cent over 1983. Market Research Africa put the average black household's monthly income in 1984 at R273, representing a 24 per cent increase.

Unemployment was increasing as the State attempted to brake inflation by discouraging consumer spending. Companies responded with production cuts and retrenchments. Many breadwinners were supporting more than six people. A grandmother in the house would contribute her pension, of course, but this was only R57 per month.[6] The price of maize, the staple food of the black population, rose by 27 per cent between January and April 1984.

The bus to Vereeniging and back cost Sharpeville residents about eighty-four cents a day,[7] and taxis were a little cheaper, at forty cents each way. Only a few of the taxis in South Africa are private, door-to-door luxuries. Most of them travel from one fixed point to another, like small, tightly packed buses, stopping anywhere along the route on demand.

There are no free schools in black areas. African parents make huge sacrifices to pay for tuition and to buy the schoolbooks and compulsory uniforms. Yet schooling is desperately inadequate and conditions unacceptable: there are brutal and arbitrary corporal punishment, non-elected prefects, widespread sexual harassment of girls by teachers, and an upper age limit. This means that the many children who must earn the means of their next year's schooling were often refused readmission because they were too old. (These and other student grievances are intrinsic to apartheid, and pupils had staged mass class boycotts at the time of the "tricameral" elections in October 1984, and have done so off and on since.)

School-leavers in the early 1980s faced a severely shrinking job market as a result of the deepening recession. Moreover, they were more numerous, and more of them held matriculation certificates, whatever these may have really been worth.[8]

The growing number of unemployable school-leavers contributed fundamentally to politicizing the issues of education and poverty. It is this feature that explains the central role of school-children and township youth in the uprising in the Vaal in September 1984.

"Although the average class in schools in this area is big – sixty pupils per teacher is not exceptional – and the facilities some-times border on the shocking, the area is streets ahead of the other regions in the quality of the education provided," ex-plained Professor Tjaart van der Walt in the report of this one-man commission of enquiry appointed by the government to investigate the school boycott in the Vaal. "The need, the hunger for education and the total inadequacy of the available facilities are evident everywhere."

But that hunger had to compete with physical hunger, and many children had to leave school so that their families might eat. Even Van der Walt acknowledged that this situation accounted for the involvement of large numbers of schoolchil-dren in the anti-rent demonstrations in August 1984, the begin-nings of resistance.

Housing, however rudimentary, was in desperate demand. Average monthly "rent"[9] in Lekoa was R62.56, R10 more than in any other black township in the country and twice the national metropolitan average for blacks. Rent for a house varied between R8.31 and R12.51, according to the age and type of house. In addition, all Lekoa householders were required to pay monthly fees totalling R51.20[10]: R39.30 in service charges, R10 for elec-tricity reticulation, and R1.90 as basic tariff for wiring of houses. The last two fees were an attempt to make all township residents (even though the majority of them were not owners but tenants) pay off the huge cost involved in originally bringing power to the townships around 1980. Electricity consumption was, of course, metered and charged on top of the base charges of R51.20.

While the black urban councils were unable to make ends meet, councillors were placed in an extraordinary position, at once very dangerous and very lucrative. They, instead of the government boards, were now imposing unpopular measures. They had to prevent squatting, deal with rent defaulters, and enforce the pass laws through housing control. They had the power to evict tenants and allot houses to whomever they chose, and nothing in South Africa is as desperate and difficult as finding – and being allowed to occupy – a house in a black urban area. They controlled lodgers' permits and the list of tenants permitted to reside in any house – and in 1984, in terms of influx control and the pass laws, these were still vital to anyone wishing to seek work in the vicinity or, indeed, to spend more than seventy-two hours in a township without breaking the law. Moreover, trading and liquor licences were theirs to allocate.

These ingredients formed a perfect recipe for corruption, and if councillors took bribes or interfered with the waiting lists, their opportunities to enrich themselves at the expense of their largely poverty-stricken communities were dazzling. Many succumbed visibly to the temptation, and new cars and improved homes flaunted questionable gains; few liquor outlets or permits to build petrol stations were granted to anyone outside council. To remain uncorrupted in such an environment was extremely difficult, particularly as it required a political astuteness one would hardly expect of persons prepared to flout community feeling and do the government's dirty-work for it.

Esau Mahlatsi, the mayor of Lekoa, lived in Sebokeng. He and his family reportedly got their hands on the lion's share of the spoils available to councillors in the area; they were reported to own fourteen of the fifteen liquor outlets, as well as various shops and supermarkets.

Our story concerns Kuzwayo Jacob Dlamini, the forty-one-year-old deputy-mayor of Lekoa and the highest-placed dignitary resident in Sharpeville.

Dlamini lived with his wife, Alice, and their three children in an ordinary Sharpeville "four-roomed." The only external sign of privilege was a garage he had put up to house his Toyota Cressida; what other spoils of office he may have reaped were not displayed. Nevertheless, a common perception in the township was that "he did not care for the people in the location." He had acquired a reputation for taking large bribes and being interested only in personal gain.

Dlamini's career in civic affairs dated back to 1977, when he became a member of the local urban council. He sat on the housing and trade committees and soon became known for the advantages he could obtain for relations and friends, to the extent that, in 1980, one of his colleagues resigned from a committee in protest.

Dlamini campaigned for the November 1983 local election on popular issues. Pensioners, he declared, should have their pensions delivered to their houses and not have to travel long distances and queue all day at the pay-out points. Residents should be consulted by their local councils, instead of having decisions imposed on them. House rents should be reduced, because the houses were "rotten."

It was true the houses were very poor and dilapidated, and, at an average of R10 a month, the rents were very high. But the councils had no say over the house rents: they were the one part of the monthly charges that still went to the boards. Besides, even if rents were scrapped, each household would still have had to pay more than R50 a month to the council. During Dlamini's own tenure in local office, since 1977, overall monthly charges in the Vaal had increased by 350 per cent.

Dlamini had been a teacher and had taught many of the young people in Sharpeville. He also managed his own local football team, and he lived in the ward he represented on the council. Perhaps he was best known in the community because he was the councillor people approached for help in getting a house. It is no secret that residents were in the habit of going to see him privately at home in connection with their housing problems. One woman said, "I heard that he evicted people from the house, but with us he helped us. He helped my mother get the house." As there were no vacant houses, no councillor could help one family to obtain a house without depriving someone else, and as a more realistic woman put it, "Councillors administered houses. Dlamini would get people out, and get you a house if he liked you."

One Sharpeville subtenant was trying to get the house he occupied transferred to his own name because the official tenant was leaving the area for good. "I had been to Mr. Dlamini's house many times to ask that I get the papers," he said. "Mrs. Dlamini was always interfering when I was speaking to her husband. She would say I was not special. She would hint that

I would have to give her money if I wanted to get the special papers. I thought this is not the way to behave. The deputy-mayor should not allow this."

Mrs. Dlamini seems to have been more actively disliked than her husband – for her loud mouth and her arrogance. She was *motho* (swaggering), people said. Someone noted during the trial that she "liked to tell everyone in court, even the interpreter, that she owned a car." People said she and her husband were always proud: "They thought they were like God."

The unfortunate woman had her own problems. Her husband had women all over Sharpeville and beyond, and this humiliating fact was common knowledge. There was, according to friends and relations, a lot of friction in the house.

Dlamini had left teaching and was employed as personnel officer at African Cables, a large Vereeniging company where, in May 1984, more than a hundred workers were, they claimed, unfairly dismissed. Many of them held the personnel officer directly responsible. What was worse, two months later the Lekoa Housing Committee, on which Dlamini sat, authorized the eviction of these unemployed men from their houses, because they had fallen behind with their rents. Even though their attorneys had provided the council with written assurances that the men would likely be rehired, the evictions went ahead.

Meanwhile, Dlamini himself had run up rent arrears of more than R800 for a petrol-station site he had been allotted in Zamdela in 1981. He had also failed to honour his agreement to build upon the site within a certain period. Needless to say, he was never penalized.

The Lekoa councillors were certainly aware of the physical dangers inherent in their position and had acquired firearms for their own protection. In July 1984, they discussed insuring themselves and their personal property against politically motivated violence. The deputy-mayor said then that councillors were easy targets for "elements" who accused them of co-operating with apartheid.

Perhaps Dlamini was corrupt and greedy, arrogant and a bully; perhaps he did side with the white authorities for short-term gain. In this there seems no reason to suppose that he was worse than many other councillors at the time. However, he does seem to have had one distinguishing feature: he was obstinate to the point of stupidity.

In August 1984, 1,500 employees were transferred to the payroll of the Lekoa council by the Orange-Vaal Development Board, following an application by the council for city status. The mayor, Mr. Mahlatsi, made the curiously provocative and inaccurate statement that the augmented staff occasioned by the change of Lekoa's status was "the only reason for increasing rents on houses."

Whatever its ostensible reasons, the Lekoa council promptly announced that service charges would be increased on September 1 by R5.90,[11] and the electricity reticulation charge would rise from R10 to R12, bringing the flat rate (excluding house rent) to R59.10. The cost of metered electricity was to rise by almost 20 per cent (from 5.2 cents to 6.2 cents per unit consumed). Simultaneously, the Evaton council announced an increase of R6 per month in residential permit fees, directly affecting all privately owned houses.[12]

It is easy to say with hindsight that it was unwise of Dlamini to announce the forthcoming increases in person at the mass meeting called by the council on August 5, 1984. And it is easy to see as symptomatic a small incident at this meeting, which people did not forget: apparently, a woman in the crowd wagged her finger at Dlamini as she protested. He became very angry and told her never to do that to him again, or else . . .

The Lekoa "rent" increase of R5.90[13] per month may seem trivial as £1.50 or $2.25 (U.S.). In fact, however, the additional burden for each household (including the R2 electricity reticulation increase) was quite steep: it was a 12.5 per cent rise, or nearly 3 per cent of the average monthly wage, a cost equivalent to that for ten days' transport or twenty loaves of brown bread. A Sharpeville resident put it very simply: "When they raised the rents, they never asked us. They wanted us to pay more rent and our houses are so small and so bad. You can't pay such rent when your wages are also so small."

Protest meetings were held in all the Vaal townships after the announcement, generally in church halls, and mostly under the auspices of the Vaal Civic Association, a popular local organization affiliated with the UDF. When the Lekoa council refused to negotiate or to scrap the increases, the people decided that they would pay what they considered an "affordable rent," R30 a month. No rent boycott was suggested.

Black councillors had been recognized as willing agents of the government and as corrupt self-enrichers at the expense of the hard-pressed township residents. Suddenly, a seemingly innocuous if ill-judged rent increase in the Vaal Triangle – not the first there or elsewhere since the councils took office – transformed all councillors from the very ordinary mortals most of them were into living symbols – visible, accessible, and vulnerable – of apartheid and economic exploitation.

The Vaal area was first to explode, perhaps because rents and other costs there were the highest, while wages were not. But the same pressures were being felt everywhere, and before the end of 1984, townships all over the country had broken out in violent protest against grinding poverty and hardship, and the people's political impotence.

PART ONE

The
Causes

❖

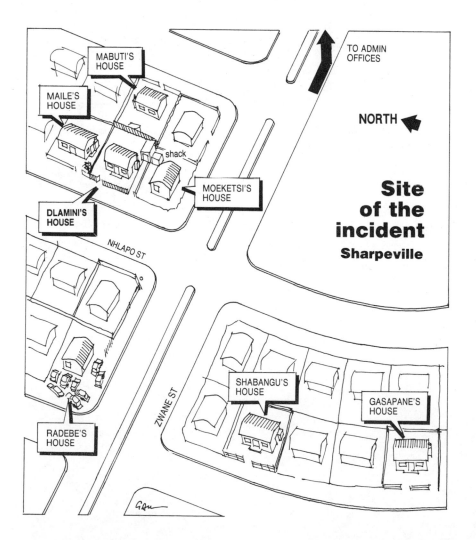

TO ADMIN
OFFICES

MABUTI'S
HOUSE

MAILE'S
HOUSE

NORTH

shack

MOEKETSI'S
HOUSE

DLAMINI'S
HOUSE

**Site
of the
incident**
Sharpeville

NHLAPO ST

ZWANE ST

SHABANGU'S
HOUSE

GASAPANE'S
HOUSE

RADEBE'S
HOUSE

The Incident

"HARENA CHELETE"
("We have no money.")
PLACARD SLOGAN

On Monday, September 3, 1984, black workers throughout the Vaal Triangle observed a stay-away in protest against the rent increases announced by the Lekoa and Evaton councils.

The stay-away was unanimous, and no buses or taxis operated. Gatherings and protest marches took place in all the black residential areas in the Vaal, but it was in Sharpeville that things first went wrong.

At about 7:30 a.m., small groups gathered in the dirt roads that criss-cross the township. Their intention was to march to the administration offices where the rents were paid and to demonstrate their opposition to the rent increase peacefully, by a strong presence.

The following are the undisputed elements of the incident that changed the lives of all the people in this book:

Zwane Street is wide and tarred, with a grassy island in the middle. The people moved towards it like tributaries flowing into a river and were soon advancing eastwards along the main road, in the direction of the offices. According to eyewitnesses, there were a few hundred marchers at most. They were singing and shouting slogans. Placards were carried high: PUPPET COUN-CILLORS RESIGN, and HARENA CHELETE ["We have no money"].

Some of the marchers were angered by the presence of passive spectators; the rent issue affected everybody, and it was important to make a united stand. Bystanders who showed reluctance to join the protest were threatened with damage to their property and injury to their person.

The marchers had their backs to that famous police station, near the beginning of Zwane Street, where the 1960 massacre took place. About two kilometres from the administration offices, they reached Nhlapo Street, a dusty little side-road like many others they had passed. As they approached from the west, those marching on the left side of Zwane Street came abreast of the house of Councillor Dlamini, second from the corner.

Someone or several people shouted, "This is the house where the sell-out Dlamini lives!" and stones were thrown at the house.

The police appeared and dispersed the crowd with tear-gas and rubber bullets. They injured at least two people. Seeing that it was not safe for Dlamini to remain in his house, they asked him to accompany them, but he refused.

The police left the scene and, within fifteen minutes, some of the crowd – according to eyewitnesses, about a hundred people – regrouped. There was more stoning of the house. Dlamini opened fire on the crowd from inside his house and injured at least one person. The crowd became incensed.

Petrol and/or petrol bombs were thrown at and into Dlamini's house, which caught fire. Dlamini came out through his kitchen door, which faced Zwane Street, and ran round the back, towards his neighbour Maile's house, the third house from the Zwane Street corner. As he reached the fence, a member or members of the crowd grappled with him for his gun and disarmed him. Stones were thrown at him. He fell down and lay unconscious near Maile's kitchen door.

Meanwhile, Dlamini's car had been pushed from its garage into Nhlapo Street, and had been rolled over onto its side and set alight. Some unidentified people – possibly three – dragged the unconscious Dlamini into the street and tried to put him onto the burning car, but he slid off. He was then drenched with petrol or covered in petrol-soaked paper and set alight.

The police were called. When they arrived at 9:00 a.m., Dlamini was dead.

Arrests[1]

**"The envelope was made of a Colgate
toothpaste box."**
SUSAN DINISO

Two months went by after the murder of Kuzwayo Jacob
Dlamini. Then, at 3:00 a.m. on November 2 (or 3), 1984,[2] a
banging on the doors and windows of their house at 8055
Sharpeville woke Mojalefa "Ja-Ja"[3] Sefatsa and his common-law
wife, Regina Morathi. "There were lots of policemen – two
white and many black. The black policemen hit him," she later
said. She did not know then, nor did Ja-Ja, that the very big
white policeman was the investigating officer in the Dlamini
murder case, Detective Warrant Officer Pieter Schoeman,
nicknamed "Hard Hitter." He had his chief black henchman
with him; but where Schoeman was trim, Sergeant Matunzi was
both huge and grossly overweight. They were asking about a
firearm.

At age twenty-nine, Ja-Ja was a successful fruit-vendor at
Vereeniging railway station, an entrepreneur in a small way. He
had several young employees at strategic points selling fruit, and
was apparently making a very good living. He needed to, as sole
breadwinner for his family, which included three younger brothers and a sister, all still at school. His parents' separation had
stopped his education when he was fourteen and in Standard 5.
His mother drank and his father used to beat her up. She left
the family and went to Cape Town, and her children hadn't seen
her since. The father went off with another woman. For a while,
some of the children lived in Bophuthatswana, a neighbouring
"homeland," with their paternal grandmother; after she died
they returned to Sharpeville.

Because of the success of his business, Ja-Ja would not have been very hard-hit by the rent increase, and politics, he said, did not interest him. He enjoyed his work, although frequent police raids and confiscation of his goods caused recurrent frustration. Stay-aways were a nuisance because of the loss of income, but otherwise of no interest to him.

His great pleasure was the cinema, and he had the looks of a romantic lead: tall, well-built, and very dark, with high cheek-bones and a confident smile displaying beautiful white teeth. He was very well liked in the township, despite his strict objection – on religious as well as health grounds – to drink, cigarettes, and drugs. He was a regular church-goer, a Methodist.

Ja-Ja and Regina had been together for nearly six years, and theirs seems to be a real and enduring love affair. They had had one baby, who died in 1980 at age eleven months; and to their great joy their second child was soon due. On that terrible morning that the police burst into her life, Regina said later, "I just kept quiet, but they also assaulted me. They hit me in the face and I cried but they said I mustn't cry. Ja-Ja and I were scared for the baby – it was born on 23 November."

The police took Ja-Ja away and held him for two days. When they released him, he thought that was that, and he wouldn't hear from them again. But the next week, in the early hours of Friday, November 9, they came again. The police car drove off with Ja-Ja in it, followed by a van whose occupants Regina could not see. She said, "I wasn't scared. I thought he would come back in the morning."

Two young people were under police guard in the back of that van. One was Christiaan Mokubung, married and father of a baby, the sole support of his family. The other was a slightly stout young woman of medium height wearing a dress over her nightdress, Theresa Ramashamola, aged twenty-four.

For as long as the occupants can remember, 8050 Sharpeville has been a house full of women. Theresa was born there on August 31, 1960, while her grandmother was the "registered tenant." During her childhood, Theresa shared one of the two bedrooms with her older sister, Violet; her grandmother, her mother, Julia, and her younger sister, Josephine, slept in the other. After the grandmother's death, Julia turned one of the bedrooms into a sitting room, and everyone slept in the other.

Violet became a nurse and moved out. Theresa was going to marry her sweetheart, Andrew Vusi Mnthali, who had paid *lobola* (the price paid by a bridegroom to the bride's family for the right to call children of the marriage by his name) to her mother in November 1981. Julia was a darkroom assistant in the X-ray department at Sebokeng Hospital. She and Theresa were just about managing, with their combined wages, to pay for food and young Josephine's education. Josephine still had five years of school ahead of her when their precarious world was turned upside-down.

Theresa had had no training beyond primary school. The first job she found was as a cook in Vereeniging, at the Oxwagon Restaurant. Her second, and last, was at the Burger Box,[4] where her monthly wages were R95.94.[5] By the time she had paid for her transport to and from work, she had R76 left: for the bus fare was forty-two cents each way, and a taxi 2 cents cheaper.

On Friday, November 9, 1984, Theresa would have set off for work at first light, but the police arrived before 3:00 a.m. in a van and a car, woke everyone up, and told her to dress. "There were four or five blacks and three whites," she said. "One was Schoeman. Matunzi said I am a bitch." They put her into the van and went on to pick up Christiaan. Then they fetched Ja-Ja out of his house, but he was put in the car.

Reid Mokoena's mother opened the door when the policemen banged on it. Schoeman and Matunzi barged through into the bedroom, shouting, "Hey you, get up. Where's the gun?" Reid, aged twenty-one, was small, thin and painfully shy; he said he did not know. Well, they said, Ja-Ja had told them Reid had the gun. They punched him in the face and body.

Mrs. Leah Mokoena was sixty-two years old then. She had been a domestic servant all her working life, and was still working part-time in Vereeniging, earning R70 a month. Her little house, a standard four-roomed, was bursting at the seams. Phillip, her eldest son, was a teacher. He was living at home and saving to get married. Next came Reid, aged twenty-one, then his younger siblings, Louis and Martha, both school-aged. Leah had also taken in the two small sons of her daughter Sarah, who had been murdered by her husband, and another grandchild, a little girl.

Reid's father, an alcoholic, had habitually assaulted Leah, and had finally abandoned the family when Reid was thirteen. Leah's devotion to all her children was warm and constant, and Reid, who was sensitive to her difficulties and conscious of her love, had tried from an early age to help her make ends meet. At sixteen he had had a part-time job, but then he had had a bad idea:

"I stole a lawnmower because I wanted to start a business and I didn't have the money. I knew it was wrong, but I did not have the money. I thought that I wouldn't be hurting them badly because they had so much money they could easily buy another one. I was not happy with the people I stole the lawnmower from. I worked for them as a gardener and they paid me R1.50 a day and I was working very hard. When I stole their lawnmower I thought that they would not know . . . because they did not know my address, but they may have seen me walking with the lawnmower all the way from Vanderbijlpark to Sharpeville." For this Reid was sentenced to six lashes. It was his only brush with the law.

He found better ways to help his mother. At the weekends and after school, and later, after work, he did odd jobs around the house, painting, repairing, and mainly gardening. He created a big, square vegetable patch at the back, which went a long way towards feeding the family. He made the front garden pretty, with paving near the gate (his middle name, "Malebo," is drawn in the concrete), shrubs, and flowers. These things are exceptional in Sharpeville.

In 1982, when his girlfriend, Dorothy Morobe, became pregnant, Reid decided he must leave school in order to support her and his baby. He got a job in Vereeniging as an unskilled machine-operator for a company making caravan parts, at a starting wage of R65 a week. By November 1984 he was earning R67 a week, and hoping to be able to marry Dorothy soon. But he was giving his mother R30 a week towards the household expenses and his siblings' schooling, and supporting his little son, so saving was barely possible. Dorothy and the child were not in the house that terrible morning – they were still living with her family.

Reid was ordered to dress, and Matunzi gripped him by the belt and shoved him outside and into the back of one of the waiting cars. His mother and sister came out into the dark street, asking the policemen what Reid had done. Mrs. Mokoena was told to go back into the house. Martha asked again why they were arresting her brother, and the black policeman replied, "I'll belt you in the face."

Oupa Diniso, a handsome man of twenty-nine, was living quietly with his wife, Susan; their little boy, Thembile, age six; and Lindiwe, their baby daughter. He was supporting them fairly easily; unlike most Sharpeville inhabitants, he did not have crippling obligations towards his wider family, though he did support his mother. He had a semi-skilled job as a quality inspector for a Vereeniging firm called Tubemakers of South Africa, checking steel tubes for length and thickness, internal and external diameter, and straightness. He was earning relatively well, R740 a month, and had various commitments that go with such a salary: two life-insurance policies, furniture bought on instalment, and so on.

Oupa was hoping to become the "registered tenant" of the standard four-roomed he was renting, so that he might buy it. He had already done a lot of work on the house: on one external corner, fancy plastering created an impression of stonework; a broad slab of highly polished red cement made a patio in front of the door; enormous copperplate numerals proclaimed "3842" across the wall above a solid wooden front door; and inside, strip-pine ceilings made the living room and bedrooms warm and attractive.

He was a keen golfer, and spent much of his free time practising his shots. His wife calls him "Scotch," from his taste for checked or plaid shirts, not from any tendency to drink. He was a strict vegetarian, something very unusual in his community.

"They knocked on the windows and at the door," said Susan. "It was 5:45. Oupa got up. When they came in, they pushed him immediately onto the furniture so that it fell over. There was a Zulu-speaking man called Matunzi. He said, 'Where's the gun? Where's the gun?' Oupa didn't say anything. He took the gun from the 'bathroom' – it was in the space where things were put in the ceiling."

"Bathroom" was a family joke. The room was more like a passage, and too small to contain any furniture. Oupa had not put in a ceiling, so that there was open access to the space above the living-room ceiling. Far from being a hiding-place, this was a much-needed storage shelf for cartons and other objects, including the zinc bath the family used every day in that "room" for their ablutions.

Matunzi had not come alone. There was also a white police sergeant called Wessels, and they had brought Ja-Ja with them. Oupa did not hesitate, argue, struggle, or try to escape; nor did he deny any knowledge of the firearm. In the presence of Ja-Ja, he simply fetched it and handed it over.

Then the police took him away.

❖

That morning of November 9, 1984, as soon as the police had gone from each house, each family left behind began its separate odyssey. Baffled and shocked, old people, young siblings, wives, and small children set off in search of those who had been picked up.

Leah and Martha Mokoena went to Vereeniging to the police station. No one had heard of Reid. They returned to the Sharpeville police station. No, no one of that name. Back again to

Vereeniging, the same day, to be told, "Those people have been released." Home, full of hope. Of course, Reid was not there.

Members of the other families also trudged from one police station to another all day, trying to find out where a husband, brother, daughter, son had been taken, and why the arrest had been made. No one in authority seemed to know or care.

Nearly all the people involved in this story lived in the section of Sharpeville they call Rooisteen, where the house numbers start with 7, or in nearby Vergenoeg, where they start with 8. Most of them knew one another, some well, some only by sight, except the Dinisos who lived in a different part of Sharpeville and were strangers to the others.

But it was Susan Diniso who found the missing group. After she had alerted her in-laws about Oupa's arrest and dropped her younger child off at her own mother's house, she rushed to Vereeniging, and she had no doubt: "I looked up to the windows of the security branch section and I saw them there. I saw my husband, and Reid Mokoena, Ja-Ja Sefatsa, Theresa Ramasha-mola, although I didn't know them at that stage. Also a few others. I saw them again, they were brought down the stairs from the third or fourth storey . . . to a van. I was in the waiting room, near where they park the cars. . . . Some SAP [South African Police] were saying they have been freed. But I saw them being taken away." That was during the afternoon of November 9. Of course, Susan had no idea where the van had gone, and no one would tell her.

Another thing she could not know was that those she had seen together were separated the same day. Theresa Ramashamola was released that afternoon and went home to her mother.

The next morning, Saturday, Regina went looking for Ja-Ja again. She said, "I met Susan at Vereeniging police station on the 10th of November – the day after the arrest. After that, we worked together. I knew I was not the only one with this problem."

She still believed Ja-Ja would be released after a day or two, as he had been the week before. But this time he did not come home to her. The days went by. People missed the young fruit-seller at the taxi rank at the station, and came to his house to ask where he was. Regina could not tell them anything. At one police station she had been told he had been released.

Two weeks after Ja-Ja vanished in the police car, Regina gave birth to his baby. She stayed at home for ten days after the confinement, because she was not well. Her sister went from one police station to the next with the other families, looking for the young people who had been picked up. Regina could not get the idea out of her mind that Ja-Ja was dead; she thought her sister had discovered this but was keeping the news from her.

When Ja-Ja had been gone for about a month, a prison warder came unofficially to see Regina, and brought her a letter. In it, Ja-Ja asked her to tell the credit controller at Joshua Doore, a furniture shop, that he would come as soon as possible to pay his hire-purchase instalment; otherwise, he said, their bedroom suite would be repossessed. And Regina must go to Groenpunt Prison, near Vereeniging, but on the other side of the Vaal River in the Orange Free State, and visit a certain prisoner there.

Regina dealt with the furniture shop as best she could, and went to Groenpunt to visit the prisoner. He told her that Ja-Ja's cell was not far from his own – he knew which one it was because he could hear his voice – and that he was all right. Ja-Ja had an urgent message for her: "Get me a lawyer before Christmas!" Regina undertook to do this, and asked the prisoner to tell Ja-Ja that his baby was a girl, and she was waiting for the name.

After Susan Diniso saw Reid, Ja-Ja, and her own husband, Oupa, being taken away from Vereeniging police station, she searched and waited. And then, she says, "The same warder [the man who came to Regina] came to me. He brought a letter made of toilet paper. The envelope was made of a Colgate toothpaste box. It said, 'Get a lawyer.' It said, 'Ask for a prisoner and give him a message.'

"I visited the prison at Christmas. I had had two letters by then. But I forgot the prisoner's name! A higher-up policeman said, 'Who said Oupa Diniso is here?' I said I had a letter from the police saying he was in Groenpunt. He said, 'That man is not here at all.'

"My heart was awfully pained. It was Christmas and they couldn't tell the truth. There were four of us. One was a friend, Gcina. She has a stronger personality. Gcina insisted that he is there. I was frightened. They might ask, 'How do you know?' They might go back to Scotch and beat him up. I was deadly scared for him. We didn't know what to say. I went home. I had to go to bed after that, the doctor said I had a heart condition.

"The warder came again to say he is there and don't forget the prisoner's name!"

Once their families had discovered by these unofficial means where the young men were being held, they applied for permission to visit them. Section 29[6], under which they were detained, explicitly denies access to detainees without permission.

"Early in 1985," says Reid's mother, "a letter came in the post, and also the detectives came. They came to say that I must go to the prison in Vereeniging. And I would see my child. I was sick at that time. I went."

Regina's experience of this first meeting since their shock separation was almost identical to Ja-Ja's. Speaking four years later, she said, "I was crying when I waited for him to come. I waited a long time. Even when he came I cried."

And Ja-Ja, also speaking four years later, but in a different place, echoed, "When I first saw her I started to cry."

He went on, "I was so happy to see her alive. I was so happy to see my baby for the first time, I cannot explain it. . . . I was allowed to hold my baby until my baby was asleep."

And Regina, "He took the baby and held her. He was so worried about the things he hadn't done for the baby."

She said, "They told us to talk so that they could hear."

He singled out the same restriction: "I wasn't allowed to talk about the situation at the prison. She keeps on asking me, 'What is wrong, Ja-Ja? I can see that you are so thin.'"

Regina went home, to wait in hope. Ja-Ja returned to the cells at Groenpunt.

Susan visited Oupa the same day. "I thought, hey, he's getting fat! Is he worrying about something? I was happy to see him. I took the children. He grabbed them in his arms. He told them he would be in court. The police were there and we couldn't talk properly. The tears were coming. Scotch talked to his mother when I was overcome with grief. I felt he's not coming back. He started crying too. This is serious, this is bigger than we thought.

"Thembile was thrilled to see his father. He cried when we were going home. We told him his dad would come home tomorrow. . . . Later Thembile went to a psychiatrist because the teacher said he's not all right at school. He has no attention. He doesn't cry, he's all pent up."

Oupa's experience of this visit contained another kind of pain. "When I saw my mother, my wife, and my children, I was shy. I felt I had embarrassed them. They knew that I have never been aggressive or violent. How can I end up in prison? When they saw me the elder child was crying. When I saw him, I did my level best to hide my hurt, my disappointment. I could only make the promise that I will be back."

Reid says of this first and only visit during his detention at Groenpunt, "When I saw my mother, she was a little bit thin. She tell me that my son is going well and that everyone is just waiting for me. She was very happy to see me because she did not know where I was and the police did not tell her where I was.

"She was with me for thirty minutes and she gave me some food parcels and then went away. I felt when I saw her if only I could get out and console her, because she was very, very worried. I felt that if the prison would release me, then I can tell my mother what the police had done to me."

Ja-Ja did not have an easy time at Groenpunt. And he had seen some things that horrified him.

"There was a prisoner, he was my front neighbour. He asked me if a person can cut himself with a razor blade, will he die? He was very unhappy there with the food and the treatment. The following day he cut his body and his chest in three lines with a razor blade. I was scared. I did not know what to do. I could not sleep but I was too afraid to call anyone. The prison authorities . . . they use a strait-jacket, they put many prisoners in it. I saw many people in it. It was very painful. Then, if the prisoner recovers, the authorities laugh at them. Those people could not move properly."

Ja-Ja had other problems too: "On my part there was a tension with Oupa Diniso at Groenpunt. There was a guy by the name of Koets. He was one of the gang called Big Fives in the prison. He was a friend of Diniso. He used to come to ask me what have I said about Diniso to the cops.

"My brother was also at Groenpunt. He was there because he was a pick-pocket. He informed me that Diniso told the people inside and outside that I am the one who pointed him out. I do not know how did Diniso get letters out because we were under intense security. The Big Fives would come to talk to him early and late in the afternoon. Oupa did not say anything to me all the time there."

Oupa was also a first-timer. He said of his Groenpunt cell, "There was no mattress on the floor. There were no mats and some blankets were in the corner. [The cell] had a smell of stale urine. The toilet is in the cell. The toilet itself was dirty. The blankets were dirty. There was a smell and there were lice in them."

The day after he arrived, Oupa complained about the blankets to a Brigadier Boshoff and the next day he and the others received clean ones.

All the prisoners and detainees objected to the food. Oupa was specific: "At 8:00 a.m. we had soft porridge and cold coffee. At twelve o'clock for lunch we had a quarter loaf of bread and powdered liquid [protein powder and water]. For supper sometimes we would get meat or fish."

The detainees took part in a hunger strike. (That was why Ja-Ja was so thin.)

Oupa says, "We did not eat for fifteen to twenty days. We drank water. It's terrible to go without food but I felt that I had to fight for it. . . . For the first few days you feel stronger because you make the decision not to eat, but later you get weak. We also got irritable with the prison warders and the security police. I did not get cross with other prisoners. In front of me the cells were empty. Next to me were convicted prisoners but I did not want to speak to them in case they passed on information.

"The detainees' inspector would tell us they would change the food, but every day I could see they didn't. There was one policeman, I think his name was Leibrandt. I think he was a lieutenant. He was a white man. He was in his early thirties and he spoke Afrikaans. He was a good man. He said we should get better food. Later they started cooking better food. We got fried meat, well-nourished vegetables, milk, fresh bread with butter and peanut butter. He also arranged with the security police that we should get one food parcel from our families. I liked him a lot; he was a friendly, caring man."

Of course, as a vegetarian Oupa missed out on some of the improvements, but his own diet also became much better.

❖

On December 5, 1984, when Ja-Ja, Reid, and Oupa had been in detention at Groenpunt for nearly four weeks, the police proceeded with another round of arrests. "Six white cops and two black cops" came at 4:00 a.m. to Joshua Khumalo's house. They were looking for his son Duma, who was there, with his younger brother Ishmael and an eleven-year-old nephew called Elias.

When the police took Duma away, this all-male household lost its emotional core, for he was the one who had held it together and made it a home. He did all the washing and cooking, looked after his father, and helped Elias with his homework. Twenty-six years old, thin and over six feet tall, Duma was a second-year student at the Sebokeng Teachers' Training College, and a breadwinner too, hawking clothing when he had time, to help his father support them all. And help was needed, as Mr. Khumalo was earning R55 a week, driving a light truck for Vereeniging Refractories,[7] where he had been employed for twenty-six years.

Duma was not told why he was being arrested. "They put me in the back seat of a car. . . . We then went to Theresa's place. They brought her and put her next to me. I knew her from long ago, from 1979 when she was a girlfriend of one of my friends. Theresa did not look scared. She said to me, 'We are here because of what happened on 3 September. . . . Don't worry, we will be back, they will let us go.'"

Duma's elder brother, Phinda, who lived in Sebokeng, called at his father's house as usual that morning and learned what had happened. He went to the police station to ask where Duma was, why he had been taken in, and when he would be released. As he says, "They said they didn't know and that they would inform us later."

Phinda met many desperate families during the next couple of weeks, as they searched for their missing people, who had been picked up around the same time as Duma. Then, he said, "The police sent a note after two or three weeks that Duma had been detained under Section 29."

Warrant Officer Schoeman was at Sebokeng police station when Duma and Theresa arrived. Duma says of him, "He asked me and shouted later, 'What do you know about the 3rd of September?' Before I could answer, he would always interrupt me. He shouted at me, 'Ons doen julle mense, julle fokken snakes. En as jy 'n snake sien, moet jy die snake op die kop skiet. Ons gaan jou toesluit en jy sal nie jou prokureur sien nie, jy sal nie jou ouers sien nie.' ["We fix you people, you fucking snakes. And if you see a snake, you have to shoot it in the head. We're going to lock you up and you won't see your lawyer, you won't see your parents."]."

Duma and Theresa were taken the same day to Vereeniging police station, and locked up in the cells there. Duma says,

"Theresa told the cop she knew to go and tell our parents where we were. Some of the police also smuggled our family in for a visit. When my girlfriend, Betty, and my family knew where we were, they brought us tracksuits and food, but I could not eat. I was too nervous. I had never been in prison before. Some of the policemen who had got our family in told me that we will be in for at least six months, while the trial was prepared."

Duma had company in his cell, for many other men had also been taken in. Theresa was alone in the female section, but, as Duma said, "Our cells were separated by a wall and at the top of the wall was a fence so that she could hear when we spoke. We tried to encourage her."

But no one could help Theresa through the next lap of her journey: "They handcuffed my foot and hands together on the way to Diepkloof.[8] I was crying. My heart was very cross. I asked them to release my hands. The warrant officer, who was white, said he can't unlock the cuffs because I will run away. I said how can I run away if the car is moving, but he did not let my hands go.

"After a long time we were in the reception. They unlocked the cuffs, then a black prison warder told me I must not be afraid, she will help me, and she said that if she gets a chance, she will phone my mother. This was very kind, because when you are detained, your family does not know where. She phoned my mother and my sister. On the way she told me that I must not tell other warders, because she is not allowed to do this.

"We went to the doctor and then I met another person who worked in the prison. . . . I knew her from Sharpeville. She told me not to worry and that anything I want, she will tell my sister and this will help me. They then took me to a cell. It was clean."

The other prisoners with Theresa were all political. All were in solitary, but at exercise they were together. "These prisoners were very nice to me."

Duma's first experience of prison was devastating: "I was put in a single cell. I was afraid when I saw the cell and when I heard the creak of the door behind. When I hear the door slam, then I just get depressed. Even today," he says, a few years and many cells later, "after so long, nothing has changed. When the door behind me closes, I become sad."

Suicide seemed the only way out. He noticed that some of his cell windows were broken. "I decided to take pieces of glass and started putting them in my mouth. This was at night. I had only been in the cell for a short time. The following day, I see when I go to the toilet that I was taking blood out from the back. I was scared of the blood."

Christiaan Mokubung had been picked up on November 9, on the same trip as Theresa's first arrest, and so had another young Sharpeville man, Gideon Mokone, only twenty years old but married and father of a two-year-old child. Both were at Diepkloof by this time, and Duma saw them during exercise and told them what he had done.

They were shocked. Duma tried to persuade them to join him in a hunger strike, but they refused. "I then asked them and some other prisoners to break my leg. I wanted to get out of this place with all my heart. . . . They tried their best to break my leg. I would sit down and keep my leg straight and they would smash a steel bucket on my leg. We did this in my cell, because during our exercise period we could enter our cells and others could come with us, if we wanted. It was very painful. They would close my mouth so I could not scream and someone pressed my back and leg to make it straighter. There were six or seven who were doing this."

Duma's leg was not broken, though it was badly cut and bruised in the attempts to crush it. But his anguish persisted, and he was unable to eat. It was finally his loss of weight that attracted the attention of the sergeant in charge, and he had Duma taken to see a Dr. Jacobs at his surgery in Johannesburg. Duma said, "I went there several times but he failed to tell me what was wrong with me. He gave me sleeping tablets. He was a nice man. He wanted to know about my case. He asked me whether I was worried. He encouraged me. He said, 'Look, Joshua, you are in prison, you must accept this. But you won't be there for the rest of your life.' He gave the security police reading material for me. This he knew I needed because I was in solitary and lonely."

In March 1985 many of the detainees in Diepkloof went on a hunger strike, not for better food but demanding to be charged or released. "After seven or eight days," said Duma, "the doctors came to investigate us. After a few days I became easily angry and easily irritable with the prison authorities. I also became easily irritable with fellow prisoners who did not participate in the hunger strike. I would get a headache every day but this also happened when I was not on hunger strike. I lost a lot of weight. . . . I could not remember things and I would only sleep for a very short period. I still to this day sleep very badly."

❖

The first seven to be arrested in connection with the Sharpeville case were detained, as we have seen, under Section 29 of the Internal Security Act. It is doubtful whether they themselves knew when they signed the papers that this meant they could be held and interrogated as long as the police saw fit; they could be kept in solitary confinement; they had no right of access to their families, private doctors, their own priests or pastors, nor to their legal advisers.

Five of them were held for six and a half months, and two for five and a half, and all were kept in solitary and denied access to anyone (except for the one family visit). But only Reid, who made a statement, and Christiaan, who, like Reid, was made to point out certain Sharpeville sites to a police officer, had any further dealings with the investigating team.

No use was made of the crucial facility provided to the police under Section 29, to interrogate detainees as long as they see fit. Each of the seven was questioned at Sebokeng police station on the day of his or her arrest, and after that not one was interrogated again. Their detention was purely punitive.

❖

Four months later, on April 10, 1985, seven months after Mr. Dlamini had been killed, Francis Mokhesi was arrested. His wife, Alinah, said, "There were five cars. But three whites and one African came in. They asked Francis, 'What's your soccer name?' He said, 'Don.' They said, 'We want you.' It was ten o'clock in the evening."

Francis was living with his wife and child, and his father and one brother at 7589 Sharpeville. He was a well-known figure in the township, because he played soccer for the popular Vaal Professionals – a very good-looking guy, not very tall, but solidly built as becomes a professional sportsman. The surprise comes when he speaks: he has an exceptionally soft voice.

He said, "They took me straight away to Sebokeng police station. There were many there who were arrested, in the charge office. I had been arrested once before. It was for possession of *dagga* [marijuana] in 1983. I knew why I was picked up. They asked me where I was on 3 September 1984."

Alinah was very surprised when her husband was taken away. And the police were behaving strangely, she thought. "They were polite. They were taking him to Randfontein for a few questions, then they were going to bring him back."

But they did not keep their word. "For two weeks I didn't know what was happening. I went to the police station in Vanderbijlpark and Vereeniging. I got sick . . . when I didn't know where he was.

"A letter arrived from Francis after two weeks, saying that he was at Krugersdorp. And that I should come to meet him there. The following day we went to see him. They said, 'Your husband has killed someone.' . . . I was astonished and couldn't understand."

Francis said, "After three days at Krugersdorp, they told me that they were charging me for the murder. So I knew about the charges. I didn't have a lawyer. I was very worried about this."

Alinah was not quite accurate about the two weeks that elapsed between Francis's arrest and the arrival of the letter. The interval must have been a little shorter, as we shall see.

CHAPTER 3

The Indictment

"Except for the names of the accused, the names of the other persons are unknown to the State."
FROM THE REPLY TO THE REQUEST FOR
FURTHER PARTICULARS ON THE INDICTMENT

On April 24, 1985, in the afternoon, the Johannesburg office of Ismail Ayob and Associates, where I practised as an attorney, received a telephone call from the police. Certain clients of ours were to appear in court the next day at Oberholzer, a small town in the Western Transvaal, not far from the deepest gold mine in the world and about a hundred kilometres from Johannesburg.

After the rent protests in the Vaal Triangle, the violence intensified and spread; the Detainees' Parents' Support Committee (DPSC) had been overwhelmed with requests from families to help find their vanished young people and arrange for their defence if they ever appeared in court. If these detainees were to be unrepresented, or if they had to accept a *pro deo* defence, they would be at a great disadvantage. Among the thousands detained at the time, only a handful could have afforded to pay for their own defence.

The DPSC had a list of law firms prepared to defend these accused, and tried to spread the growing burden among them.

Our partnership was on the committee's list, and we had agreed to act on behalf of a number of detainees held in connection with various incidents that occurred in the Vaal townships at the very beginning of the protest nearly eight months earlier.

On the hot morning of April 25, I drove down to Oberholzer. All my clients had been held incommunicado under Section 29, so this was my first meeting with them. There were the eight from Sharpeville, and three other sets of accused appearing on charges arising out of the killing of town councillors in the Vaal unrest of September 3, 1984. I was acting in three of the four separate cases (the Sharpeville eight and the murders of councillors Jacob Chakane of Sebokeng and Philemon Diphoko of Eraton) and representing twenty accused.

I received copies of the indictments, and went down to the court cells. My clients were very happy to see me and to know that they were going to be represented in court. Since their arrest, the Sharpeville detainees had had one family visit only, and no other contact with the outside world. They showed no signs of fear or anxiety at their impending court appearance, perhaps because of their long solitary confinement, or simply because they were relieved to be charged at last.

But I had to tell them all that the main charge against them was murder. They couldn't believe it. Each one exclaimed, "But I didn't kill . . . !"

Unsatisfactory as it was for all of us, I could only say we would discuss the whole question later, and go into the detail of each and every one's case, and in the meantime they should leave everything to me and try not to worry.

Nearly all the accused had family members sitting in the courtroom, waiting to hear what charges would be brought against their husband, son, daughter, brother, sister, sweetheart.

The court appearance itself was very brief. There was a gasp from their families when the Sharpeville eight were accused of the murder of Kuzwayo Jacob Dlamini. The subversion charge followed, with its two alternative charges of malicious damage to property, and arson.

In the indictment, the murder charge was straightforward: "In that the accused on or about 3 September 1984 and at or near Sharpeville in the district of Vereeniging unlawfully and intentionally killed Kuzwayo Jacob Dlamini, a black man."

This is South Africa: identity is established by name, colour, and sex.

The subversion charge ran: "the accused and other persons jointly and/or severally on or about 3 September 1984 and at or near Sharpeville in the district of Vereeniging acting with a common purpose unlawfully and with the intention to achieve any of the following objects . . . [to influence the government of the Republic and/or to intimidate, demoralize or persuade members of the public to do or not to do something] . . . caused general dislocation or disorder in the black townships in the Vaal Triangle in the districts of Vereeniging and Vanderbijlpark, or impeded or complicated the maintenance of law and order in the specified area or attempted so to do, or enticed, incited, ordered, assisted, advised, encouraged or procured other persons to do this, by committing one or more of the deeds or acts as set out in the schedule hereto."

The two charges alternative to subversion – malicious damage to property, and arson – alleged that the accused set fire to Dlamini's car and to his house, with the object of damaging or destroying them.

The Schedule to the subversion charge gave the State's version of the incident: what happened, who intended it to happen, and who caused it to happen.

1. On 3 September 1984 mobs formed processions in certain black residential areas in the Vaal Triangle which moved inter alia to the houses of councillors of the Lekoa Town Council. Concentrations of persons occurred in front of these houses. The accused were jointly responsible for the formation of a procession in the residential area of Sharpeville or they later joined the group or they had already gathered at the home of Councillor Kuzwayo Jacob Dlamini when the procession arrived there.

2. At the house of Councillor Kuzwayo Jacob Dlamini (hereafter called the deceased) the mob, including the accused, made noise and shouted in a disorderly way and threw stones at the abovementioned house.

3. The mob, including the accused, also set fire to the house with the help of petrol or similar inflammable fuel in consequence of which the house was destroyed.

4. The mob, amongst whom the accused, also pushed the deceased's vehicle off his erf [plot or stand of land] and set fire to it in the same way in consequence of which it was destroyed.

5. The mob, amongst whom the accused, assaulted the deceased by hitting him, by removing from him the firearm with which he attempted to defend himself, throwing stones at him, taking him into the street, throwing his body onto his burning vehicle and thereafter throwing petrol or similar inflammable fuel on him and setting fire to him in consequence of which he died.

The Schedule looked more straightforward than it was.

In paragraph 1, it did not seem to matter whether the accused were "jointly responsible for the formation of a procession" or whether they "later joined the group" or whether they had "already gathered at the home of Councillor Dlamini when the procession arrived there."

Paragraphs 2 to 5 merely described certain events. But the subject of every verb (the perpetrators of the crimes) had become "the crowd, including the accused."

Somewhere between paragraphs 1 and 2, the eight accused had lost their individual identities and acquired instead the alleged intention of the mob and total responsibility for its actions.

The accused were not asked to plead and the case was remanded for further investigation. The Attorney-General had issued a certificate that precluded our bringing an application for bail.

The forthcoming trial had become political, loaded by three factors: the detention of the accused under Section 29 of the Internal Security Act; the Attorney-General's intervention; and the charge of subversion. The victim was a deputy-mayor and the murder had occurred during a rent protest, but neither of these aspects made a political trial mandatory. That was the State's choice.

The other two groups of accused whom I represented – and the third group who were clients of another attorney – were all charged identically with murder and subversion and with similar alternative charges. They were also denied bail.

❖

None of the accused really understood what was happening. Francis said, "I was happy when I saw Prakash and he will be our lawyer. I never expected anyone to be there so I was very happy when he told us. I thought we would get bail. It was very painful. We were hurt very much by us not getting bail. The magistrate didn't refuse directly, he just postponed the case."

Reid said, "I thought that I would be charged for assault as I had admitted that I had stoned Dlamini. . . . I thought my mother would be my lawyer, because when I was arrested for stealing a lawnmower, my mother defended me. It was in a magistrate's court, and I thought she would help me again because this is also a magistrate's court. . . . Mr. Prakash explained to us what is happening in the case. I felt that as I did not kill Dlamini and I have a lawyer, the judge or magistrate will understand my argument. But I was worried because what if they did not accept my reasoning."

Ja-Ja said, "I thought when I got there I would be charged for the Malachia case.[1] I thought that I was being charged for being in the group. Malachia was a member of the special branch. They started hitting his house with stones. He tried to escape with his firearm. They disarmed him of his firearm."

When he was told he was being charged with Dlamini's murder, he was shocked. "I did not know anything about the Dlamini case. I was surprised because I was not there. I thought if we go to court maybe I would be freed. We got to court and when the magistrate said that we could not have bail, it was very painful."

Oupa also expected something quite different; he had not understood the charge. When I first asked him what his plea would be, if he had to plead, "Guilty," he said. "Why?" "Because

I was in possession of a gun"—meaning, of course, a gun without a licence.

About the murder charge Duma said, "I was greatly shocked, but when I began to think about it, I was also a bit happy. I knew that justice would be done. I would be free soon. This was because our demand to be charged was met and I knew that I would get bail.

"I was not worried about not having a lawyer, because our family had a lawyer. When I saw Prakash at the court he explained to us everything. Then I realized that it would be difficult for our family lawyer to take this case. I accepted him."

Theresa said, "I only knew when I got to Oberholzer what I was being charged with. I did not understand why they took me to Oberholzer. I thought they were taking me to court to release me. I was shocked when they charged me with murder. I asked myself why they charge me with murder. I know that I did not kill him."

She had no idea how events would proceed. "I was afraid when the magistrate said that I was being charged with murder and subversion. I thought I did not do this and my lawyer will defend me. I thought the trial would start immediately and then they will sentence us. The others told me not to worry, they could charge us but they will not sentence us because we did not do it. Then I felt much better."

Francis, who had only been away from home for two weeks, found it very painful to see his wife, Alinah, in the court. "I can't stand it, for so long being without her," he said. "My whole family was there. I had never been away from my wife for such a long time. During this time I use to think much about my child. Her name is Ruth Mamodise—the name means 'somebody who cares for animals.' My heart was very sore, when I think about her. I didn't sleep those nights and all the time at Krugersdorp and before Oberholzer. I was worried that my wife was caring properly for the child, because she was alone."

Duma had no visitors. "That day at the court was the most painful day. I will never forget it because some of the accused saw their family, but mine were not there. They were waiting for formal information from my family lawyer, but he never got any information from the authorities, and my co-accused, their parents had gone to the meetings of the Detainees' Parents' [Support] Committee. They had been well informed about their children and so knew about the court. The magistrate not giving us bail was another painful thing for me that day. My co-accused and I, there were tears in our eyes. Christiaan was crying and some of the parents were crying."

Theresa was very happy to see her family. "They were crying. I cried. All of us were crying. The police allowed us to spend an hour with them. They allowed our family to buy food and anything they wanted to buy for us."

After her family left, she overheard Detective Warrant Officer Schoeman talking to some of his friends, other policemen. "He said in Afrikaans, 'The bloody fucking coolie, he thinks the people will get out. They won't get out.'" Theresa understood what he said, and interrupted, "You must not say this. How do you know we will not be released?" (The group I was standing in nearby heard all this. Someone retaliated: "Don't say we are bloody fucking coolies, you are a bloody fucking Boer.")

Theresa went on, "Schoeman then said he was only joking. Then he asked us whether we wanted to see our families again. We said, 'If you want to let us then that is okay.' Then he went to call our families."

The four sets of prisoners from the Vaal Triangle were remanded in custody as awaiting-trial prisoners. They were taken the same day to Potchefstroom in the Western Transvaal, about 120 kilometres from Johannesburg and 100 kilometres due west of Sharpeville.

That was where I consulted with my clients, and we began to get to know each other. For the first six weeks, while we were preparing the case, I saw them every other day, except weekends. After that, when most of the work was done, I was there once a week.

It was very difficult to explain that they were being charged not with "direct" murder but with "indirect" murder; that it was not alleged that they had caused the death, but that they had been part of the crowd, associated with the crowd by one act or another, and were therefore individually responsible for the murder that was perpetrated by unidentified people in the crowd.

Nevertheless, I enjoyed these meetings. The eight from Sharpeville were easy to talk to, and all of them spoke some English or Afrikaans, so that we could manage without an interpreter. They were alert at most times and answered my questions openly and frankly. I felt I had their full co-operation and trust. They believed that when the court heard their case, properly explained by their advocate, that would be the end of their troubles.

If they were not too worried about their own position, the prisoners were extremely anxious about their families' plight. Oupa Diniso and Ja-Ja Sefatsa were the only breadwinners in their households, and all the rest were important contributors to the running of their homes. It was not only money that worried them. Young wives with small children were on their own to cope with day-to-day problems. Several of the prisoners had younger brothers and sisters at risk because they were attending school or elderly parents who depended on them. There was more violence than ever in the black townships, and the police and the army were everywhere, not necessarily contributing to law and order or the safety of the civilian population.

Now that they had been charged, my clients were no longer Section 29 detainees with no rights, but ordinary awaiting-trial prisoners who could receive visits from their families, food parcels, and clothing. None of their close relations had cars and the public transport between Sharpeville and Potchefstroom is infrequent and expensive. Fortunately the defence team was able to arrange for the families to be brought to the prison twice a week.

The seven Sharpeville men – and eleven others – were together in one cell. Some, like Reid, felt this had its advantages. "In Potchefstroom we used to talk to each other a lot. We spoke about what if this happens and what if that happens. It was not so painful there because we were together and we could speak to everyone."

But as Duma admitted, "Our coming together brought suspicion amongst ourselves. I did not know why I was in prison. I wanted to know who pointed me out to the police. Myself and Don [Francis], we did not have a good relationship when we were outside and because I was arrested first, he thought I'm the one who identified him to the police. So something like that can be more painful than even the prison itself. We could not talk openly with each other. We had to hide our feelings, we did not always speak what was on our mind."

The police had told both Reid and Oupa that Ja-Ja had said they had Dlamini's gun.

Ja-Ja liked his co-accused. "We were in this case and facing one charge," he said. "I thought they had been picked up like me and will also be free one day.

"And then, at Potchefstroom, my wife came with news that all the people outside said that I am the one who made Oupa to be caught. When his sisters used to come to visit him, they used to look at me badly. My wife said I must not say anything to him because if I do have a quarrel we will fight. I also felt like this because I do not like to fight, I then must leave him alone.

"The tension was there in the cell. We would talk about outside things but not about what he said. Sometimes even now there is tension. He would talk to others, but not to me."

Reid was also angry with Ja-Ja, for the same reason. "The way you know people are cross, because one person would not eat your food. Say, for example, Ja-Ja he did not want to eat the food from my food parcels. There was no physical fighting between us.

"I am not cross because he [Ja-Ja] confessed after being tortured, that he said I have the gun. I am cross because he does not admit this to me or to the lawyers."

Francis hated Potchefstroom. "I took that prison as a school. It learnt me the life of being a prisoner. It was my first time being in the prison. [He had not been jailed for his *dagga* offence.] I find that I had to teach myself to endure the pain that I had."

"This prison was very different to Diepkloof," said Duma. "We were put in cells with ordinary criminals. The blankets were dirty and the food was poor." That was not all. Within the prison he and his co-accused encountered gang rule, sodomy, theft among prisoners, corruption. Being young and nearly all first-timers, they were shocked and sometimes frightened. Years later, he said, "The five of us that are here now, each of us needed each other even then. We did not want to be separated. You can love and hate at the same time. We decided to form our own group at Potchefstroom and to create some discipline. We needed this, because amongst the ordinary criminals, there were many problems. People were being robbed of their watches and of their money and we wanted to get the watches back and to take them to the owners and by doing so, some of the other prisoners began to respect us.

"There was a gang called the Twenty-eight [a notorious gang present in prisons all over South Africa]. They planned to attack us. But one of them informed us and the authorities in the prison that the Twenty-eight gang would use weapons against us. So the authorities did a strip search and confiscated those weapons."

Complaints about dirty blankets and about a terrible stench met with a reasonable response, Duma said, as did a request to open the tuck shop.

"One day we refused to go back to our cells unless they would open the tuck shop. The tuck shop was always closed and we could not buy things there. Then because we did not want to go in the warders and the major confronted us. The others were carrying batons. One of us explained to the major why we were refusing to go back to our cell. The major understood our problem. He then told them to open up the tuck shop."

At the end of August 1985, some of the suspicion among the prisoners was allayed when further particulars were furnished by the prosecution. Francis could see then that it was not Duma who had pointed him out. "We could all see that none of us were to be blamed."

But when they saw the precise allegations against them, some of my clients realized – perhaps for the first time – what they were really up against. In Duma's case it was dramatic: "While we were still at Potchefstroom and before going to court, Prakash brought us an indictment [the reply to the Request for Further Particulars on the Indictment] from the Attorney-General. It said that I poured petrol while the deceased was inside the house. I then became very afraid. . . . Prakash could see the change in me because he immediately started telling me that I must not worry."

Theresa, of course, was separated from the men. She said later, "It was a prison like any other. It was clean. I was in a cell by myself. There were awaiting-trial and convicted prisoners that I was with. They were all right these prisoners, they would give me their food and when I got, I would give them. When I got there, my cell had a new sheet and a new blanket. The prison warders were good. I told the white prison warder that I did not have money and my lawyer will only bring me money later. She said that it was not a problem, I can buy from the tuck shop on credit and when I get the money, I can pay. And she even got me things from the tuck shop herself.

"I was feeling all right. I was getting visits twice a week from my mother and my sister Josephine. Whenever I requested boiling water during the night, they would give it to me.

"I was worried about the charge of murder but I wasn't so worried because I know I did not kill Mr. Dlamini and they would release me."

But she did feel lonely away from her co-accused. "I did not know what they were talking about, but sometimes when Prakash came, I would spend the whole day with them and we would speak."

❖

Morris Basslian,[2] junior counsel for the Sharpeville accused, had drawn up a detailed Request for Further Particulars on the Indictment, and the reply the defence team received from the prosecution shed a lot of light on the principles involved in the case.

Our request was written in English. The reply came in Afrikaans. This is not unusual in South Africa; both languages are official.

On Count 1, the murder charge, we asked whether all eight accused were alleged to have killed the deceased, and if not all, which of them. Our second question was, in what manner were the accused alleged to have killed the deceased?

"It is alleged that all eight of the accused and the rest of the group who assaulted the deceased on his property had a common purpose to kill the deceased, although he was not necessarily assaulted by all of them and although the assault by an individual member of the group may not *per se* have caused the death of the deceased."

Certain of the accused had assaulted the deceased, it was alleged, and in this manner killed him:

ACCUSED NO. 1: [Ja-Ja] threw stones at the deceased; hit him with his fist and grabbed hold of him in order to disarm him of the firearm with which he was defending himself; threw him over a fence.

ACCUSED NO. 2: [Reid] threw at least one stone at the deceased.

ACCUSED NO. 3: [Oupa] grabbed hold of the deceased in order to take away from him the firearm with which he was defending himself.

ACCUSED NO. 4: [Theresa] incited others to kill the deceased (she screamed that the deceased must be killed and in that way incited . . . , etc., others to kill him).

ACCUSED NO. 7: [Duma] threw stones at the deceased.

Counsel had asked when and where the common purpose was formed, if that was what the State was relying on.

It was "inferred" to have been when they gathered on the morning of September 3, 1984, or when they joined the mob that was at the house of the deceased or on its way there.

The State was asked to furnish the full names of each and every member of the alleged common purpose.

The reply we received to this question is fundamental to any understanding of this case: "Except the names of the accused, the names of the other members are unknown." In its deceptive simplicity it lies at the root of the tragedy of the Six.

No doubt the full truth will never be known, but it seems about a dozen names came into the State's possession. For whatever reasons, certain people were prepared to implicate certain other people. It is curious that citizens who lived and had attended school right in the area where the murder occurred, among the very people who apparently formed the crowd, were able or willing to identify so few. Or is it curious that anyone was named at all?

To me, as the attorney for the Sharpeville accused, it is impossible to find an explanation for the indictment of so few, if it is accepted that a crowd of at least a hundred people killed Mr. Dlamini. As for the members of that crowd who never came to court, I cannot imagine why all escaped scot-free, for however one looks at it, someone killed Dlamini.

The defence asked, what was the purpose of the "common purpose" and how was it to be achieved?

This, the reply said, was to commit the offences as set out in the Schedule to the indictment.

On Count 2, in which subversion by "the accused and/or other persons jointly and/or severally" was alleged, we asked for the names of each and every other person referred to. The same crucial response: "Except for the names of the accused, the names of the other persons are unknown to the State." And the same replies about common purpose as given for the murder charge.

Counsel asked what the accused and others separately and/or severally wanted the government of the Republic of South Africa to do or not to do.

The reply alleged they wanted the government to abandon its policy concerning black local authorities (such as the Lekoa town council); they wanted the councillors serving in these to be induced to resign; and they wanted these bodies not to raise service charges, in particular to withdraw the R5.90 increase that was to come into force on September 1, 1984.

In what manner was it alleged that each of the accused interfered with the administration of law and order, or attempted so to do?

They committed one or more or all of the acts attributed to them as set out in the Schedule, and so transformed a situation where calm and obedience to the law had prevailed into one in which unrest, rebellion, and violent offences were committed. Furthermore, they committed these acts against the person and property of the deputy-mayor of the Lekoa town council.

And finally, "the mob, including the accused, after being dispersed at a certain stage by members of the South African Police, went ahead with their action after the police had left."

We asked in precisely what manner it was alleged that each of the accused had enticed, incited, ordered, assisted, advised, encouraged, or procured[3] others to do something.

Theresa screamed during the incident that the deceased must be killed.

Duma handed out bottles of inflammable fuel to other members of the mob.

Francis screamed to members of the mob to throw inflammable fuel on all sides of the deceased's house. And he further "enticed, incited, ordered, advised, encouraged or procured one J.M. Manete to join the mob that was on the way to the house of the deceased."

Was it alleged that all of the accused set fire to the car and the house of Mr. Dlamini?

It was alleged that all the accused were responsible for the burning of the vehicle and of the house on the basis of a common purpose. In particular, however, it was alleged that Duma and Francis and other unknown members of the mob were responsible for burning the car, and that Duma had thrown inflammable fuel at the kitchen and set fire to it, and had also handed out fuel to others. Francis had screamed at other members of the mob to throw fuel onto the house and to set fire to it.

Concerning the Schedule to Charge 2, the State's version of the incident, we asked precisely where it was alleged that people had congregated. The answer was that it was unknown precisely where all the gatherings had formed, but in this case groups had approached the house of the deceased and had milled around in front of the house as alleged.

We asked for the full name of each and every person who gathered. "Unknown except for those of the accused."

Where had each of the people and, more particularly, each of the accused gathered? "More precise information than what has already been furnished cannot be provided."

What was each of the accused alleged to have done in forming or creating a gathering, alternatively, in getting people to gather? "The accused and others gathered in front of the house as alleged." Particular mention was made of Francis's behaviour towards J.M. Manete.

Was it alleged that each of the accused threw stones at the house? "Each of the accused had a common purpose to stone the house. In particular however the following accused threw stones at the house: 1, 5, 6 and 7 [Ja-Ja, Christiaan, Gideon, and Duma]."

Precisely how many stones was each of the accused alleged to have thrown at the house? "Unknown."

Referring to the reply implicating Duma in the throwing of petrol at the kitchen, counsel asked, Was it alleged that each of the accused poured petrol over the house, and if not, which accused were alleged to have done so? "It is alleged that each of the accused had a common purpose with those who threw petrol onto the house."

Did the accused push the vehicle off the property? "Each of the accused had a common purpose to do so. In particular, however, it is alleged that accused No. 7 and No. 8 [Duma and Francis] and other unknown members of the group were responsible for doing so."

Did each of the accused set the car alight? If not, which of them was alleged to have done so. "All the accused on the basis of a common purpose. In particular . . . accused No. 7 and

No. 8 and other unknown members of the mob were responsible for it."

Was it alleged that each of the accused assaulted the deceased? "Each was responsible through common purpose."

In what manner? Here the reply was the same given to our question as to how the accused were alleged to have killed the deceased, singling out accused Nos. 1, 2, 3, 4, and 7 (Ja-Ja, Reid, Oupa, Theresa, and Duma).

Who took the firearm from the deceased? "No. 1 and No. 3 [Ja-Ja and Oupa]."

Who dragged the deceased into the street, who put him on the burning car, who poured petrol over him? "All unknown."

We asked for copies of any statements any of the accused were alleged to have made to any members of the South African Police or to a magistrate, and details of any oral statements alleged to have been made by any of the accused.

"It is alleged that No. 1 [Ja-Ja] told Det.-Sgt. P.J. Wessels of the SAP, Krugersdorp, on 9 November 1984, that the deceased's firearm was in the possession of No. 3 [Oupa] (and pointed out the house of the above accused No. 3 to Det.-Sgt. Wessels.) (The State will rely on this statement.)

"It is alleged that accused No. 3 admitted on that occasion to Det.-Sgt. Wessels that he was in possession of the firearm (and handed it over to him). Accused No. 3 explained his possession of the weapon with words to the effect that on 3 September 1984 he had taken it away from children who were playing with it. He stated that he had not taken it to the police because he was afraid they would believe he was involved in the murder of the deceased. (The State intends to lead this evidence.)

"It is alleged that Accused No. 2 and No. 5 [Reid and Christiaan] pointed out certain places to Lt. H.J. Roux of the SAP, Randfontein. Photos were taken of the places pointed out and will be furnished as soon as they are available."

No videos, tape-recordings, or drawings would be relied on. The documents and photos mentioned above as well as a photo showing the damage to the deceased's house and car and also the deceased's body lying next to the burned-out car would be tendered as evidence.

Five months passed before a court was available to hear the case. We waited. About the end of August 1985, just after we received the replies quoted above, the eight were moved to Pretoria Central Prison, and there counsel consulted with them, with me in attendance, twice a week until September 23, when the trial began.

CHAPTER 4

A Statement to an Attorney

"These names were given to me. . . . "
J.M. MANETE

Something very interesting had happened in Johannesburg during the awaiting-trial period. On May 11, 1985, one Joseph Manete of Sharpeville called at our offices and consulted one of my partners, Mr. A. Soman. Manete had been referred to us by his priest.

Of course, when Mr. Soman took these instructions, he had no idea that Francis and Duma were my clients. The nervous young man talked and talked, and Mr. Soman wrote down what he said.

> **Name:** JOSEPH MANETE
> **Date:** 11/5/85
> **Address:** 2339 Sharpeville
> **Referred by:** Father Lennon of Sebokeng
> 2 hrs
>
> I am 20 years old and I am presently living with my aunt 65/3 Evaton Road. My permanent address is 2339. I am still a student at FUBA [Federated Union of Black Artists] doing speech and drama. I completed my matric in 1983 at Mohlodi High School, Sharpeville.
>
> In November 1984 I was arrested by the Security Police of Sebokeng. I was detained for two days and then released. I was questioned about the death of one of the Councillors of Sharpeville, a Mr. Dhlamini [sic]. I did not tell the police

anything. I refused. I was assaulted, I was pushed against the wall, kicked and punched on my face. The policemen who interrogated me were policemen dressed in camouflage outfits. I cannot recognise them now. I made no statement and I was released.

On my release I was told to report the following Monday to the Sebokeng Police Station. I went as instructed to. I cannot remember the date.

When I arrived at the Police Station I was told to wait for the Security Police from John Vorster Square [Johannesburg Police Headquarters]. I waited for three (3) hours but they did not arrive. I took a taxi home and I was followed home by the Security Police at Sebokeng. I went to Shaledi's motel and I played chess. While playing chess three White policemen approached me and asked me to go to the Police Station. I refused because I had already been there. They left me after telling me not to talk with the people. I was again detained in April 1985 by Krugersdorp Security Police. I was taken to Krugersdorp Police Station. I was assaulted and forced to write a statement about the Councillor Dhlamini [sic]. They wanted to know about the people who killed Mr. Dhlamini [sic]. I made a statement and I mentioned Don [Francis] Mokhesi and Duma Khumalo's names. These names were given to [me] by the police and I was forced to write these names in the statement.

I was forced to say that Rev. Moselane and other UDF leaders held meetings and influenced people to protest against high rentals. All these names were furnished to me by the police. I was questioned by two policemen and one was Schoeman. I was assaulted by the other policemen and not Schoeman. I was punched about three times on the head. I was held for a day only (about a few hours) and I was released after I made a statement as above.

Don Mokhesi and Duma Khumalo are still in detention.

It is possible I may be called as a State witness.

When I was detained in November 1984 the police took my books and poems which I had written.

BOOKS
1. Forced Landing by Mothobi Mutloatse
2. Cry the Beloved Country by Alan Paton
3. The Black Hermit by Ngugi Wa Thiong'o
4. Let My People Go by Albert Luthuli
5. The Trial of Brother Gero by Wole Soyinka
6. Things Fall Apart by Chinua Achebe
Also: 75 poems written by me.

The date Manete was rearrested and questioned by the Krugersdorp police, referred to as "April 1985," is significant. It was April 9.[1] The very next day, Francis Mokhesi, who had been going about his business undisturbed for seven months since Dlamini was killed, was arrested and held at Krugersdorp.

Joseph Manete came again to our offices in September 1985, before the trial started, with a subpoena served on him by the police, calling him as a state witness. Mr. Soman told him that the firm could not act for him because we were representing the accused and there would be a conflict of interest. Manete then consulted another attorney, Mohamed Suliman Bham.

So it had come about that long before the trial opened, the defence knew what Manete had told Mr. Soman. And it was also clear that it would not be possible to use the statement in court, unless Manete agreed to waive the client/attorney privilege with regard to the statement.

When he gave evidence, the defence was naturally aware that he was under pressure to implicate Duma and Francis, and that it was probable he was not telling the truth.

The judge, the assessors, the accused and their families, the defence team and the prosecution – all were to hear far more than they ever wished to hear of Mr. Manete, a victim like many others.

CHAPTER 5

Rents and Riots

"Trust me, I am your friend."
SOUTH AFRICAN DEFENCE FORCE STICKER

September 3, 1984, the day of the Vaal Triangle stay-away and the murder of Councillor Dlamini, was only a beginning. The year that followed saw protest and repression push each other to new extremes, so that, by the time the trial of the Sharpeville Eight began, the country was close to chaos. Black schooling and black local government had almost completely broken down, and the security forces were unable to control the townships.

The Lekoa council received no rent payments after September 3. The police descended heavily on opposition groups, notably the Vaal Civic Association and the Sharpeville Anti-Rent Committee, and many community leaders were arrested or went into hiding. So there was very little organizational presence in the area when the rent boycott actually began.

Two weeks after the outbreak of violence, the Lekoa council announced that the increases were to be withdrawn, but it was too late.

The rent boycott proved particularly resilient in the face of repressive methods. It was of direct material benefit to the residents, who consequently had a financial stake in its continuation. And the longer it lasted, the more expensive it would have been for them to end it. The result was that, whether rent-boycott "organizers" existed or not, in or out of detention, the boycott's own momentum carried it along.

The State, in its usual tragic way, refused to recognize that anger and inability to pay had set off the protests. Resistance was attributed to "lack of understanding of the reasons for the increases," and active protest was blamed on agitators.

All meetings in the Vaal townships were banned. The authorities tried to control the protest that was spreading to black townships all over the country by making sweeping arrests. People disappeared and the police denied all knowledge of them.

Just before midnight on October 23, 1984, the South African Defence Force sealed off Sebokeng, using Saracen and "Hippo" troop carriers, tanks, and helicopters. Then the soldiers moved in – about seven thousand of them – and in groups of eight they surrounded and searched each house.

"At about midnight I saw there were soldiers all over the streets," said a resident. "I never thought they were going to make house-to-house searches. But, at about four o'clock, they knocked on the door as if they wanted to kick it in. When I opened, they didn't greet me or ask if they could search. They just asked for the house permit, then walked past me into the room where my mother and father and younger brother were sleeping. They switched on the light and demanded to know who they were. Then they said, 'We have come in peace.' Before they left, they took a sticker and stuck it on a cupboard. It said, 'Trust me, I am your friend.'"

Another resident of Sebokeng said, "Early in the morning we heard this aeroplane [a helicopter?] with a loudspeaker, saying that we are your friends, trust us, and so on. People just said that is the mayor speaking in that aeroplane, that is Mahlatsi inside."

By sunrise, 384 people had been arrested and taken away. When the army finished in Sebokeng, it moved on to Sharpeville.

Soldiers stuck stickers saying: "Co-operation for peace and security" onto those cars and houses that had been searched. Pamphlets were distributed: "We are here to promote normal social life, continued education, safe travel, stability, a healthy community and the delivery of food."

At the same time police with loud-hailers were moving around, ordering people to pay their rent, and electricity and water bills; otherwise services would be cut off.

This unprecedented act of intimidation of popular opposition made world headlines, but it did not quell the violence or bring in the council's revenue.

The Minister of Police assured the public that the military action in the Vaal townships was justified, for "revolutionary and criminal elements" would be found. The soldiers stayed there for two days, but most of the people they arrested were charged with petty crimes such as pass-law offences, trespass, and possession of marijuana.

Only a fortnight later, early in November 1984, Vaal residents gave overwhelming support to a two-day stay-away called by Transvaal student and trade-union organizations. One of the demands behind the stay-away was the removal of troops from the townships. Yet, all over the province, more soldiers occupied black townships, urging people to go to work and to school.

In another attempt to defuse anger against the State and rein-force the buffer role of the black town councils, it was announced that these would acquire their own police forces, "to ensure the safety of residents, maintain law and order, prevent crime, and see to the implementation of council decisions."

The Lekoa council decided to employ 289 men, and in February 1985 the first 40 began their "training." The unit would cost the council – and therefore the residents – about R2.7 million a year. Very soon these *kitskonstabels* ("instant" constables) or "greenbeans" were unleashed upon the townships, and were particularly hated for their brutality.

During 1985, ninety-six black townships were invaded by more than thirty-five thousand soldiers of the SADF. In many townships they stayed on as an occupying force.[1]

At the end of March, all meetings of the United Democratic Front and twenty-eight other organizations were banned in eighteen districts for three months. In June, these restrictions were renewed for another six months and extended so that sixty-four youth and community organizations as well as the Detainees' Parents' Support Committee and the Azanian

People's Organization were prohibited from holding meetings in thirty areas.

But the violence continued, and on July 21, 1985, a state of emergency was declared in thirty-six magisterial districts, including, naturally, Vereeniging and Vanderbijlpark.

The Congress of South African Students (COSAS) was banned outright on August 28, 1985, because the authorities held it responsible for the widespread school boycotts.

By September 1985, all gatherings except sports meetings were illegal, in or out of doors.

September saw an explosion of violence in the Cape, including its white suburbs. In one week, 27 died, 60 were injured, and 238 were arrested. Schools were petrol-bombed in Natal, and between March and November there were 145 arson attacks on schools in the Port Elizabeth townships alone.

It was another year of funerals watched by hostile police and very often exploding into anger and more death. Counting and monitoring the casualties was not easy because of the restrictions on the media. According to the Minister of Police, the year's total of "unrest-related" deaths was 824, of which 570 were by gunshot.[2] Another source (South African Institute of Race Relations) puts the total at 879, of which 441 were caused by the security forces. "Necklacings" (killing by burning, with a petrol-filled tire around the victim's neck) accounted for nearly 200. There were 18,966 arrests for "unrest offences." More than 7,000 people were detained without trial under emergency regulations, and another 2,436 under permanent security legislation. Many of the detainees were under age twenty, some were children.

Against this background the trial of the Sharpeville Eight began. It was still running on November 2, when the authorities put a total clamp on the reporting of "unrest," and on November 13, 1985, when a mob at Upington murdered a policeman. End-of-year examinations were boycotted by black scholars and students across the country. In Mamelodi, near Pretoria, during a stay-away on November 21 in protest against the presence of the army in the townships, restrictions on funerals, and high rents, police shot into a crowd, killing thirteen people and injuring seventy-nine.

Repression in the townships was in the hands of the SADF, the police, and vigilante groups.

Father Smangaliso Mkhatshwa, general secretary of the Catholic Bishops' Conference, said the security forces were terrorizing township residents and the situation had all the characteristics of a civil war.

PART TWO

The Trial

CHAPTER 6

Opening Statements

**"I know the black people,
I think I know them well."**
COL. G.J. VILJOEN

A huge statue of Paul Kruger, last President of the South African Republic, and probably Afrikanerdom's greatest leader, stands on Church Square, Pretoria, one of the symbolic centres of apartheid. The old Boer president, in top hat and tasselled sash of office, stares stolidly across the square at the Palace of Justice, which houses the Transvaal Provincial Division of the Supreme Court of South Africa.

On the morning of September 23, 1985, Court C was full to capacity for the opening of State *v.* Mojalefa Reginald Sefatsa and Others.

The prosecutor was Eben Jordaan,[1] a neat, bespectacled Afrikaner in his late thirties, courteous and highly competent. He was to earn considerable respect from the defence team as the trial progressed. With Mr. Jordaan were various police officers and other officials.

The defence team was led by Jack Unterhalter SC,[2] a well-known liberal advocate with a long experience of political trials. Junior counsel was Adv. Ismail Hussain; I was the instructing attorney.

It was five months since the accused had been indicted for murder in the court at Oberholzer. There was relief among their families that at last the case would be heard, and it would be clearly shown that they were not assassins.

Sharpeville is 140 kilometres from Pretoria. There is no direct bus route, and at that time the train journey from Vereeniging was expensive and cumbersome.[3] Fortunately for the families of the accused, private transport had been sponsored so that they might attend the trial every day.

The spectators – friends, well-wishers, members of various political groups, observers from foreign legations – knew they must arrive early to be sure of getting a seat. The forthcoming trial had sparked a good deal of local and international interest in legal and political circles, because of the use of "common purpose" as the basis of a murder charge in a mob situation, especially in view of the penalty attaching to murder in South Africa. It was already evident that more was at stake than the fate of the eight accused, and that if they were found guilty of murder, there would be a precedent to convict members of mobs in many a trial to come.

By 9:45 a.m., the public gallery was packed, and local and foreign reporters filled the press galleries on either side of the court.

Just before ten o'clock, the eight accused were led in, and took their places in the dock, backs to the gallery.

The "Warrant to Summon Accused and Serve Notice of Trial in the Supreme Court of South Africa" (issued in Afrikaans only) gave the date of the trial as "23 September 1985 to 7 October 1985" – underestimating its duration by about nine weeks, as it turned out. There was not enough space on the printed form for the particulars of all the accused:

ANNEXURE[3]
Accused:
1. Mojalefa Reginald Sefatsa
2. Reid Malebo Mokoena
3. Oupa Moses Diniso
4. Theresa Ramashamola
5. Motseki Christiaan Mokubung
6. Motsiri Gideon Mokone
7. Duma Josua [*sic*] Khumalo
8. Francis Don Mokgesi[5]

Address:
1. 8055 Sharpeville

2. 8317 Sharpeville
3. 3842 Sharpeville
4. 8050 Sharpeville
5. 7197 Sharpeville
6. 7537 Sharpeville
7. 7589 Sharpeville
8. 8485 Sharpeville

Sex:
ALL MALE[6]

Race:
ALL BLACK

Age:
1. 30
2. 22
3. 30
4. 24
5. 23
6. 21
7. 26
8. 28

The Court Orderly gave the customary injunction: "Stilte in die Hof!" ("Silence in the Court!") and the judge and two assessors, Dr. Hertzog and Mr. Grindley-Ferris, both of them advocates, made their entry.

Mr. Acting Justice Wessel Johannes Human was seventy-two years old at the time of the trial. With the exception of a few years' practice at the Bar, most of his long career had been in the public service, as a State advocate, i.e., public prosecutor, in the Attorney-General's Department. Thus his experience had been largely on the side of the prosecution. He was appointed to the bench in the Transvaal Division in 1968, and had retired in 1983, after which time he had served as an acting judge.[7]

The trial, like many in South Africa, had perforce to be conducted in a multitude of tongues. All the accused, except Oupa, who is Xhosa-speaking, and Duma, whose mother-tongue is

Zulu, spoke South Sotho. The judge and the prosecutor, though proficient in English, preferred Afrikaans; defence counsel was much happier in English. All the white policemen and the district surgeon and other civil servants chose to testify in Afrikaans, most of them being agreeable to being questioned in English and responding in Afrikaans. The only witnesses, black or white, defence or prosecution, to choose English were Jantjie Mabuti, Francis's uncle Dr. Mokhesi, and Professor Tyson. All the other black witnesses elected to speak through an interpreter, in Zulu or South Sotho. The interpreters are always black when African languages are involved, and they are usually able to move easily among several of these, and in and out of the two official (white) languages, the languages of the Court.

> JUDGE *(in English)*: Who is appearing for the State?
> PROSECUTOR *(in Afrikaans)*: May it please Your Lordship. I am appearing on behalf of the State.
> DEFENCE COUNSEL *(in English)*: I appear, My Lord, for the accused with My Learned Friend, Mr Hussain.

All the charges were then put to the accused. All the accused pleaded not guilty.

> JUDGE *(in English)*: On all charges?
> (Interpreter: Yes, My Lord.)

Proceedings opened with formal evidence from the district surgeon for Vereeniging, the Town Clerk of Lekoa, and the police officer who was called to the scene after the murder.

Dr. H.A. Church, who had performed the autopsy on Mr. Dlamini, testified that the cause of death was either brain injury resulting from a blow to the back of the head or burning. Mr. Dlamini, he said, would have died from the brain injury even if he had not been set alight. It had not been possible to establish the exact time of death.

The Town Clerk of the Council of Lekoa, Mr. N.P. Louw, gave evidence to the effect that on September 3, 1984, the entire Lekoa area was in revolt. Motor vehicles were stoned, including buses belonging to the Vaal Transport Company, and twenty-five community councillors' houses were attacked and some burned. Damage to buildings, shops, administrative offices, and houses in the area was estimated at R13 million.

Moreover, people were still refusing to pay any rent[8] at all, and so far the rent boycott[9] had cost the Lekoa town council R18.4 million. Cross-examined by the defence, Mr. Louw confirmed that the central government was not subsidizing the local authorities, which were totally dependent on their own financial resources, ultimately the township residents, for there were no industries or businesses operating in the townships to shoulder the main burden of rates.

Mr. Louw conceded that the Lekoa council had resorted to a Proclamation[10] permitting it to serve garnishee orders on employers of people who owed money to the council. Most employers had resisted this demand, and organized industry had, in fact, made successful representations to the Minister to have the Proclamation revoked, to avoid massive labour unrest.

Central government, the town clerk admitted, was neither able nor willing to subsidize the local authorities. He testified, however, that it was central government's intention to move the entire population of Bophelong, possibly the best developed of the Lekoa townships, to Sebokeng at a cost of R30 million, because 32 of the 1,406 Bophelong houses lay in the path of a projected highway.[11]

On September 18, 1984, he said, the rent increases that had sparked the stay-away had been suspended. Later, seven community councillors had resigned. As a result, by-elections had been set for May 20, 1985, but no candidates had been nominated.

Asked about the current situation in the area, and whether sporadic incidents were still occurring, Mr. Louw replied, "every three weeks, they stone a bus or an office, but on an *ad hoc* basis – and I get the impression that it is no longer organized. 3 September was an organized thing, but the *ad hoc* unrest conditions we are getting now are very *ad hoc*, it's a low profile. . . . "

Cross-examined about the causes of the Vaal unrest, Mr. Louw had no hesitation in blaming politics rather than the service-charge increase: "And the R5.90 . . . had never been the crux

of the matter why there had been riots, because after 18 days –
15 days after the 3rd, the 18th – we have had a special meeting
and the R5.90 had been revoked,[12] but still the people had kept
on with the riots. . . . It was a political thing which had brought
the problem to the Vaal Triangle and elsewhere in the country,
up in the Eastern Cape. . . . It is the fourth cameral, the fourth-
chamber problem which had not been provided for at that time."

Mr. Louw was referring to the new tricameral parliament,
whose advent had so firmly closed the doors of central government to blacks. By "fourth," he meant "black." His words seem
to imply that the matter of parliamentary representation for
blacks, a "fourth chamber," had not been "provided for" in
September 1984, but that a year later, at the time of speaking,
it had.[13] Needless to say, it had not.

Lieutenant Bezuidenhout, then of the Vanderbijlpark Murder
and Robbery Squad, testified that when he and his men arrived
at Mr. Dlamini's house at 9:00 a.m., in response to a call, Mr.
Dlamini was already dead.

❖

The prosecution now called the first of its eyewitnesses to the
incident. This was Joseph Lekone, father-in-law of Mr. Dlamini.
He had heard that Dlamini's house had been damaged the previous evening, and arrived there about 8:00 a.m., on September
3, 1984, to find both front windows had been shattered.

Lekone thought he had been at the house for about an hour
when a "great crowd of blacks," men and women (too many
for him to estimate the number), arrived and began to stone the
house. They screamed, "Let us break, let us break, let us break
the house and set it on fire!" When the police arrived, Mr.
Lekone was standing with Dlamini, outside in the yard, urging
him to go away. The police scattered the crowd with rubber
bullets and *sjamboks* (whips with long thongs). Dlamini declared,
"I am not getting [going] anywhere. If I have to die, this is it, I
am dying here."

Lekone then fled to the house next door. When the prosecutor asked him whether he had heard a shot at any time during the attack, he replied that he had, once, from the neighbour's; it sounded as if it came from inside his son-in-law's house; yes, he said, that was where Dlamini was at the time, and he was armed. Exhibit 1, the pistol alleged to be Dlamini's, was shown to Lekone, who said that the gun he saw that morning had been "something like that."

Lekone told the Court how the house had been set alight, and how Dlamini's car had been pushed out of its garage and into the street, and turned onto its side and set alight.

Lekone saw Dlamini run out of his house and attempt to reach the neighbour's place, where he himself and his daughter had already gone for shelter. Then he saw him fall into "a deep hole or trench" on the neighbour's stand, where foundations had been dug. He did not see him being assaulted as he ran. Dlamini had blood on his head, and lay face-down in the trench, about two metres from where Lekone was standing at a small window on the south side of Maile's house. The crowd threw stones at Dlamini as he lay in the ditch. That was the last Lekone ever saw of him.

The crowd was demanding that Lekone and his daughter come out of Maile's house. Lekone fled. The judge asked him five times where he ran to. Finally he answered: home.

Lekone saw stones in the hands of members of the crowd; no petrol bombs.

When the judge asked him if he could identify any of the attackers, he said he could not.

Judge: Do you know these people before the Court here? Can you see them? Nos. 1, 2, 3, 4, 5, 6, 7 and 8?

Lekone: My Lord, I seem to think I know this woman. . . . She seems to be a person that I had seen about in the township . . .

Judge: But did you see her on this particular day in the crowd?

Lekone: No, I did not.

Dr. Hertzog, the assessor, asked whether the crowd seemed to be organized, and Mr. Lekone said it did, because "their protestation or whatever they said was the same."

The second State eyewitness was Stoffel Maile, the Dlaminis' next-door neighbour, of 7485 Sharpeville. It was to his house that Mrs. Dlamini and her father had fled, and Mr. Dlamini had attempted to flee.

Mr. Maile testified that he was at home on September 3, 1984, and observed certain things, especially from his kitchen, which faced the side of the Dlamini house. He said Mr. Dlamini came through the fence that separated the two houses, had no energy left, and fell very near his (Maile's) kitchen door – about half a metre away.

Mr. Lekone's evidence had been different, and cross-examination of Maile proceeded as follows:

> **DEFENCE COUNSEL:** He [the father-in-law] also says that the deceased[14] was lying in a trench or *sloot* [ditch] as he calls it, something to do with the foundation. You said that the ground was level upon which he was lying.
>
> **MAILE:** Oh no, wait a minute. No, no.
>
> **DEFENCE COUNSEL:** Is the father-in-law mistaken in regard to that, eh?
>
> **MAILE:** Very mistaken. I haven't got a foundation. There is not any foundation there.
>
> **JUDGE:** Or no *sloots* there where the deceased was lying?
>
> **MAILE:** Not at all, My Lord. It is a level *stoep*.[15]

Maile was nearer to Mr. Dlamini at the crucial moments of the incident than anyone, except perhaps Mrs. Dlamini. Yet it will be seen that many aspects insisted on by later State witnesses who were not nearly as close to the action were absent from his evidence, or contradicted it.

Questioned by the judge, and by defence counsel, Maile stated that he did not recognize any one of the accused. He affirmed that he had seen people pouring petrol over the body of Mr.

Dlamini, and burning it, and that if any of the accused had been among those people, he would have recognized them in court.

❖

When the Court resumed on September 26, 1985, the judge strongly rebuked the reporter for an Afrikaans-language daily, *Die Beeld*, for totally misrepresenting Mr. Maile. The paper had reported that Mr. Maile had identified all the accused as being among those who set Mr. Dlamini alight. Maile, as we know, had clearly stated that he did not recognize any of the accused. Junior counsel for the defence, Mr. Hussain, pointed out through Mr. Unterhalter that the same dangerously incorrect report had appeared in the English-language daily *The Citizen*.

> JUDGE: It puts his [Maile's] life in danger and [the reporter] must immediately correct it. If it is not corrected in tomorrow's *Beeld* I shall deal with him.

Later in the day the judge asked whether the reporter for *Die Beeld* was in court, and made him stand up. He was duly castigated for causing erroneous and damaging information to be published, and when asked, admitted responsibility for the appearance of the same report in *The Citizen*. It was incomprehensible, the judge said, that a reporter could have made such a mistake, when Mr. Maile had said, "I don't know any of them."

> JUDGE: I want to see in the papers tomorrow, in both papers, that this mistake has been corrected and that your apology indicates why the mistake was made. . . . Is that clear? If it happens again there will be big trouble.

It appeared the reporter had misunderstood the evidence.

Various policemen testified for the State. The most senior of them was Colonel Viljoen, the police officer commanding the

Unrest and Reaction Units of the West Rand division, which covered the Vaal Triangle.

> **PROSECUTOR:** . . . He is at this stage not yet in court. He indicated this morning to the investigating official that he had to make a quick call at the Motlakeng black township where there are problems, unrest problems. May I ask for a short adjournment. He said he would be here between 10:00 and 10:30. It is now already 10:30. So it should not be long. I hope it won't be long. May I ask for a short adjournment until he arrives?

Col. Viljoen appeared the next morning. His evidence provided the answer to a crucial question. Why did the police, who were present when Dlamini's house was being attacked, fail to take action to prevent the tragedy?

The colonel testified that on September 2, 1984, late in the evening, he himself had brought men from Krugersdorp and Roodepoort to reinforce the police presence in the Vaal Triangle, where serious unrest had already broken out.

On the morning of September 3, at 6:20, he received information that the lives of members of the force in Sharpeville were in danger and that they could not handle the situation. With reinforcements from Sebokeng, he went to Sharpeville.

At 7:20 a radio message came through that Councillor Dlamini's house was being attacked. Viljoen was not far away, and arrived there five minutes later, to find one of his vehicles already on the scene and a crowd of people running away from the house in different directions. Mr. Dlamini was in front of his house, in possession of a pistol, and said he had fired on the crowd. Col. Viljoen tried in vain to persuade him to leave with the police, arguing that a house and furniture are replaceable, but that a person's life is not.

A Lieutenant du Plooy was there, and he took the weapon from Mr. Dlamini and made it safe by unloading it so that it had no bullet in the chamber and would need to be cocked before it could be fired, for Dlamini was standing there, swinging it around, and the colonel was afraid he might injure innocent people.

Col. Viljoen then patrolled the neighbourhood to find out whether anyone had been hit by the deceased's fire, and whether a regrouping of the crowd was taking place. It was absolutely impossible, he said, to leave a guard at Dlamini's house because there were so many incidents demanding police attention. Also, in that type of unrest, no dogs could protect anyone.

The colonel could not estimate, even approximately, how many incidents occurred in the area on September 3, 1984, but when he had to put in a report, he said, "I calculated that every 11.5 minutes of that day we had an incident to attend to." He had been involved in the control of "unrest" since 1959 but this was the worst he had seen in his life, and the best-organized uprising he had ever had to deal with.

In cross-examination he explained that this opinion was based on the fact that certain targets had been singled out for attack: the houses of councillors, their business premises, the homes of police officials, and also the property of the Administration Board, which by then, he said, was called the Development Board. By contrast, in 1976, at the start of the unrest in Soweto, there had been no specific targets.

This was a very curious remark. The 1976 destruction was noteworthy from the start, even to casual observers, for its clear targetting.

Col. Viljoen was in the neighbourhood of Dlamini's house "with the patrols and so on" until about 8:56 a.m., he said.

JUDGE: But you could surely not see what was happening at his house?

VILJOEN: No, I didn't go and stand next to his dwelling.

DEFENCE COUNSEL: You cannot say whether an attack was in process at that particular time against Mr. Dlamini's house or can you?

VILJOEN: No, I cannot.

DEFENCE COUNSEL: You do not know.

The assessor, Dr. Hertzog reminded the colonel that he had mentioned negotiations he had had with leaders, and wanted to know who they were.

VILJOEN: There were a couple of clergymen involved and in the first instance, if I remember rightly, a black woman, but it was mainly clergymen. I have their names, but I can't remember them at the moment.

HERTZOG: Were they white clergymen or black clergymen?

VILJOEN: Black clergymen.

HERTZOG: Was it about the reasons for the protest?

VILJOEN: Just for a bit of background, when I drove into Sharpeville on the morning of the 5th, the community was running around with this peace sign. I know the black people, I think I know them well. So I inferred that they had something to say. I stopped beside a group where I was informed through a spokesman that they didn't want to fight any more, that they wanted to talk. This caused me to withdraw my members from the area, and to say to this spokesman that they must come together at a certain place where I would then speak to them. This place was near the council office in Sharpeville.

Here the prosecutor interrupted to ask the colonel to slow down a bit, as the interpreter–who was translating the colonel's Afrikaans into South Sotho for the benefit of the accused – couldn't keep up.

VILJOEN: There I approached the group and asked for a group of between five and ten with whom discussions could be held.

HERTZOG: Yes, now these reasons for the unrest, namely the rent increase, the question of the councillors who must resign and the police who must withdraw, did you get this information from them, or where did you get it?

VILJOEN: We got it from the group with whom we had discussions.

HERTZOG: Was it said anywhere why there was insistence on the fact that the police must withdraw?

VILJOEN: They did not say why, but they alleged that the police presence would cause there to be no end to the unrest. That was their argument. My answer to that was that the police would move out as soon as conditions returned to law and order.

HERTZOG: So in your opinion were these uprisings aimed, I mean against the councillors and the rent increases or against the police presence or against both?

VILJOEN: Not against the presence of the police. The unrest was simply the reason why the police had to be there. There was unrest as a result of which the police had to intervene.

HERTZOG: What I really want to know, was it politically inspired or economically inspired or both, in your opinion . . . ?

VILJOEN: As I deduced it, politically inspired.

HERTZOG: You said it was the best organized you had ever seen. Have you knowledge of any organizations that were behind it, or do you not know anything about that?

VILJOEN: I know about it. There were many organizations behind it.

HERTZOG: You don't want to name names?

VILJOEN: Not at this stage.

DEFENCE COUNSEL: I am sorry, I did not get the Learned Assessor's last question to which the colonel replied "nie op daardie stadium nie."[16] What was the question?

JUDGE: He said there were many organizations that supported the unrest, but the names of these organizations were not mentioned.

DEFENCE COUNSEL: I thought the colonel said "not at that stage." I may have misunderstood. Perhaps the colonel could perhaps say what he intended?

VILJOEN: Yes, the question to me was whether I wanted to name them, and briefly, I said no.

The judge now asked whether many places had been set on fire that morning, whether general chaos prevailed that day.

VILJOEN: Total.

JUDGE: And I understand that during the time you were there, various people were murdered there in the Triangle?

VILJOEN: Correct.

JUDGE: Black people murdered?

VILJOEN: Yes.

JUDGE: They were all councillors?

VILJOEN: Yes.

❖

The State applied for the evidence of four witnesses to be heard *in camera* for their own protection, as they would implicate certain of the accused. To support the application, Captain Pieter Kruger of the Security Branch in Krugersdorp gave lengthy evidence about threats made to witnesses who implicated parties in court, and about the murder of one such witness.

The defence submitted that there was no reason to fear for the safety of these people and that, in the interests of justice, the public should be allowed to hear their testimony, in case any person was able to rebut or contradict it.

The judge ruled that the public, including family members of the accused, would not be allowed into court during this evidence. Journalists were admitted, but they were ordered not to disclose the identities of the witnesses. Ironically, since the names of the four – Mrs. Alice Dlamini, widow of Mr. Dlamini; Mr. Jantjie Mabuti; Mr. Joseph Manete; and Mr. Johannes Mongaule – appear in the Court's judgments and the published Appellate Division judgment, which are all public documents, it is widely known who they were. To date, no harm has befallen them.

But the accused were harmed by the decision to hear this evidence *in camera*. For the Court seemed to them a fortress for the protection of these witnesses, a hostile environment instead of a neutral one, intimidating in the absence of their families. There was no one to check on these witnesses, no public to measure their evidence against its own knowledge of certain facts, and against common sense. There is a validity in the saying that justice must be seen to be done, and for the public, justice was being done behind closed doors.

CHAPTER 7

Ja-Ja

**"The streets were full of people
as well as police."**
J. MABUTI

Mrs. Alice Dlamini testified that, on the morning of September 3, 1984, she was busy clearing up broken glass in her house – stones had shattered all her windows the night before – when she heard a noise. Her husband was also in the house. Suddenly, stones landed on the roof, and in their backyard. She and her husband went outside and she saw a crowd of more than a hundred people, the nearest of them being about eight and a half paces away. Mrs. Dlamini heard some of the people scream, "We're after you, Dlamini, sell-out, who has a lot to do with whites – white people – and who eats with them!" She and her husband went back into the house.

When she went outside again, her husband remained standing in the doorway. She heard a young man scream, "He got me!" (the interpreter said this could also be translated as "He shot me!"). She said she did not understand what this young man meant. She saw her husband with a gun in his hand, but she couldn't say whether he had fired a shot, although she was very near him. When the young man screamed that he had been struck, the couple went indoors.

She went out again, leaving her husband inside, and saw that there was smoke in the house. She fled to her neighbour, Mr. Maile. While Mrs. Dlamini stood on the *stoep* next to Maile's kitchen door, Mr. Dlamini came out of his house, which was on fire.

MRS. DLAMINI: He attempted to come towards me. Before he could reach me, that is before he came to the fence, he was approached from behind by a young black man who grabbed hold of him, and a struggle ensued between the two for possession of the firearm. Now, at my small gate, the front one, there was a group of young men and women. While the struggle went on for possession of the gun, between the deceased and this guy, the young chap succeeded in getting the firearm from the deceased, but at that point some of the group who were standing at the front gate – that little group I mentioned – started to throw stones.

PROSECUTOR: Where to? Or rather, at what?

MRS. DLAMINI: You see, some were afraid, hesitant to throw stones, but nevertheless there was a young man, black, whom I noticed.

PROSECUTOR: Who did what?

MRS. DLAMINI: It was at this stage, as my husband tried to get over the fence, that this young man threw a stone that struck the deceased in the face. It made him fall down.

The widow said the young man was six paces from her husband when he threw the stone. She indicated the forehead or the face as the place where the stone struck her husband.

MRS. DLAMINI: After the deceased had fallen, some of the group jumped over into Stoffel's *erf*. I was busy getting the deceased up. The deceased called out, "Ja-Ja, what are you doing?"

JUDGE: Was he asking you what you were doing?

PROSECUTOR: No. To whom did he say, "Ja-Ja, what are you doing?"

MRS. DLAMINI: "Ja-Ja, what are you doing?"

PROSECUTOR: To whom did he say it?

MRS. DLAMINI: I was not familiar with that name. I did not know that person, Ja-Ja. I did not know who he was referring to.

PROSECUTOR: Yes?

MRS. DLAMINI: But that person who threw the stone that hit the deceased and made him fall, I am certain about him.

JUDGE: Who is it? Look, there are 1, 2, 3, 4, 5, 6, 7 and 8, which one is it?

MRS. DLAMINI: It is Accused 1.

PROSECUTOR: This Accused 1, did you know him from before?

MRS. DLAMINI: I knew him from before. I saw him often before. . . . Some days when I went to work, we were in the same taxi.

Mrs. Dlamini could not estimate how many times she had seen Accused 1 before. She said, "It was on various occasions, but I did not know his name."

PROSECUTOR: What happened after the deceased used these words, "Ja-Ja what are you doing?"

MRS. DLAMINI: It was then, at that stage, that those who had come over onto Stoffel's *erf* threw stones at the deceased and hacked him with stones. . . .

JUDGE: These were now the people in Stoffel's yard?

MRS. DLAMINI: Yes.

PROSECUTOR: And was the deceased now on Stoffel's *erf*?

MRS. DLAMINI: Yes, that was where he fell.

Mrs. Dlamini went into Stoffel's house and looked out through the dining-room window until Stoffel pulled her away and took her outside to where her husband lay near the kitchen. She saw that he was "full of blood" and that he had a "knife wound." His jersey was torn at the back. She went back into the house.

MRS. DLAMINI: While I was in the house, the next thing I saw was that the deceased was lying in the street.

PROSECUTOR: Outside the stand, or where?

MRS. DLAMINI: Yes, outside Stoffel's *erf*. It was near where the car burned.

The widow had not seen how her husband had reached that position near the car. But while she stood looking, some of the young men there picked him up and tried to throw him onto the burning car, but they did not succeed, and he landed next to the car.

The judge intervened to ask whether the witness recognized any of the young men who tried to put her husband onto the burning car. No, she said, it was too chaotic there. The judge asked what happened after that.

Mrs. Dlamini said she stood at the window and saw young men pick up paper, spread it on her husband, and set it alight. She could not identify the people who did this.

Mr. Dlamini had owned the house.[1] It was entirely destroyed, the widow said. "There is no longer a house there." She did not know whether her husband had insured it. Certainly she had received no payment for the damage to the building. She had been paid R11,000 by her insurance company for the clothes and furniture, all of which were destroyed.

Before cross-examination began, the judge asked Mrs. Dlamini whether, when she went outside and thought her husband had been stabbed in the back, there was anyone else near him. No, only herself and Stoffel.

Defence counsel asked whether Mr. Dlamini had alerted the police on the evening of Sunday, September 2, 1984, when his house was stoned. Yes, said the widow, he had phoned Mr. Louw, expecting him to pass on his message to the police: "It is bad. Send in security." But no help arrived that night.

Mrs. Dlamini's memory of how and when her three children left the house and went to her father was extremely confused. She thought her father had arrived at her house on the morning of September 3, at about seven o'clock, bringing the children with him. They seem to have left again on their own.

It was around 8:00 a.m. that she heard a noise, looked out and saw a crowd approaching along Zwane Street. Her husband wanted to go outside, but she persuaded him not to. "He was walking around in circles inside the house."

Later, when the shot was fired, the young man who got hit was on the corner, she said, of Nhlapo and Zwane streets, facing her house.

On defence counsel's suggestion, Mrs. Dlamini was allowed to take a break, for she had become very distressed.

The next day, when the Court resumed, counsel requested that the numbers be removed from in front of the accused, so that if a witness had been told to go into the court and implicate, say, No. 1 or No. 2 or whomever, he would not be able to do so. Counsel was not suggesting for a moment, he said, that this would happen, but there was a possibility. The prosecutor having no objection, the numbers were removed.

Cross-examination continued. Did Mrs. Dlamini go out and use her tap in the yard that morning? No.

Now how did Mr. Dlamini make his way towards Maile's house?

DEFENCE COUNSEL: Through which part of your house did he come out?

MRS. DLAMINI: Through the kitchen door.

DEFENCE COUNSEL: And can you tell us how he made his way to Stoffel's *erf*?

MRS. DLAMINI: Well, he came running.

JUDGE: But did he reach the fence?

MRS. DLAMINI: He ran up to a distance between the side wall of my house and the fence and this is where they grabbed him.

DEFENCE COUNSEL: A black man grabbed hold of him?

MRS. DLAMINI: This is where they grabbed him.

DEFENCE COUNSEL: They grabbed him? . . . There is more than one person you say?

MRS. DLAMINI: Well, firstly one grabbed hold of him, at first.

DEFENCE COUNSEL: You had a clear view of this, did you?

MRS. DLAMINI: Yes.

JUDGE: This man grabbed hold of him before he reached the fence?

MRS. DLAMINI: That is so.

JUDGE: Can you identify this man?

MRS. DLAMINI: At this point I cannot seem to see this person.

The fence in question, that separated Dlamini's stand from Maile's, consisted of three slack horizontal strands of plain wire. Visually, it could not have been an obstruction; neither was it in any way difficult to get through or over. It served simply to demarcate the boundary between the stands.

After the struggle for the firearm, near the fence, Alice Dlamini did not see what happened to the young man who got the gun, or where he went.

> **DEFENCE COUNSEL:** This was the only man who was engaged in the struggle with your husband for the firearm?
>
> **MRS. DLAMINI:** The others feared to get nearer. So it was only the two and they were in the struggle for the possession.

Then Mr. Dlamini was struck in the face by a stone thrown at him as he tried to get through the fence sideways, facing Nhlapo Street.

Where was the person who threw the stone at him?

> **MRS. DLAMINI:** I have two gates, a big one and a small one. Now my small gate is next to Stoffel's fence. . . . There was a young man at my gate, the small gate, quite a tall chap, this young one. . . . Before he [the deceased] managed to get his one leg over the fence to get onto Stoffel's *erf*, then he was struck. He was felled by this stone thrown by this tall chap.
>
> **JUDGE:** Who was this tall chap?
>
> **MRS. DLAMINI:** The first accused.
>
> **DEFENCE COUNSEL:** Now, the person whom you saw grabbing hold of your husband was on your *erf* at that stage?
>
> **MRS. DLAMINI:** Yes.
>
> **DEFENCE COUNSEL:** Have you seen how he had come onto your *erf*?
>
> **MRS. DLAMINI:** He came from the backyard. He was approaching the deceased from behind him.
>
> **DEFENCE COUNSEL:** So the Court is to understand that this man did not come through the fence or the gate on Nhlapo Street,

which I call the front of your house? You are saying that he approached your husband from the back of your house?

MRS. DLAMINI: Yes, from behind.

Counsel asked the witness whether – before the stone was thrown – she had noticed the young man who had thrown it.

JUDGE: Well, we know it is Accused no. 1 now, we might as well refer to him as Accused 1. Did you see Accused 1 before he threw the stone, or did you only see him at the time he threw the stone, or what is the position?

MRS. DLAMINI: Well, I saw him for the first time in that group, it was when he threw the stone.

DEFENCE COUNSEL: Now are you quite sure that the person you are identifying is Accused 1?

MRS. DLAMINI: I am positive.

DEFENCE COUNSEL: Can you describe how he was dressed?

MRS. DLAMINI: He was wearing a white spotty sun hat.

JUDGE: Wearing a what?

MRS. DLAMINI: A white spotty . . .

JUDGE: What is a spotty?

MRS. DLAMINI: A spot is a hat, sun hat.

JUDGE: Spotted?

MRS. DLAMINI: No, no, it is spotty.

DEFENCE COUNSEL: A spotty is a hat, you say?

MRS. DLAMINI: Yes.

JUDGE: He was wearing a white hat?

DEFENCE COUNSEL: A white hat. Did it have a brim?

MRS. DLAMINI: It had a brim. I did not notice the other items of clothing he had on.

This whole absurd interchange derived no doubt from a problem with the interpreter's pronunciation of English. His translation of Mrs. Dlamini's word was almost certainly "sporty," but to the white men it sounded like "spotty."[2]

The witness described how her husband mumbled something as she tried to lift him up, after he was felled by the stone. That, she said, was when he cried out those words: "Ja-Ja, what are you doing?"

JUDGE: He cried out?
MRS. DLAMINI: "Ja-Ja, what are you doing?"
JUDGE: You are not known by the name of Ja-Ja, are you?
MRS. DLAMINI: I did not know that name.
JUDGE: He never called you that before?
MRS. DLAMINI: No.

What was the position in which Dlamini lay after he fell at the fence?

> **MRS. DLAMINI:** He fell on his backside on the buttocks on the ground . . . in a sitting position.

Then, she said, when stones were rained on him, and she had retreated into Maile's house again, her husband was lying on his stomach, with his head facing towards Maile's kitchen.

❖

Jantjie Mabuti was the key witness for the prosecution. He was a married black in his late twenties, with a Standard 9 (the penultimate school year) education, and worked for an electrician. His house was back to back with Dlamini's, facing east onto a nameless road parallel to Nhlapo Street. A wire-mesh fence and the back wall of a shack in Mabuti's yard separated his stand from Dlamini's.

Mabuti elected to give evidence in English. He testified that he had vigilantly observed the occurrence of September 3, 1984, with the sole purpose of giving information to the police. He denied under cross-examination that he was or ever had been a police informer, though it was rumoured in Sharpeville that he was.[3] In any event the police called him "Jantjie," but in the township he was known as "Skelm" (sly crook), not an affectionate nickname.[4]

Mabuti stated that he had telephoned the police on the evening of September 3, 1984, and told them he had watched the entire incident and had information for them. The police had called on him the next day and taken a statement in which he disclosed the identities of six people he said he had seen performing various acts in the course of the incident. The six whose names he gave were Ja-Ja, Theresa, Christiaan, Gideon, Duma, and Francis.

This information about the behaviour of the other main participants in the drama was extremely interesting to the defence. The police first: if Mabuti was to be believed, they were in possession of these people's names for two months before they arrested any of them, and during that time they left the "suspects" entirely to their own devices. They did offer an explanation: they were under pressure because of the escalating unrest.

And what did these six people do with the two months' grace? Absolutely nothing. Those who had regular jobs went to work, the others continued to go about their normal business, all slept at home, none went into hiding. Police and soldiers were all over Sharpeville, off and on, and it was well known the authorities viewed the murder of councillors in an extremely serious light.

Ja-Ja was picked up early in November, questioned, and released. Why, if Mabuti saw him disarm Dlamini? And why was he given several days to pass the word to anyone he might have incriminated during his first interrogation? If he knew where the gun was, why did it not disappear after his first release? The questions must be raised, whatever answers may be imagined.

Theresa was picked up on November 9 and released the same day. She was at large for four weeks before her re-arrest, and she knew exactly what the police were after. Duma, who had also been named and seriously implicated, so Mabuti said, on September 4, had three months' liberty before his arrest, and Francis, similarly implicated, no less than seven months.

❖

Mabuti was up early on September 3, 1984. He walked from his house along his nameless road to the corner of Zwane Street, and saw that the streets were full of "police and people." There was a large crowd, he said, armed with stones, approaching along Zwane Street and singing as they marched. When they reached Nhlapo Street, the people moved around, screaming and shouting; picked up stones; and started stoning Dlamini's house. The police dispersed the crowd once, with tear-gas and rubber bullets, and left the scene. The crowd, or some of the crowd, regrouped after a short time and continued to attack Dlamini's house.

Mabuti saw Christiaan and Gideon in the group that was throwing stones, but he did not see them throw any. Dlamini fired into the crowd and wounded Gideon, who was on Zwane Street, at the corner of Nhlapo. Some people picked Gideon up and fled with him.

Many of the people withdrew to "the motor wrecks." This was the property of the Radebes, motor mechanics, whose yard was always full of cars, some awaiting repair, some beyond it. The Radebe house is second on the right, past the corner of Nhlapo Street, looking west down Zwane Street from where Mabuti stood. He saw some of the crowd "opening the boots [sic] of the motor vehicles and tapping petrol."

The next step in Mabuti's evidence was an interlude never mentioned by Mrs. Dlamini or Mr. Lekone. Mabuti said he went to Mr. Dlamini, who was with his wife, and told them to flee because the crowd was coming to burn down their house. Dlamini asked him to take his wife and car away, but Mrs. Dlamini refused to leave, and, anyway, Mabuti felt it would be too dangerous to be seen in Dlamini's car in the township.

Mabuti said he then observed Duma and Francis, together with others, pushing Dlamini's car into the street. Someone set it alight. Then, he said, he saw Dlamini come out of his house through the kitchen door and go around the back of the house.

He saw Ja-Ja, together with a group, tackle Dlamini and wrestle with him at the fence between his stand and Maile's for possession of his gun. In the struggle, Ja-Ja got hold of Dlamini's one leg and lifted or pushed him over the fence: "he jacked his leg and the deceased went over the fence." A stone then struck Dlamini on the back of the head, and he fell down.

The prosecutor asked Mabuti whether he had said Dlamini was hit with a stone as weapon, or with a stone as missile. The witness replied that a thrown stone had felled Dlamini, but he did not know who had thrown it.

> **JUDGE:** Where did the stone hit the deceased?
> **MABUTI:** On the head.
> **PROSECUTOR:** Point out – would you point out again, please, I didn't see. Where did it hit him?
> **JUDGE:** He is pointing to the back of his head.

Alice Dlamini and Jantjie Mabuti, the only two eyewitnesses who implicated Ja-Ja, contradicted each other fundamentally. If the evidence of both is to be accepted, we have to believe that Ja-Ja, hatless, went around behind the house, attacked Dlamini, wrestled with him without being recognized by Mrs. Dlamini, dispossessed Dlamini of his firearm, vanished, got hold of a sporty sun hat, and within seconds reappeared at Dlamini's front gate, found a stone, aimed at Dlamini and struck him in the face, causing him to fall. We also have to believe that, as Ja-Ja's stone struck Dlamini in the face, another stone from someone else in Nhlapo Street struck him on the back of the head, and that each of these was the single stone that made Dlamini fall.

The State was supposed to prove its case against each accused, the test being proof beyond all reasonable doubt. If any doubt subsists as to the guilt of an accused, he is to be given the benefit of that doubt and found not guilty and acquitted. This is elementary law.

Mabuti's evidence was the single thread running through the prosecution case. We shall have to return to him again and again.

❖

The State called Joseph Manete, also described as an eyewitness to the events on the day in question. There is no need to introduce this young man: he was the one who made a statement to my partner Soman four months before the trial began. Some of his evidence contradicted Mabuti's, and some was seen to corroborate it. What he had to say touched only indirectly on Ja-Ja's case.

Manete testified that Dlamini succeeded in getting over the fence and that, when people grappled with him, he was already on Maile's property and about to enter Maile's house. Later in his evidence, he said Dlamini ran out of his kitchen, reached the fence, put his hands on it and jumped over; this was not easy, as he had to wrest himself free from two or three people who were pulling at him.

Manete said he himself was standing at Dlamini's gate on Nhlapo Street during this episode, and saw a knife in the hand of an attacker who stabbed Dlamini several times in the neck. None of the previous witnesses nor the district surgeon supported any evidence of stab wounds in the neck.

Manete claimed that he had a clear view of Dlamini approaching the fence. Yet unlike other eyewitnesses, he did not mention the struggle for the gun at the fence.

> **DEFENCE COUNSEL:** So, I will then put to you again what I put earlier: having only seen that he [Dlamini] had the weapon in his hand and not having described as the other witnesses have, that there was a fight with him to dispossess him of that weapon, is the Court to understand that if other people gave evidence of that fight and you did not see that fight, those other witnesses are wrong in their evidence?
>
> **MANETE:** Probably that did happen without my noticing it, why, because he was surrounded by a crowd of people. Now I could not see the extra movements of individual people with the deceased in the crowd. I could not see through the crowd. It could have happened without me not seeing it. That is why I did not say or talk about it.

Mabuti, of course, had claimed that he could see Dlamini at this moment, and had given detailed evidence on what he saw.

We shall return to Manete later in connection with Duma and Francis, whom he implicated.

❖

Johannes Mongaule was twenty-five years old and had completed his schooling to matric level. He lived about five hundred metres from Dlamini, at house no. 7385. He was called as a State eyewitness, and seemed to be a reluctant one. At his first appearance, he said he could not give evidence, as he had just come off night shift. He was excused for the day.

The next day, Mongaule told the Court that he knew Ja-Ja Sefatsa as a fruit-vendor at the railway station and that he had worked with Oupa Diniso at Tubemakers of South Africa. He implicated them both as having dispossessed Dlamini of his firearm.

> DEFENCE COUNSEL: And you claim to identify Accused no. 1 as one of those persons who grappled with the deceased for the gun . . . you have no doubt about it?
>
> MONGAULE: There is room for doubt.
>
> JUDGE: There is room for doubt?
>
> MONGAULE: Yes, My Lord.
>
> JUDGE: Were those his words?
>
> (Interpreter: Yes, My Lord.)
>
> JUDGE: Do you mean to say that you may not be certain that it was Accused no. 1 and 3 who tackled the deceased?
>
> MONGAULE: Yes, My Lord.

Mongaule recounted events in a sequence that did not accord with previous evidence. For example, he said Dlamini was dragged into the street before his car was pushed out there and set alight. As well:

> MONGAULE: . . . [the police] kept on putting in an appearance and then the crowd would disperse, then they would start all over again . . .
>
> JUDGE: Oh, you mean the police came quite a number of times?[5] Do you want to question him any further?
>
> DEFENCE COUNSEL: My Lord, there is a certain aspect that has a general bearing and perhaps, with the Court's leave, I should do it.

JUDGE: You say the police came several times? Are you sure you were there?

MONGAULE: Yes. I was there.

DEFENCE COUNSEL: Well now, His Lordship has asked you a question: are you sure that you were there? You understand what His Lordship has said?

MONGAULE: Yes.

DEFENCE COUNSEL: You know that His Lordship, the judge, is here to protect every witness?

MONGAULE: Yes.

DEFENCE COUNSEL: It is for that reason that His Lordship, the judge, has ordered that this evidence be heard *in camera* and that your identity should not be revealed.

MONGAULE: I see.

DEFENCE COUNSEL: And I want to say to you, if there is anything that you want to tell the judge, the judge will protect you.

MONGAULE: Yes.

DEFENCE COUNSEL: Now, isn't it a fact that you were in fact injured by a rubber bullet and you were taken to your home and you do not know what happened after you were injured by the rubber bullet fired by the police?

MONGAULE: Oh yes, I did suffer injury, but I am not prepared to say that I was shot.

JUDGE: What injury did you suffer?

MONGAULE: I do not know, My Lord. Something happened to my right ear and the next thing that I was dizzy and dazed. What happened I do not know. Something must have hit me.

DEFENCE COUNSEL: And you agree, do you not, that the next thing you knew is you woke up in your own home?

MONGAULE: That is true, very true.

The urgent, disquieting question arises: if Mongaule did not see any of the things he described in his evidence-in-chief, who told him what to say in court?

> **DEFENCE COUNSEL:** You were arrested, were you not?
>
> **MONGAULE:** Yes, I was taken into custody. I was taken to Randfontein.
>
> **DEFENCE COUNSEL:** Do you remember sharing a cell with a man called Johannes Radebe whose name is also Zulu?
>
> **MONGAULE:** I remember him, yes.
>
> **DEFENCE COUNSEL:** Do you remember discussing your situation with him? And do you remember telling him that you knew nothing about Dlamini's death?
>
> **MONGAULE:** Yes, that is true.
>
> **JUDGE:** You did?
>
> **MONGAULE:** Yes, during conversation.

This man Zulu was a client of ours, an accused in the murder of another councillor. Monguale had told Zulu, when they were together in a cell, that the police had assaulted him and instructed him to give evidence to implicate Ja-Ja Sefatsa and Oupa Diniso.

Mongaule's cross-examination ended like this:

> **DEFENCE COUNSEL:** You see, I want to put this to you, Mr. Mongaule, your version differs in so many respects from the details given by others that it suggests that you have made it up or that someone has told you to tell it and that you were not there and you are putting in this version although you do not really know what happened. What do you want to say to that?
>
> **MONGAULE:** I have no comment to make in that regard.
>
> **DEFENCE COUNSEL:** Well, do you deny that it was suggested to you that you should tell this story?
>
> **MONGAULE:** No.
>
> **DEFENCE COUNSEL:** Were you assaulted while you were in custody?
>
> **MONGAULE:** Yes, I was manhandled and assaulted when they fetched me initially and brought me into custody.
>
> **JUDGE:** By whom?
>
> **MONGAULE:** My Lord, I cannot remember, but it was a number of white policemen . . .

> **DEFENCE COUNSEL:** Did you show the police where Manete's house is?
>
> **MONGAULE:** Yes, when they were beating me up I did that.

Mongaule was the last of the eyewitnesses on behalf of the prosecution.

For the prosecution, Mongaule was quite a disappointment, and they showed it. The police had brought him with the other State witnesses from Sharpeville to Pretoria, but after he had given evidence that day, they took their other witnesses home, and simply abandoned Mongaule at the court. He got a lift back to Sharpeville with families of the accused.

From the defence point of view, Mongaule was very important. The suspicion was developing that the State's case was not strong enough to stand on its own without police interference.

The judge found him to be a very unreliable witness, and attached no weight to his evidence. But he made the unfortunate choice of ignoring its possible implications.

One other piece of evidence implicated Ja-Ja. Sergeant Petrus Wessels of the Krugersdorp Murder and Robbery Squad, who had assisted Warrant Officer Schoeman in murder investigations in Sebokeng and Sharpeville, testified that Ja-Ja led him to Oupa Diniso's house in response to the question, "Where is Dlamini's gun?" The gun was found there, and the prosecution reasoned that if Ja-Ja knew where the gun was, he must have been at the scene of the crime, and he and Oupa Diniso must have grappled with the deceased for possession of the firearm.

There is no doubt there was a rumour in the township that someone called Oupa had Dlamini's gun. The police questioned many people, including Reid Mokoena and at least one other Sharpeville Oupa, about this firearm, before they came across Oupa Diniso.

❖

Ja-Ja's story was that he directed the police to Oupa Diniso's house in response to a different question, namely "Where does Oupa live, the one who plays golf?" He maintained that he did not inform them that Oupa Diniso had the gun, because that was something he did not know himself.

Ja-Ja's main defence was an alibi. He said that on the morning of September 3, 1984, he was in the Vuka section of Sharpeville, quite a distance from his own house, which was in the area they call Vergenoeg. Dlamini lived in Rooisteen, adjacent to Vergenoeg on the opposite side from Vuka.

Ja-Ja said he was visiting his grandmother,[6] Tante Sefatsa. (This woman was in fact his aunt, but it is not unusual in African society to call an older female relation "grandmother," whether she be cousin, aunt, or great-aunt.)

Because of the stay-away, no public transport was functioning, and he couldn't go to Vereeniging railway station, his usual place of work. Furthermore, he knew there would be no customers around to buy his fruit.

While he was with his cousins, at his aunt's house, they heard a noise and went to investigate. A black security policeman, Warrant Officer Malachia, was being attacked. They went to his assistance.

To support Ja-Ja's alibi, his story about Malachia was investigated by Mohamed Ameen Jassat, an attorney practising in Vereeniging. Malachia told Jassat that he was attacked and injured on that day and that he did receive help from some people, but he was unable to say with certainty that Ja-Ja was one of them.

When it was disclosed to the Court that Ja-Ja was going to say he had gone to help Malachia, the prosecution immediately had Malachia called as a witness on their behalf. Whereas Malachia Mmotong had had a very vague recollection of the details when he spoke to Jassat, in court he was able to testify that he worked night duty on September 2, 1984, knocked off at 1:30 a.m., woke up at about 9:00 a.m. on September 3, 1984, had something to eat, went outside the house at about 10:00 a.m., heard a noise at about 11:00, whereupon his house and he were attacked.

Malachia went on to state in his evidence-in-chief that "no one came to my assistance," later changing that to, "I do not know if anyone tried to help me." Under cross-examination he admitted that he had had a terrifying experience, but denied that Tante Sefatsa, Ja-Ja's "grandmother," wiped the blood off his face. Arrogantly, he said he had forgotten nothing. He also stated that Jassat had not questioned him about times, which of course was absurd, for time was of the greatest importance to Ja-Ja's alibi.

Under pressure in cross-examination, Malachia admitted that "some of this group helped me to my house where I lay on the grass." But soon after that, not wanting to make any concessions to the defence, he stated that "nobody helped me get back to my house."

Tante Sefatsa and her son Dokki (Ja-Ja's aunt and his cousin), Piet Phamotse (known as "Peks"), and Stoffel Heqwa were called to support Ja-Ja in his alibi defence. All of them testified that they had helped Malachia to fend off his attackers, and that Ja-Ja had been one of their group and had also helped.

Sometimes, because of linguistic confusion, people spoke at cross-purposes in this trial. We have already seen evidence of this in connection with a sun hat. But sometimes, when people were at cross-purposes, it was not because of linguistic confusion.

Piet Phamotse's evidence, given in South Sotho through an interpreter, started like this:

> **DEFENCE COUNSEL:** Do you also have the nickname "Peks"?
> **PIET PHAMOTSE:** Yes.
> **JUDGE:** Do you know what "Peks" stands for?
> **PIET PHAMOTSE:** It is an abbreviation of Phamotse.
> **JUDGE:** It is the Latin for "peace."
> **PIET PHAMOTSE:** Yes.

Only then could counsel proceed.

On a less amusing note, during Peks's cross-examination, this occurred:

> PROSECUTOR: Who are these "we" who now took him [Malachia] to Malachia's house?
>
> PIET PHAMOTSE: Hoffman Theme, Dokki Sefatsa, Stoffel, Machwachwa,[7] and Ja-Ja.
>
> PROSECUTOR: Five people?
>
> PIET PHAMOTSE: It was me . . .
>
> JUDGE: Yes, well, he has named five people: Hoffman, Dokki, Stoffel, Machwachwa, and him, that is five.
>
> DEFENCE COUNSEL: And Ja-Ja.
>
> JUDGE: And Ja-Ja.
>
> PROSECUTOR: Yes, go on.
>
> JUDGE: Six.
>
> PIET PHAMOTSE: We were six.

Not long after this exchange, Peks was shown a statement he had made on September 13, 1984; it had been taken down by a policeman at Sebokeng. The prosecutor, a polite and self-controlled man, did not mince his words about the policeman's performance: "My Lord, I took the liberty of having it [the statement] typed this morning, because I had terrible difficulty in deciphering it. . . . There is a typing error here and there which I shall point out to the Court, but it is much more legible than it was, for it was hideously badly written [*geweldig lelik geskrywe*]. . . . "

Peks's appearances were littered with minor incidents. During re-examination, defence counsel asked him whether he and his two friends were together when they made their statements, or whether each was taken away separately to make his statement privately to the policeman.

> PIET PHAMOTSE: . . . the three of us were before each policeman and the policeman was taking a statement of each and every one of us.
>
> JUDGE: The same policeman or different policemen?
>
> PIET PHAMOTSE: Three different policemen.
>
> JUDGE: Who are the three of you?
>
> PIET PHAMOTSE:: Hoffman Theme, Dokki Sefatsa, and Piet Phamotse.

JUDGE: And ourself?[8]

PIET PHAMOTSE: I am Piet Phamotse, yes.

Ja-Ja said that after helping Malachia, he heard about Dlamini being attacked, and went to Nhlapo Street, but when he got there everything was over and the police had been on the scene for some time.

CHAPTER 8

Reid

**"In those days I was a small guy.
I did not know anything."**
REID MALEBO MOKOENA

The only evidence against Reid Mokoena was his own, the confession that he made to a magistrate on November 21, 1984. No eyewitness placed him at the scene of the crime, and no one directly linked him with the murder.

Reid challenged the admissibility of his confession on the grounds that it was not made freely and voluntarily, but extracted from him under duress. This challenge constituted the substance of a trial-within-a-trial.

In a trial-within-a-trial, the roles played in the main trial are reversed. The prosecution has to defend itself against an allegation made by the defendant. Therefore the defendant's case is put first, and the prosecution's case must answer it. The defendant has to establish – on a balance of probability – that his allegation is valid. It is common practice in our courts to deal with a challenge to certain evidence by conducting a trial-within-a-trial.

When the prosecutor called Mr. John Leonard Muller, the Vanderbijlpark magistrate who had taken the statements of certain prisoners from Groenpunt Prison on November 21, 1984, he informed the Court that there would be a trial-within-a-trial, but that the magistrate would not be giving evidence on that aspect. He would have been called later if he had not wanted to go on holiday.

Mr. Muller's evidence began with confirmation that the interpreter on duty on November 21, 1984, was an experienced one. The judge intervened immediately:

JUDGE: Aren't you going ahead with the – the assessors are sitting with me.

PROSECUTOR: Yes, My Lord.

JUDGE: And I decide to hear argument on the admissibility of these statements, it can just as well – have you any objection to the assessors being with me?

[Defence counsel had no objection.]

JUDGE: Why can't we hear the contents of the statement now?

DEFENCE COUNSEL: That, My Lord, is challenged.

JUDGE: Well, you can challenge it, yes, but that does not prohibit the State from tendering the contents of the statement now because it is not going to be a secret to us.

At this point defence counsel informed the Court that the challenge of the contents of the statement made by Reid Mokoena would take place with the trial-within-a-trial.

JUDGE: Well, you say if it is admissible. If we rule that it is admissible you will have no objection to the State Prosecutor reading the statement instead of the magistrate?

Defence counsel pointed out that the magistrate was going on holiday, so he would hardly insist he read it.

Mr. Muller then testified that on November 21, 1984, at 12:00 noon at Vanderbijlpark there had appeared before him,[1] in the presence of T.E. Nazo, an interpreter, and no one else, Malebo Reid Mokoena, a black man aged twenty-one, apparently of sound mind. After warning him that he was not obliged to make any statement, Mr. Muller had asked Reid all the mandatory questions, notably:

"Were you assaulted or forced by any person with the purpose of influencing you to make a statement?

"Were you encouraged by any person to make a statement?

"Were any promises made to you in order to influence you to make a statement?"

To all these, Reid had answered, "No."

In cross-examination, counsel asked Mr. Muller whether he felt that these questions were adequate safeguards to establish that the deponent of a statement was indeed making it freely and voluntarily. Supposing a policeman had warned a prisoner not to say he had been coerced into making a statement, and supposing that policeman had added that anything the prisoner said to the magistrate would be read by the police, how would the magistrate satisfy himself that a "No" to these questions was a true response?

MULLER: I don't know what the police do beforehand and what they do afterwards, but experience has taught me to look at the man who is [to make] the statement, I look whether he has any marks on his face or whatever. If he has I note it on my statement and if he has not then naturally I don't note it, but if I notice that he has in fact got marks then I'll note it.

And if the prisoner had been assaulted in a way that left no visible marks, what guarantee would the magistrate have that he had not been threatened after an assault?

MULLER: No well, I haven't got it, a guarantee of that, but as I say according to the questions I ask him – I just go according to the questions that I ask him.

DEFENCE COUNSEL: In other words you accept what he says even though he may be lying to you?

MULLER: That can be, yes.

DEFENCE COUNSEL: It is for that reason I am putting it to you that it is an inadequate system for testing the – for satisfying yourself . . .

JUDGE: But surely you are not suggesting that the witness who takes the statement, he must investigate what had happened to this man whilst he was in custody of the police? Surely that is not his function?

Counsel persisted, asking what could be done about a prisoner who had received electric shocks that left no mark, and who had been threatened that if he told the magistrate about the shocks he would get more of the same treatment.

The judge intervened again, saying the magistrate would not know whether the person before him had been shocked or threatened by the police.

Counsel asked Mr. Muller whether it had occurred to him that the people[2] he had before him had been in police custody for twelve days, and that any injuries they might have sustained at the beginning of their detention could well have disappeared by this time.

> **MULLER:** It could be so, My Lord, I don't know.
> **DEFENCE COUNSEL:** No, the thought did not cross your mind?
> **MULLER:** No, no.

Counsel asked for the name of the inspector of detainees operating in his area, and in particular at Groenpunt Prison. Mr. Muller did not know. Neither could he say which magistrate would visit prisoners at Groenpunt, for that was under Vereeniging's jurisdiction.

The magistrate would be aware, counsel said, that an accused who was going back to the police, knowing they would read what he had said, could be afraid to tell him anything that had happened to him. Had Mr. Muller thought of finding out from the inspector of detainees and the magistrate whether they had received any complaints of assault from that particular accused, before he took his statement?

> **MULLER:** I did not consider it necessary, My Lord.
> **JUDGE:** No, this Court has to decide whether the statements
> were made freely and voluntarily, not this witness.

The judge defended the magistrate through a few more interchanges. Then counsel asked Muller why he had not thought the precaution he had suggested would be a wise one to take, and he replied, "My Lord, I only do the necessary which is permitted to me to do." Again the judge intervened, and there followed an extraordinary duet:

JUDGE: Is it your duty?

MULLER: It is only my duty . . .

JUDGE: To start an investigation whether he was or was not indeed assaulted?

MULLER: It is not my duty.

JUDGE: If he says to you, "I was not assaulted," is it your duty?

MULLER: It is not my duty to . . .

JUDGE: To institute further investigation . . .

MULLER: Not to institute investigation.

JUDGE: To institute a great investigation whether he was assaulted or not, is that your duty?

MULLER: It is not my duty.

DEFENCE COUNSEL: . . . to satisfy yourself so that the Court can be satisfied that the statement made to you is freely and voluntarily given. Do you agree that that is primarily your task?

MULLER: My Lord, it is my duty, and after I have asked him these questions, I don't then see that I should make enquiries at a prison or at the investigating officer's – to include that too.

DEFENCE COUNSEL: But why not? . . .

MULLER: It is my duty to ask him this set of questions, which I did indeed do, and to look whether he has any signs of assault, and I did that, and I cannot see what else I must do.

JUDGE: If an accused, if a man who wants to make a statement before you says he was indeed assaulted by the police, will you go ahead with the taking of that statement?

MULLER: I will note it and I will not go ahead with the statement.

Counsel asked why one of the people making a declaration was recorded as "Reit Malevo Mokoena" when in fact the name in the charge sheet was "Reid Malebo Mokoena."

MULLER: I can't say. That is how I got it and wrote it.

JUDGE: Who gave you the name?

MULLER: The interpreter.

Mr. Nazo, the interpreter, confirmed that he had translated Reid's statement, and translated it back to him after it had been taken down.

To support Reid's allegation of coercion, the defence announced its intention to call other assault victims, whereupon the judge remarked, "But then we will be here for years." He need not have worried, however, for only Ja-Ja and Theresa were asked to testify; they alleged similar police assaults at the same time and place.

The Trial-Within-a-Trial

"No, My Lord, I am very frightened of electricity."
WARRANT OFFICER P.S. SCHOEMAN

The trial-within-a-trial began on October 18, 1985, and ended on October 29, 1985, when the judge gave his ruling.

Reid's evidence was that on November 9, 1984, at about 4:00 a.m., a knocking on the window woke him up. Two policemen, one black and one white, came into the bedroom he shared with his older brother. The white one, Detective Warrant Officer Schoeman, slapped his face and asked where Dlamini's firearm was. Reid did not know. Did he know Ja-Ja? Yes. Well, Ja-Ja had said Reid had the firearm.

Sergeant Matunzi punched Reid on the right ear and asked him where the firearm was. Reid said he did not know anything about it. Matunzi hit him for the second time with his clenched fist, causing Reid to stagger.

All this happened in the presence of Reid's mother, Leah; his elder brother Phillip; and his younger sister Martha, who gave evidence in support of Reid.

Reid was hustled out to a waiting car, where he found Theresa in the back seat. He got in and sat between her and Matunzi.

Schoeman drove, and another black policeman sat in front with him. Matunzi continued to ask Reid about Dlamini's gun, and Reid said he knew nothing about it. Matunzi hit him on the mouth with his right elbow, and then on the knees with his torch. Schoeman slowed down, and told Matunzi that Reid had better tell the truth, there and then, about the whereabouts of the firearm, for they would not be able to go back later to find it. But, of course, Reid could not oblige.

They went to the mortuary at Sebokeng, where extra accommodation had been made available to the police, for since early September the police station next door had been overburdened and overcrowded. In an office, Reid saw Ja-Ja standing against the wall. Matunzi asked if he knew him, and Reid said he did.

> REID: . . . When I was pulled to the second office it was Schoeman with us and Matunzi was with us. Matunzi was still holding me behind my neck by my clothing. . . . There was nobody else in the room when I entered the room. There were a wooden table and chairs, also of wood. Matunzi then asked me to sit down. I was then told to turn my chair away from the table, so that it does not face the table. I was then looking at the door, sitting on this chair. At that stage Schoeman and Matunzi were to my back. A white rag was then tied around my face, mouth and around my nose. Whilst seated I felt something hot getting onto my body [indicates] behind my shoulders. . . . It was something like wire. . . . It was something that made me shaking as if I was trembling. . . . Whilst I was burnt this way I was continuously asked the question "Where is Dlamini's firearm?" I could not speak at that stage because the cloth was round my mouth. I then indicated by lifting my arms up and down that I know nothing. I tried to get these burning things off my shoulder, but my arms were turned away from my shoulder. This burning feeling took quite a while on my body. When they stopped choking me I fell down.
>
> DEFENCE COUNSEL: Do you say choking or shocking? I am not sure.
>
> (Interpreter: He used the word choking.)

DEFENCE COUNSEL: Oh, I see. Shocking and choking is the same word, is it?

(Interpreter: As the Court pleases.)

JUDGE: I was choking.

DEFENCE COUNSEL: But by that do you mean shock?

REID: I mean shock.

Reid said he fell off the chair when the shocks ceased, and Matunzi kicked him and asked again where the firearm was. Then he noticed that a policeman they called Piet (this was Detective Sergeant Petrus Wessels) was also present.

Schoeman left, apparently to fetch Ja-Ja from somewhere nearby, and the next encounter was in a passage.

REID: . . . Schoeman and Accused no. 1 came towards me from the front. When we were almost near each other – whilst we were near each other Matunzi still held me behind my neck by my clothing and Schoeman then held Accused no. 1 behind his neck by his clothing. . . . Our heads were bumped three times against each other.

Farther along the passage, Reid said, Matunzi pushed him into a hole in the wall, near the fire hose, and asked again about Dlamini's gun. Reid knew no more of it then than he ever had before, and said so. Matunzi punched him in the stomach.

The constant questioning and manhandling of Reid in connection with the whereabouts of Dlamini's firearm, at a time when the police were about to find it at Oupa's house (and allege that Ja-Ja had led them to it), is relevant to the case of all three of them.

Reid did not know, at about eight or nine o'clock in the morning when he was taken with various other men to Vereeniging police station, that Oupa's presence among them signified the gun had been found.

Soon after they arrived, Schoeman called Reid into a room where he saw Sergeant Piet Wessels and two black policemen.

REID: He told me that I did hit Dlamini on his back with a stone, and that I put his house on fire.

DEFENCE COUNSEL: What did you say in reply to that?

REID: I denied that.

DEFENCE COUNSEL: Did anything happen when you denied it?

REID: Piet then struck me with his clenched fist . . .

Reid described how he fell forward onto Schoeman, who lifted him up. Reid by this stage was extremely frightened.

DEFENCE COUNSEL: Following on your fear, did you do or say anything?

REID: I then admitted that I did throw a stone at Dlamini and I did put his house on fire.

What Schoeman wrote down then was not read back to Reid, nor did Reid sign anything. He waited in another room, under strict instructions not to say a word to anybody. Schoeman called him in again, and asked him again what he had done on September 3.

REID: When I told him what I did he denied it, Schoeman. He said to me, "You did throw a stone at Dlamini and you did put his house on fire."

JUDGE: But I thought you had already admitted that?

REID: Yes.

JUDGE: So why did he want to hear it again? Did you think it sounded better to him?

REID: I believed so.

DEFENCE COUNSEL: Was a statement placed in front of you on the second occasion, were you asked to sign it?

REID: Yes.

DEFENCE COUNSEL: And did you sign it?

REID: Yes.

Reid was taken to Groenpunt Prison near Vereeniging. He said he made complaints through the proper channels about the assaults. A doctor saw him, and a magistrate and an inspector of detainees. Pain-killers were procured for him, three days after he had complained.

The experiences of two of Reid's co-accused, Ja-Ja and Theresa, on the same morning, at the same hands, and in the same place, were admissible as evidence.

Theresa alleged that she was questioned by Schoeman at the mortuary at Sebokeng with no one else present. Earlier, she said, she had seen Ja-Ja holding his mouth and nose and observed that his face looked slightly swollen. She was scared.

She said Schoeman asked her if she knew Ja-Ja, Malebo (Reid), Motsiri (Gideon), and Oupa Kopsiek Mariletsi, and she said she did.

The inclusion of Oupa Mariletsi must be noted, because it indicated that the police were still following up information that someone called Oupa might be in possession of the gun. Neither "Kopsiek" nor "Mariletsi" is one of Oupa Diniso's names, and the inclusion of "Mariletsi" showed that the police had not yet reached "Diniso" on their list of Oupa suspects. It reinforces the possibility that Ja-Ja was telling the truth when he said he had merely directed the police to the house of the Oupa who played golf.

> **JUDGE:** Yes, and then?
> **THERESA:** And Mr. Schoeman said to me there is something that you know about these men. And then I said no.
> **JUDGE:** Yes, and then?
> **THERESA:** And he hit me with an open hand.
> **JUDGE:** Where?
> **THERESA:** On this side [she shows the left cheek], because I was looking that way. And he asked me, "Do you see these papers lying here? I have got full evidence about you, what you did on 3 September." And he said to me, "You do not want to speak, but I will make you to speak."
> **JUDGE:** But I will make you speak?
> **THERESA:** Yes, he said, I will make you speak. Then he said to me, you must undress.
> **JUDGE:** He said you must undress?

THERESA: Yes.

JUDGE: Well, it seems to me your counsel is taken a bit aback at what you are telling the Court now.

DEFENCE COUNSEL: I am not. It is just that I feel in the circumstances we should let her tell her story. Your Lordship has put certain questions and I told her to tell it in her own words.

JUDGE: Well, very well, carry on. Carry on, tell us now what happened. He said you must undress. Did you take off your dress?

THERESA: I was wearing a dress and a nightdress. I took off the dress, which was on top of the nightdress. And I remained in the nightdress. Then he asked me, "Why is the nightdress remaining? Why do you not take it off?"

But the judge could not desist at this stage.

JUDGE: What did you have on underneath?

THERESA: I had on a panty, because he woke me up whilst I was sleeping.

JUDGE: I had only a panty on underneath?

THERESA: Yes.

JUDGE: And a bra?

THERESA: I was not wearing a bra, because they arrived whilst I was sleeping . . .

JUDGE: Was he alone with you?

THERESA: Yes, we were only two. And then he came and stood behind me.

DEFENCE COUNSEL: Carry on.

THERESA: And then he brought one of his hands over my left shoulder, I remember well, round my neck.

DEFENCE COUNSEL: Did he touch your breasts?

THERESA: Yes, he touched this breast [she indicates the left breast].

DEFENCE COUNSEL: Carry on.

THERESA: Well, because I was scared, I just left him alone to do what he wanted to do with me.

JUDGE: What, did you think he was going to rape you or what?

THERESA: Yes, the way he had ordered me to undress, I assumed that perhaps he wanted to have sex with me.

DEFENCE COUNSEL: Now, while you were standing there, naked, except for your panty, and he was behind you, Mr. Schoeman, was anything else done?

THERESA: He tied round a wide bandage covering my face and my eyes, he covered my whole face.

DEFENCE COUNSEL: And did anything happen?

THERESA: I felt that he had placed two objects here in me [she indicates on both shoulders] and these objects came up to the points of my breasts and gripped the points of my breasts.

JUDGE: These objects touched the points of your breasts?

THERESA: Yes, they touched the points of my breasts, but it was not a hard grip, but something into which the points of my breasts got into.

JUDGE: You mean your nipples? The nipples of your breasts?

THERESA: Yes, the nipples of my breast.

DEFENCE COUNSEL: How did you feel? Did you experience anything, once these points were in position on the nipples of your breasts?

THERESA: My whole body was hot and I felt pains. . . . I thought that was a way of shocking me, because it was like a kettle when somebody puts an object onto a kettle and then I felt that there was such a shock on me . . .

[After that the bandage was removed, and Theresa got dressed again. Her counsel asked her if anything else was required of her.]

THERESA: Yes, there is. Mr. Schoeman asked me who had taken Dlamini's firearm. . . . My reply was, "I do not know. I was already shot. I did not see."

Schoeman then required Theresa to take him to Reid's house, and they went there in a car, with Matunzi and a tall policeman whose name Theresa did not know. She described to the court how Reid was brought out of his house and put into the car, on the back seat between herself and Matunzi.

> THERESA: He struck Reid with his elbow in the mouth and Reid felt lots of pain. . . . Matunzi also struck Reid on his knee with a torch.
>
> DEFENCE COUNSEL: And when he struck him with the torch, had he asked him any questions?
>
> THERESA: When he hit him with the torch, he asked him only one question and he said, "Young man, where is the firearm?"
>
> DEFENCE COUNSEL: And did Accused 2 reply?
>
> THERESA: He said, "I do not know about it." He was crying.

In cross-examination, Theresa said she was released the same day, November 9.

> PROSECUTOR: Was that because at that stage you had indicated that you wanted to become a State witness?
>
> THERESA: No, it was not me that made that suggestion, it was Mr. Schoeman who told me that.
>
> JUDGE: You did not suggest becoming a State witness?
>
> THERESA: No.
>
> PROSECUTOR: Now what did Warrant Officer Schoeman say to you in that connection?
>
> THERESA: Mr. Schoeman said to me, "Look, in connection with those four people that I asked you about, I will tell you what to say," and then I said to him, "No, I refuse, I will not do it, I will not agree with what you tell me to say, because at that stage I was already shot."

Was the following a deliberate diversion, an attempt to make Theresa's words ridiculous, a joke?

> JUDGE: You were shot?
>
> THERESA: Yes, I was shot.
>
> JUDGE: Did Mr. Schoeman shoot you?
>
> THERESA: No.
>
> JUDGE: Who shot you? Matunzi?
>
> THERESA: No.
>
> PROSECUTOR: Where were you shot?

THERESA: I was shot in the head.

PROSECUTOR: Yes, but where? In Sharpeville or Sebokeng or where?

THERESA: I was shot in Sharpeville on 3 September.

JUDGE: I was shot on 3 September in Sharpeville. By whom?

THERESA: Yes, the soldiers shot me.

JUDGE: I only want to know whether Matunzi or Mr. Schoeman shot you. I did not understand where you were shot.

THERESA: It was not them.

PROSECUTOR: In any case, he wanted you to become a State witness, that is what you told me?

THERESA: Yes.

PROSECUTOR: Was it before or after you were slapped?

THERESA: It was after, it was also after he shocked me.

JUDGE: After he shocked you?

PROSECUTOR: Shocked.

THERESA: Yes.

PROSECUTOR: So first he assaults you and does all sorts of things to you, and then he says you must become a State witness?

THERESA: Everything I have said here is what he himself said with his own lips.

Ja-Ja alleged that he was assaulted by Schoeman and Matunzi at his house in the early hours of November 9, 1984, and his wife, Regina, supported his evidence.

Ja-Ja told the court the two policemen continued their assault on him at the Sebokeng police station. They took him into a little office with a chair and a table in it. Matunzi wrapped his face in a bandage that covered his eyes. He then felt certain things "poking" him, like a torch with two leads pointing like tongues. He felt great pain, and crept under the table, removed the bandage, and saw Schoeman bending towards him. He grabbed the instrument and broke it. Schoeman became very angry and took off his watch and ring, and both he and Matunzi hit Ja-Ja with their fists. While Ja-Ja was on the floor, Matunzi trod on his foot. (Matunzi by his own admission weighed 230 pounds.)

In his cross-examination of Schoeman, defence counsel had said that Ja-Ja's evidence would be that he was made to sit on a chair and felt shocks, and that Schoeman was responsible for this.

SCHOEMAN: I don't understand what type of shocks, My Lord.
DEFENCE COUNSEL: Electric shocks.
SCHOEMAN: No, My Lord, I am very frightened of electricity. I don't play with that sort of thing.

A little later, this exchange occurred:

DEFENCE COUNSEL: . . . It is important, is it not, to try to get information from people whom one suspects? It would be valuable. It would help the police, wouldn't it, to get information?
SCHOEMAN: That is right, My Lord. We work mainly with information.
DEFENCE COUNSEL: And again, just talking generally, some people if they are tortured or shocked, are so anxious not to have this continue that they will talk. You will agree with that as a general proposition?
SCHOEMAN: Well, I cannot speak of that. I have never yet had that experience. I don't know . . .
DEFENCE COUNSEL: I want to put it to you that the infliction of pain on people who are in the custody of the police could be a means of getting those people to speak, correct?
SCHOEMAN: Now I don't understand what he says, My Lord.
JUDGE: He says if you cause someone pain he may possibly talk, if it is through the police's action that he feels the pain.
SCHOEMAN: Well, it is a possibility, My Lord. As I say I have never yet made that discovery. I don't know whether–what happens then.

❖

Dr. Izak Petrus van der Westhuizen, district surgeon of Bloemfontein, examined Reid and Ja-Ja on November 13, 1984, at Groenpunt Prison, in response to complaints. Dr. van der Westhuizen testified that "in the case of an assault, we never ask how the assault occurred, except when we find that there are serious complications. Then we like to have the exact cause of the injury."

In Reid's case, he noted a complaint about headaches and pain in the chest as a result of an alleged assault on November 9, 1984, and said the chest pains were quite consistent with having been caused by electric shocks, which may give rise to muscular spasms. He also found tenderness at the back of the neck, consistent with shocks, or with a blow to the head.

Dr. van der Westhuizen noted that Ja-Ja complained that his chin was sore and that he could not hear in his left ear as a result of an assault by the police on November 9, 1984, the date he was arrested.

The doctor's records[3] showed symmetrical lesions on the forearms, and also in the third rib-space left and right of the sternum. These could have been caused by an instrument with electrodes through which current was passed. Also noted were lesions on the front of the left shin, consistent with a kick, and on the outside of the left ankle; some swelling, caused by a blow or a fall (not by an infection) in the left cheekbone; and a fresh perforation of the left eardrum, with diminished hearing.

The prosecutor suggested to the doctor that Reid could have had tenderness in the back of his neck and shoulder because he had been sleeping on a bed that he was not used to, and that Ja-Ja could have received his injuries, for example, in a soccer game or some other contact sport, and the perforated eardrum could have resulted from blowing his nose very hard. The doctor conceded that these things were possible. The defence contended none was probable, and the symmetry of the chest and arm injuries was not suggestive of sports injuries.

The doctor could not say with certainty whether the injuries were sustained five days before he saw them (pre-arrest) or four or fewer days before (post-arrest).

No doctor saw Theresa. Counsel told the court that he knew his Learned Friend (the prosecutor) would submit that, if she had not made a complaint, it was highly improbable that anything had happened to her. The defence would argue that she did in fact make a complaint, to her mother, and Mrs. Julia Ramashamola confirmed this.

> **DEFENCE COUNSEL:** Did you yourself as the mother decide to go to the police and lay a complaint?
> **MRS. RAMASHAMOLA:** No.
> **DEFENCE COUNSEL:** Will you tell His Lordship and the Court why you decided not to do that?
> **MRS. RAMASHAMOLA:** We know that we blacks we have no right. If there is something done to a black person, that black person can't go to the Law, that is the police, and lay a charge against the police. We know that, we have been told about that many times.
> **JUDGE:** What? The police do not take notice of any complaints by you, the black people? Is that so?
> **MRS. RAMASHAMOLA:** We grow up knowing about that.

The judge refuted this emphatically, with examples known to him personally.

> **MRS. RAMASHAMOLA:** I said that if a person had been a detainee, a person who has been assaulted by the police, and that person goes and lays a charge against the police, we know, we grow up knowing that the police will ask you, do you come and lay a charge against the Law to the Law?
> **JUDGE:** That is absolute nonsense.

Reid described in evidence his next experience, in which Detective Sergeant Gillmer came to Groenpunt Prison to interview him on November 20, 1984. In the presence of a Lieutenant Mynhardt and a black man called Bokkie Eland, Gillmer asked Reid where he was on September 3, 1984.

> **REID:** . . . When I told him where I was on 3 September he denied [contradicted] it. He then said to me, "You know where you were on 3 September and you also know what you did," he has not come here to play, I must not talk nonsense. I then asked him, "What kind of truth must I tell you?" He then again said to me, "You know you did throw a stone at Dlamini and you did put his house on fire." . . . I was very frightened.
>
> **JUDGE:** Did he assault you?
>
> **REID:** No.
>
> **DEFENCE COUNSEL:** Why were you frightened?
>
> **REID:** I was afraid that the repetition of the shocking and the assaults would take place again on me.

Gillmer and Mynhardt gave evidence to the effect that they had in no way persuaded, forced, or intimidated Reid into making a statement.

Reid informed the court that he made a statement and signed it, and the next day he was taken to a magistrate, who asked him if he had been assaulted, threatened, or promised any reward. He said the police had warned him not to mention anything of that sort, and to say he had come of his own free will. They said they always saw reports of what people told the magistrate, and if he didn't do as they said, they would know about it and deal with him later.

That was why he did not tell the magistrate that he had been assaulted, nor that the police had promised that if he carried out instructions, he would be free within three days.

Then he made a statement, written in Afrikaans.

The prosecutor announced his intention to read it out to the Court, because he wanted to establish that in it Reid had made no reference whatever to setting the house on fire.

JUDGE: Well, you are entitled now to cross-examine him, because he says the police told him what to say, so you are entitled to cross-examine on the contents of this statement.

The prosecutor then read Reid's statement aloud to the Court:

It was plus/minus seven o'clock in the morning. I was standing by the gate when a group of people came along. About nine of them jumped over the fence and took me into the street and said, "Come let's go to Dlamini's house." They told me they would burn down my parents' house. I went with them. When we got to Dlamini's house we threw stones at it. The police appeared and threw tear-gas at us. I ran into another property to wash my face. The police moved on and I went back to Dlamini's house. I stood outside and his house was on fire [the prosecutor apologizes for misreading] he stood outside and his house was on fire. I threw a stone at his back. The police came back and we ran to the shops where we also threw stones. We went to the beerhall. We also threw stones at that. We went to the bar near Sharpeville police station. The police expected us [the prosecutor interjects: "I don't know if that is correctly typed"] and we went home. On 9-11-84 the police arrested me. They took me to Sebokeng where they asked me about Dlamini's firearm. I went to Vereeniging and then to Groenpunt prison where I was held. That is all.

Asked if he agreed that there was not one word in the statement about his setting Dlamini's house on fire, Reid said, "Yes, I agree. I heard."

Cross-examination went on for some time about that, and about why the confession did not include it. The prosecutor made the point that the police seemed to have been satisfied with very little.

Defence counsel pointed out that Reid's mention of Dlamini standing outside his house while it was on fire contradicted all other evidence and suggested that Reid did not witness these events.

Reid's statement, known as the confession, was put to him point-by-point by defence counsel, and Reid formally denied each point.

On October 28, 1985, the defence and the prosecution addressed the court on the merits of the case in the trial-within-a-trial.

The next day the court resumed to hear the ruling[4]:

> **JUDGE:** The Court has unanimously decided that the statement made by Accused 2 before magistrate, Mr. Muller, on 21 November 1984, will be admissible as evidence against him. The reasons for our decision will be given at a later date.

Reid's statement was handed up as Exhibit AA, and the trial-within-a-trial was over.

❖

Lieutenant Roux of the Randfontein police gave evidence for the State in the course of the main trial. He had been instructed to collect Reid from Groenpunt Prison on December 18, 1984, and take him on a tour of the sites mentioned in the statement he had made before the magistrate. Reid was to point out specific landmarks, which a police photographer who accompanied them then photographed. Roux gave evidence at some length about this tour, and about the notes he had made in a "sort of album" he had put together.

He said Reid informed him that he had stood at the gate of Dlamini's house and thrown a stone that broke the right-hand window.

Poor Reid. He seems to have been ready to admit to anything, unless Roux was fabricating. He could not possibly have broken a window in Dlamini's house on September 3, for every one of them had been smashed the night before, according to Mrs. Dlamini.

Then, Roux went on, after the police had tear-gassed the crowd, Reid ran away to a nearby house to wash his face, and returned to the scene to find Dlamini's house burned down and Dlamini standing outside the house.

Defence counsel objected that what Reid had allegedly said to Roux was not admissible as evidence, and the judge agreed that it was not, but with this in mind, Roux carried on reading Reid's alleged words from his album.

"Dlamini was standing then outside his house on his stand. I then threw a stone at his back. I stood by the gate when I threw the stone at him. Dlamini fell, and then a lot of police appeared. I ran away with the group . . . to Sipho's[5] shop."

If Reid said this, was he there in fact? No police arrived at the point when Dlamini fell. But this was not evidence; one could only hear it and put it out of one's mind, as the judge had undertaken to do.

Roux denied that any pressure had been brought to bear on Reid to speak. On the contrary, he said, he had had to ask the prisoner to speak more slowly, so that he could write down his words.

When Reid was cross-examined about the tour, he said Roux consulted a piece of paper he had with him, and as they moved around in the car, he read from it and questioned Reid. When he was asked whether Roux had threatened him, he said he had.

> PROSECUTOR: By doing what?
>
> REID: That I must say what he read out to me from that paper, and I must only say that.
>
> PROSECUTOR: Did he threaten to hit you or what did he threaten?
>
> REID: He threatened me in the manner in which he spoke to me when he was speaking to me . . . that he was in possession of that statement and I must only say what was written there.

The prosecutor asked if the document Roux had with him in the car was the statement Reid had made to the magistrate. Reid did not know. Roux had looked at the document and then told Reid what to say.

PROSECUTOR: Did he ever tell you must say you had smashed a window with a stone?

REID: Yes.

PROSECUTOR: Did you ever tell the police in any statement that you had smashed a window with a stone?

REID: No.

PROSECUTOR: Now where could he have come by that story?

REID: He just deduced it from the fact that, when I said that I had thrown stones at Dlamini's house and he just kind of thought I must have smashed a window.

The questioning went on, running rings around Reid. Did he know Dlamini? Yes. Did he know he was a councillor? No. What did Reid know of him then, how had he got to know him? When he was a teacher, he taught two of Reid's brothers. Did Reid know where Dlamini lived? No. So how could he point out his house to Roux? Reid said he had found out where it was after September 3. When? He couldn't remember but it was a couple of days after September 3.

PROSECUTOR: I put it to you that Lieutenant Roux in no way forced you to point anything out.

REID: The State prosecutor cannot put that to me, because he was not there, I was there. Those things were done to me.

The prosecutor asked Reid how he had managed to point anything out when his hands were tied behind his back. Reid said he had pointed with his head.

Reid's evidence began with his own version of what he did on September 3, 1984. He was in his house in the early morning when he heard a noise and went outside. There were many people there, singing and saying that people must go to the office. They were not marching, but "just mixed up and going along." One of them asked Reid why he was standing at the gate, and he said he was on his way to work. He was told that "today people must not go to work, we are getting to the office to go and find out about the rent." This person was not speaking in a friendly way – he was "in a fighting mood." Reid was then told that if he didn't join the crowd that was going to the office, his mother's house would be burned down. He got scared, and went along.

On the way, he said, at the corner of Sefatsa and Kodisang streets, the police appeared and "started shooting, throwing tear-gas and shooting with rubber bullets." Reid ran to a nearby house to wash his face at a tap. And then he went home.

He never arrived at the house of Mr. Dlamini.

Exhibit R was another nail Reid had forged for his own coffin. It was a letter he had written, in Afrikaans, to the Minister of Law and Order.

What happened to Reid during his stay at Groenpunt? He seems to have lost his head completely, or else he was given advice entirely against his interests. He made his statement to the magistrate, he admitted whatever Lt. Roux suggested to him on the pointing-out tour, and then he put pen to paper again. In his desperation to get out and go home, he was ready to confess to anything. The pathos of the naive, bullied, frightened young man Reid then was, destroying himself with his own evidence, is one of the more terrible aspects of this story.

The letter to the Minister was dated December 21, 1984, three days after the pointing-out tour with Lt. Roux.

In it Reid told how he joined the crowd under threats, went with them to Dlamini's house, threw a stone at a window, ran away to wash his face when the police tear-gassed the crowd; returned to the house, saw Dlamini lying on his stomach, threw a stone at his back; and when the police appeared, ran away with the crowd to Seepoint shop, and threw a stone there.

In an attempt to show that the above behaviour was not politically motivated, he went on, "I am nothing in the location. I haven't a group of UDF/COSAS and I am not a member of them.

I will never walk together with them. I am only a member of SEAWUSA [Steel Engineering and Allied Workers' Union of South Africa] at the factory."

He described his arrest on November 9, 1984, but mentioned no assault in his house. Of Sebokeng police station, he wrote, "I was well and truly beaten there."

He was taken to Vereeniging police station, where "I wrote my first statements till I [*sic*] to the magistrate in Vanderbijlpark to go and write the same statement. I did not *gevosier* [(forced?) has been inserted in the typed copy of Exhibit R] to do so. I am held at Groenpunt under Section 29.

"Now I see my king that I have made a mistake. I heard it from the prisoners. I will not, please *Morena* [Lord, Master], to do so. It was my first and the last I do so. I shall never again. I am now tired of being alone. I ask my king please I go home. Although I made a mistake; it was not my aim to do so. I was just scared to let my mother's house not burn. I only *gevosieer* [*sic*] to go there. Is true my king I threw a stone. Please I want to go home to live with my family and go to work for mother, because I have no father. Please *Morena*."

> **PROSECUTOR:** Did anyone ever tell you what happened at Dlamini's place . . . ?
> **REID:** No.
> **PROSECUTOR:** You could not have known for example that he fell on the ground at one stage and lay there and the people then stoned him?
> **REID:** That is correct . . .
> **PROSECUTOR:** . . . How did you know Dlamini was lying down while he was stoned?
> **REID:** It is Mr. Schoeman who told me that I could throw a stone at his back when he was lying on the ground.
> **PROSECUTOR:** You just told me no one told you that the deceased lay on the ground.
> **REID:** It is Mr. Schoeman who told me that I threw a stone at his back, that means that he was lying on his stomach where he fell.

> PROSECUTOR: Did Mr. Schoeman tell you he lay on his stomach?
>
> REID: No.
>
> PROSECUTOR: Now where do you come by—why do you think this bit out in your letter, where do you come by the idea that he was lying down?
>
> REID: That is how Mr. Schoeman told me, that if I threw a stone at his back, it must be that he was lying on his stomach.
>
> JUDGE: Did Mr. Schoeman tell you he was lying on his stomach?
>
> REID: No.
>
> JUDGE: Then I don't understand your evidence any more. How did you know Dlamini was lying on his back when he was stoned – on his stomach at least?
>
> REID: No, I would not have known about that, because it was something that was said to me, that I threw a stone at him.

The judge and the prosecutor carried on with this point, taking turns to ask Reid the same thing, how he could have known Dlamini was lying face-down if he was not at the scene, and Reid persisted in his reply, that Schoeman had told him he had thrown a stone at Dlamini's back while he (Dlamini) was lying down, and Reid had deduced from that that Dlamini had been lying on his stomach.

> PROSECUTOR: And just by chance, it tallies with the evidence of the State witnesses.

The judge said Reid must have been there because otherwise how could he have known he was lying on his stomach.

> REID: No, I was not there, it is something that was said to me, that I threw a stone at his back and I just sort of deduced that he must have been lying on his stomach.
>
> JUDGE: Who told you that you threw a stone at his back?
>
> REID: Mr. Schoeman.

JUDGE: He just came out of the blue and said you threw a stone at the back of the deceased?

REID: Mr. Schoeman said these things to me because he could not find a firearm in my possession.

Reid was asked whether he had pointed out to Lt. Roux the house where he had washed the tear-gas off his face.

REID: No, that is not the house I pointed out.

Roux had given the number of the house, 7483, and had had it photographed. But now Reid was saying he had not pointed out the house to Roux?

REID: I showed him, but it was not the house.
[The judge intervened. Had he or had he not pointed out a house to Lt. Roux?]

REID: I would like the Court to understand me. I showed him a house, but it was not the house where I washed my face.

JUDGE: Now what house was it?

REID: It was just a house in that street, Dlamini's street, but it was not a house that I went into.

JUDGE: Now what did you point out that house to him for?

REID: He told me I must point out to him a house where I washed my face.

JUDGE: And then you pointed out that house?

REID: Yes.

JUDGE: Now why did you point that house out to him?

REID: They just wanted to talk me into a trap that I was there in Dlamini's street in that house.

PROSECUTOR: You wanted to talk yourself into a trap, is that what you say?

REID: They wanted to talk me into a trap.

PROSECUTOR: Oh, they wanted to, I see. Now tell me, you did in fact wash your face that morning?

REID: Not at that house.

PROSECUTOR: You washed your face that morning, yes or no?

REID: Yes.

PROSECUTOR: At what house did you wash your face?

REID: It was a house in Sefatsa Street.

[Why had Reid not pointed out that house to Roux? Because that house was far from Dlamini's place.]

PROSECUTOR: But why didn't you show him that house, then everyone could see that you were far from Dlamini's house?

REID: No, they wanted everything I said to fit with Dlamini's street, to show that I was in fact there in Dlamini's place.

During cross-examination Reid was asked what the crowd was going to do at the rent office, and before he could answer the judge made an important comment. He seemed to have formed an opinion, though Reid was only the second accused to give evidence on the events of September 3, 1984.

JUDGE: But those people who told you you had to walk with them, we know now from all the evidence, which you have also heard, that those people were not on the way to the municipal offices, they were on the way to Dlamini's house in order to burn it down and to burn him to death, these people that you were walking with. Did they not say to you, look, we have to go to Dlamini's house now, and set it on fire and kill him?

REID: No.

Cross-examination went on:

PROSECUTOR: It's very easy to get away from a crowd of five hundred people, isn't it?

REID: Yes.

PROSECUTOR: And you didn't have to go with them?

REID: No, I didn't have to go with them, because I didn't know that the rent had been raised or not.

Reid was asked how long he had lived in Sharpeville. All his life, he replied.

JUDGE: How old are you now?

REID: Twenty-two.

PROSECUTOR: The house you live in there, is it your parents' house?

REID: It is my mother's house.

PROSECUTOR: And who normally pays the monthly rent?

REID: I have a brother, and we put the money in together to go and pay.

JUDGE: Were you working at the time?

REID: I started work in 1982.

JUDGE: I'm asking if you worked that day, on that day what work did you do?

REID: Yes.

JUDGE: Where?

REID: At a certain firm[6] in Vereeniging.

JUDGE: Weren't you supposed to go to work that day?

REID: I was.

JUDGE: Why didn't you go?

REID: There was no transport.

PROSECUTOR: How did you know, you were at your house?

REID: Because that morning I went to the bus stop and when I got there I heard from the people that there was no transport.

[The court adjourned for tea.]

PROSECUTOR: You say you were part-responsible for the payment of your rent?

REID: Yes.

PROSECUTOR: So you had certainly heard that there was talk, in your house too, that you would now have to put more money together to pay the rent?

REID: Yes.

PROSECUTOR: So you knew before 3 September about this rise in the rent?

REID: Yes.

PROSECUTOR: Why did you say before the tea break that you didn't know anything about it?

REID: No, I didn't know about the R5.90. I only heard that the rent would be raised.

PROSECUTOR: Were you satisfied with it?

REID: No, I can't say that I was satisfied or not satisfied, because it was not yet – the rise was not yet paid at that time.
PROSECUTOR: Would you be content to pay it when the day came?
REID: Yes.

That letter to the Minister was not yet finished with.

PROSECUTOR: You were not instructed to write that letter?
REID: I was told to.
PROSECUTOR: By whom?
REID: Johan Meyer, policeman by the name of Johan Meyer.
PROSECUTOR: And did this person, whoever he may be, tell you you must say this that and the other in the letter?
REID: Yes.

The judge asked whether Meyer had dictated while Reid wrote. Reid said no, Meyer had told him what to say, and left him.

Reid had drawn a street plan, and wanted to show the Court where the crowd had walked, and the route he himself had taken, but the judge scorned it, saying he didn't want any more drawings and plans.

Finally defence counsel, re-examining, gave Reid a chance to produce the plan, and asked him to point out which was the house where he washed his face.

Reid's plan was handed up as Exhibit EE.

JUDGE: You are a good draughtsman and you have got a nice handwriting too.
REID: Yes.
JUDGE: What standard did you reach at school?
REID: Form 3.[7]

When Dr. Hertzog, the assessor, asked Reid exactly what he meant by "hit" Dlamini with a stone, whether he intended it as hit by throwing the stone, or hit with a stone which he was holding, Reid could not answer, because, as he said, he didn't do either, and he didn't know which meaning Schoeman had intended, but he had been told to say he had thrown the stone.

There is one more factor in Reid's case. Mabuti, the State witness who claimed to have seen every aspect of the incident, stated categorically in cross-examination that he knew Reid as well as he knew all the other accused (except Oupa, whom he did not know at all). Reid was the only one of the accused known to Mabuti who was not implicated by him. It seems Mabuti did not see Reid throw that stone – in fact, he did not see him at the scene of the murder.

CHAPTER 9

Oupa

"A thing that didn't work."
OUPA MOSES DINISO

The case against Oupa Diniso was based on circumstantial evidence alone: he was found in possession of Dlamini's gun.

None of the eyewitnesses who appeared for the State – except the discredited "Yster," Johannes Mongaule – saw him at the scene of the crime. Mongaule claimed to have seen Oupa and Ja-Ja divest Dlamini of his gun. Soon, without much persuasion, he admitted that there was room for doubt about their identity, and that he had been injured at the scene and had not seen anything of the incident.

Nevertheless the judge's memory played tricks on him during Oupa's testimony.

> **DEFENCE COUNSEL:** Evidence was given by one person to the effect that you were on the scene on the day when Mr. Dlamini was attacked at his house.
> **JUDGE** (intervenes): It is Mabuti, Mabuti gave that evidence.
> **DEFENCE COUNSEL:** No, not Mabuti, it is that very last witness, Yster.
> **JUDGE:** Mabuti said, "No. 1 got hold of the deceased in the back yard."
> **DEFENCE COUNSEL:** No. 1, but this is No. 3. It is Yster . . . who said this.
> **JUDGE:** Yes, you are correct.

Later, cross-examining Oupa, the prosecutor asked him whether he knew Mongaule. Yes, said Oupa, we worked together. Did they often talk to each other? No.

The judge intervened here, asking Oupa where he worked. The reply was Stewarts and Lloyds, then a listed company and almost a household name in the steel industry in South Africa.

JUDGE: Stewarts and Lloyds?
OUPA: Yes.
JUDGE: You only work at night?
OUPA: We alternate. For two weeks we do night shift and for two weeks it's day shift.
JUDGE: What do you manufacture? I thought you were insurance company people?
OUPA: No, it is Tubemakers.
JUDGE: Oh, Tubemakers.
PROSECUTOR: Lloyds is an insurance company, but Stewarts and Lloyds . . .
JUDGE: Yes, but it doesn't matter now.

And the court adjourned for lunch. So much for Mongaule.

Oupa's case fell into four unequal parts. One was the connection between him and Ja-Ja, crucial to both of them. It involved the question of the various Oupas who lived in Sharpeville, and whether Ja-Ja led the police to the house of "the Oupa who plays golf," as he claimed he did, or whether he led them to Dlamini's gun, as the police insisted.

Another portion, the shortest, concerned what Oupa did on the day of the murder, September 3, 1984. He said he went to St. Cyprian's Church in Sharpeville for a meeting about the higher rents, waited around until it was evident the meeting would not take place, then went home and spent the rest of the day there.

A third part comprised the events of the next day, September 4, and Oupa's explanation of how he came to be in possession of the gun.

The fourth section concerned November 9, 1984. The crux of the matter here was the discrepancy between what Oupa said he told the police when they came to his house and arrested him, and what the police said Oupa told them on that occasion.

❖

Sergeant Wessels, of the Krugersdorp Murder and Robbery Squad, testified that on November 9, 1984, at around 5:45 a.m., at Sebokeng, Warrant Officer Schoeman handed over to him Accused no. 1, who conducted Wessels to an address in Sharpeville. There he found Accused no. 3.

> **WESSELS:** I asked him if he knew anything about this firearm which was alleged to be in his possession. The man said yes and he said to me that he would give it to me. . . . In the passage of the house in question, at that address, there is an opening in the ceiling. The man climbed up there and took a firearm out. It was a 9-mm Star pistol.
>
> **PROSECUTOR:** I point out to you Exhibit 1 in this case, a firearm, Star pistol, 9 mm. Do you recogize it?
>
> **WESSELS:** It is the same weapon. I asked the man if he had permission to own the weapon, whether he could show me a licence for it. He could not, and I asked him for an explanation, and he made a report to me.

Defence counsel, cross-examining Wessels, asked him whether he knew that Ja-Ja Sefatsa had been, at one point, in a cell at Krugersdorp with Oupa Mariletsi. Wessels had no recollection of that. Did he know of any reference to a person accompanying Accused no. 1 bearing the name "Oupa"? Wessels did not know.

> **DEFENCE COUNSEL:** You do not know the name, that one of the names of Accused no. 3 is Oupa?
>
> **WESSELS:** My Lord, I know him as Blackman with surname "Diniso." His surname is Diniso.
>
> **DEFENCE COUNSEL:** And you do not recollect the use of the word "Oupa" in connection with him?
>
> **WESSELS:** It is possible that he may be called Oupa. I don't know.
>
> **DEFENCE COUNSEL:** You see, the evidence of Accused no. 1 is going to be that you saw him in a cell at Krugersdorp in the company of a man called Mariletsi and that on that

occasion you took him out of the cell and you questioned him about the possession of a firearm.

WESSELS: My Lord, no. I did not – I never at any time took Accused no. 1 out of a cell and questioned him about this firearm.

DEFENCE COUNSEL: Do you perhaps remember that he might have been shackled on his leg and that you removed the shackle?

WESSELS: My Lord, if reference is made to shackles, I don't know about anything like that.

DEFENCE COUNSEL: And he did not say to you, in respect of a question about the firearm, that the only one he knew was Malachia's firearm?

WESSELS: My Lord, I did not question that man. I got that man from Warrant Officer Schoeman on 9 November . . . [Counsel now discussed the events of November 9.]

DEFENCE COUNSEL: Is it not correct that you were actually sitting in a motor car in the early morning at Sebokeng police station and Accused no. 1 was brought down by a black policeman called Matunzi?

WESSELS: My Lord, Matunzi may have brought the man, but I received my instructions from Warrant Officer Schoeman and not from any black member.

Wessels insisted that Ja-Ja had shown them the way, in that car, to Oupa Diniso's house. Defence counsel said Ja-Ja's evidence would be that the house was found by means other than information given by him.

DEFENCE COUNSEL: Now when you arrived at that house, was Accused no. 1 brought into the house with you?

WESSELS: Correct, My Lord. He had to point out to us the man who was supposed to be in possession of the firearm, and after we knocked, Accused no. 3 opened the door and he pointed him out to us and said this is the man who is in possession of the firearm.

DEFENCE COUNSEL: Now in your evidence-in-chief you said

that Accused no. 1 would point out a person who was possibly in possession of a firearm.

WESSELS: That is correct. That is what I said.

DEFENCE COUNSEL: How did you come to get the information that Accused no. 3 would be possibly a person in possession of a firearm?

[Wessels stated that these had been Schoeman's words.]

DEFENCE COUNSEL: Now, is it not correct that when you came to the house a question was put to Accused no. 3 in connection with the firearm?

WESSELS: My Lord, I could . . .

JUDGE: What question was put?

WESSELS: Questions may have been put. I do not know, My Lord.

JUDGE: What question was put? To no. 3?

DEFENCE COUNSEL: Let me put it to you this way, Mr. Wessels, did you ask Accused no. 3 if he is Oupa "who plays golf"?

JUDGE: Who does what?

DEFENCE COUNSEL: "Who plays golf."

JUDGE: Oh, plays golf.

DEFENCE COUNSEL: Yes, did you . . .

WESSELS: My Lord, yes, the game of golf did come into the discussion. I know we were looking for a man who played golf. If I remember rightly the man also told us later that he was a golf-player. Accused no. 1 also told us that the man who was in possession of the firearm was, or he said it to Warrant Officer Schoeman – it is now hearsay, it is what I heard from him later – that he was a golfer and his name was Oupa. That's right, My Lord. I can remember it now.

DEFENCE COUNSEL: So that the name "Oupa" was used?

WESSELS: That is correct, My Lord, "Oupa" is much used, but I know in this case the name "Oupa" was also used.

DEFENCE COUNSEL: Because the evidence of Accused no. 3 is going to be that he was asked by you, "Are you the Oupa who plays golf?" Is it possible that you could have put that question to him?

> **WESSELS:** My Lord, I may have asked him that. It is possible that I asked that. After the man had been pointed out to us, I could have asked him that, but I cannot say specifically that I did ask him that, but it is possible.
>
> **DEFENCE COUNSEL:** Is there any possibility, Mr. Wessels, as far as you are concerned that there was any confusion between the Oupa Mariletsi, to whom I have referred earlier . . . , and this Oupa whose name is Oupa Diniso?

Remember that when Theresa was at Sebokeng police station, two or three hours before Oupa's arrest, Schoeman had asked her if she knew Ja-Ja, Malebo (Reid), Motsiri (Gideon), and Oupa Kopsiek Mariletsi, and she had replied that she did. So, at that stage, the police – who had information that someone called Oupa was in possession of the gun – were still unsure as to which of several Sharpeville Oupas that might be, and were going through a process of elimination.

Wessels denied all knowledge of Mariletsi.

Counsel asked Wessels if he thought a look at his occurrence-book might help with this aspect of the enquiry. Wessels thought not, because such a matter would not be important enough to have been entered. Where was the book? In Krugersdorp, possibly in the major's office.

Cross-examination moved on to the morning of Oupa's arrest. Sergeant Wessels had testified as follows: "He said to me that on the third of the ninth month he had taken the firearm in question from a group of children who were behaving in a disorderly or riotous manner in the street, and that this was near the house of Councillor Dlamini."

Counsel told the witness that Oupa's evidence would be that he had given Wessels no date, and that he had not told him he met the children near Dlamini's house. But Wessels stuck to his version.

> **DEFENCE COUNSEL:** Now, this was a very important piece of information, was it not?
>
> **WESSELS:** Yes, My Lord, it was. I wrote it down in my statement.

DEFENCE COUNSEL: And can the Court assume that because of its importance when he told you it at the time, you recorded that in your occurrence-book?

WESSELS: My Lord, yes, it was written down in my statement.

DEFENCE COUNSEL: No, not statement, in your occurrence-book.

WESSELS: It is possible.

JUDGE: Pocket-book.

DEFENCE COUNSEL: In your pocket-book, yes.

WESSELS: It is possible. It is possible that I may have written it down.

DEFENCE COUNSEL: Well, I am going to ask his Lordship, because of the importance of this aspect, to request you please to bring the book so that it may be checked. If His Lordship gives the order will you assist us in bringing the book?

WESSELS: My Lord, I shall try to get hold of the book. I cannot guarantee that I will get it, but it is usually locked up in our office, in our section commander's office. . . . I shall first have to get hold of him in order to hear where the book is, and if the books are not filed at some other place, or what, but I think – if the book is available I shall certainly bring it.

Asked about the terms of Oupa's arrest, Wessels denied telling him he was being arrested for being in possession of an unlicensed firearm, and claimed he had arrested him for murder.

Discussion followed about the identity of the firearm, and whether it was in fact the one that Oupa Diniso had handed over to Wessels, for Oupa would say that the handle of the one he had had was brownish, and that of Exhibit 1 was black. Wessels had not made a note immediately of the particulars of the gun.

DEFENCE COUNSEL: So, no notes were made in your occurrence-book while you were in the house of Accused no. 3?

WESSELS: My Lord, no, I did not stand there making notes.

DEFENCE COUNSEL: Can you remember where you wrote the notes in your occurrence-book?

WESSELS: My Lord, the book consists, I think, of seventy-eight pages. I do not know. It is somewhere in that book.

Counsel was sorry, his question had not been put clearly enough. Not where in the book, but at what place – police station, house, or where? Wessels couldn't remember.

This Wessels was the man known as Piet who, according to Reid, assaulted him at Vereeniging. After questioning him about this, counsel reminded the judge about the pocket-book.

JUDGE: Would you perhaps just try and see whether you can lay hands on the pocket-book?

With Wessels's assurance that if he got hold of the pocket-book, he would certainly produce it in court, and that he would try his best to get it, cross-examination of this witness ended.

Police regulations are specific: a pocket-book, when full, is to be kept in a place of safety in the care and custody of the police-station commander.

Sergeant Wessels's pocket-book was never produced.

❖

Oupa gave evidence in Xhosa, so there had to be "double translation" – Sesotho for his co-accused, as well as one or other of the official languages. He testified that on September 4, 1984, the day after the murder of Dlamini, the unrest continued, and again there was no public transport. Knowing that no other blacks would show up at work, he decided to take his golf clubs and go and practise his shots.

On his way home, he came across three young boys who were totally unknown to him. They were arguing over something, and one seemed to be trying to hide an object, unsuccessfully, for Oupa saw that it was a firearm. He asked the oldest of the boys if he was not afraid of injuring the others with it. The youngest said to him, "Brother, I picked up this thing from the scrap motors." The boys then handed over a gun to Oupa, and he took it and put it into his golf bag because he felt it would be dangerous to leave it with these boys.

At home, he took out the gun and examined it. This was the first time that he had ever held a real gun. He noticed at once that there was a "hole" under the handle of the gun. This was evidently where the magazine is inserted, but Oupa did not know that. Because there was no magazine, the trigger was jammed. Oupa assumed that the firearm was broken, "a thing that didn't work," as he said. He thought he would give it to his son to play with, but the boy was staying with an uncle in Sebokeng because he attended school there, and Oupa put it into his toolbox and forgot about it.

On November 9, when the police woke him up in the early hours of the morning, asking about a firearm, he went straight to his toolbox, took out the gun, and handed it over. Oupa described the place where the box was stored as a high shelf where he kept his tools. Wessels said it was an opening in the ceiling in the passage. It was, as we have seen, that open place under the roof – standard storage space in Oupa's type of Sharpeville house – where the family kept the zinc bath they washed themselves in, and all sorts of other cumbersome goods and chattels. It was nothing like a hiding-place.

Without apparent reason, Oupa said, the police assaulted him. They asked him whether he had a licence to possess a firearm. He replied that he had not, and was told he was being arrested because he had a gun in his possession, and no licence. He was not questioned about any murder, nor told about any murder charge.

Oupa said he had told Sergeant Wessels exactly the same story as he had just given the court, about the manner in which he had acquired the gun, except that he had not specified the date of his encounter with the three boys.

So Wessels's account of what Oupa said at the time of his arrest differed from Oupa's in three important aspects: date and place of acquisition of the gun, and demeanour of the children from whom he got it.

CHAPTER 10

Theresa

"Do you say she was there?"
MR. ACTING JUSTICE WESSEL JOHANNES HUMAN TO
STATE WITNESS J. MABUTI

Theresa Ramashamola was implicated in the murder by one witness, uncorroborated.

Jantjie Mabuti gave evidence at considerable length on the making of petrol bombs by members of the crowd. He described how petrol was poured at Dlamini's kitchen door and set alight, and how someone inside the house put out the flames. Then, he said, Dlamini shot into the crowd from inside his house. At this point, he heard someone shout, "He is shooting at us, let us kill him!"

Mabuti assured the Court that this person was Theresa, and that he heard her shout these words several times.

By Mabuti's own admission, the crowd was screaming, shouting, singing, and throwing stones. Dlamini was shooting. More than a hundred people were milling about, probably raising a great deal of dust, for Nhlapo Street is not tarred and the dry Transvaal winter is not over by September. Mabuti was adamant: he had heard the words clearly, and he had seen who had uttered them.

After Dlamini had been disarmed, and his car had been pushed into the road and set alight, Mabuti said he saw three people – whom he did not identify – drag the unconscious Dlamini to the street and try to put him on the car. He slid off, then petrol was thrown over him and matches were lit. "Now," said Mabuti, "one of the people, a woman there, screamed: 'Take him away from the burning car, don't burn him!' " He could not identify this woman.

> **PROSECUTOR:** Yes, and then, what happened then?
> **MABUTI:** That woman was hit, she was slapped.
> **PROSECUTOR:** By whom?
> **MABUTI:** By this same woman here, Accused 4.
> **JUDGE:** By No. 4?
> **MABUTI:** Yes.
> **PROSECUTOR:** Where did she slap the woman?
> **MABUTI:** In the face.

Counsel had been cross-examining Mabuti for some time before he came to the acts Theresa was alleged to have perpetrated.

> **DEFENCE COUNSEL:** Now, you said that this woman shouted, "Do not burn him!" With all that noise going on, those large numbers of people and the singing of the songs and the distance that you were away from the house of the deceased, could you hear this woman say these words?
> **MABUTI:** I think, My Lord, you will have to pardon me for not saying that my position had now changed from the fourth house to the third . . . the house opposite to Mr. Stoffel, in the same street, Nhlapo.
> **DEFENCE COUNSEL:** Why didn't you tell us that before, that you changed your position and you moved nearer the deceased's house?
> **MABUTI:** My Lord, as I am listening to what is going on, My Lord, I answer a question and so on, then I cannot come to that, My Lord. I am sorry for that, but that is what happened.

A large amount of Mabuti's evidence and cross-examination was concerned with where he was standing, or said he was standing, at various stages in the course of the incident.

> **DEFENCE COUNSEL:** And in this very large crowd of a hundred people, was it possible for you to see what you have just

described, that No. 4 accused did to this woman?

MABUTI: It was quite clear, My Lord. . . . It was quite clear for me to see that for I was there.

DEFENCE COUNSEL: You see, her evidence is going to be a complete denial of this. She is going to say that she was not there. What do you say to that?

MABUTI: Oh well, My Lord, I would not say anything but I say on my statement she was there, My Lord.

DEFENCE COUNSEL: Do you know anything about her having been injured by receiving a rubber bullet on her head?

MABUTI: Yes, sure, My Lord. I know that.

DEFENCE COUNSEL: How do you come to have that knowledge? How do you know about that?

MABUTI: How do I know about that, My Lord?

DEFENCE COUNSEL: Yes.

MABUTI: No, well, she came down – when she was in Zwane Street she had what you call a *doek* [head-scarf] on her head.

JUDGE: A *doek*?

MABUTI: A *doek*, and it was stained with blood.

JUDGE: Was that before the police came or after the police left?

MABUTI: No, when she was in Zwane Street . . .

JUDGE: After the regrouping?

MABUTI: Yes, My Lord.

JUDGE: Accused No. 4 had a *doek* around her head which was blood-stained?

MABUTI: Yes, My Lord.

DEFENCE COUNSEL: It is quite an important piece of evidence this, as to a woman wearing a blood-stained *doek* on that occasion, isn't it?

MABUTI: Pardon?

DEFENCE COUNSEL: It is an important piece of evidence this, that there is this woman with the blood-stained *doek* in the crowd. It is important, isn't it?

MABUTI: No, well.

DEFENCE COUNSEL: You do not know?

MABUTI: I do not know, My Lord.

DEFENCE COUNSEL: My question is, why didn't you mention this to His Lordship and the Gentlemen Assessors when you gave your evidence-in-chief, that the woman was standing there and she had a blood-stained *doek*?

MABUTI: I think I made it clear to the police who came to take my statement that she was shot.

JUDGE: No, but the question was why didn't you tell me that when you gave your evidence-in-chief?

MABUTI: Yes, My Lord.

JUDGE: You did not tell me that.

MABUTI: No, My Lord.

JUDGE: Now why didn't you? That is the question.

MABUTI: Oh, why didn't I tell, My Lord. No, well, it should have slipped my mind.

DEFENCE COUNSEL: She is going to deny that she wore a blood-stained *doek*.

MABUTI: Well, if she denies that I do not know if she will also deny that she has got a rubber-bullet mark on her head.

DEFENCE COUNSEL: No, she is going to say that she was injured by the police with the rubber bullet.

This went on for a while, with counsel stating Theresa's case, that she had gone to a house for treatment, and Mabuti sticking to his story that she was there as he had described, until finally the judge intervened.

JUDGE: What do you say? Do you say she was there?

MABUTI: I say she was at Mr. Dlamini's . . .

JUDGE: Or wasn't she there?

MABUTI: I said she was in Nhlapo Street at – when the incident took place.

JUDGE: That is after the police had left and she was coming along with the regrouped crowd?

MABUTI: That is right, My Lord.

❖

Theresa's defence was that on the morning of September 3, 1984, she heard a noise in the street outside and went to see what was happening. A large group of people were walking down the street, singing, and some of them asked her what she was standing there for, and whether she did not know that people had to go to the office. "They said I must go with them. If I do not they are going to burn the house." She was very frightened and decided to go with them.

There was in fact considerable evidence from the police and other witnesses, both defence and prosecution, of intimidation by the crowd.

Theresa said she was made to carry a placard that read: HARENA CHELETE ("We have no money").

In cross-examination, the prosecutor asked her what the crowd was singing.

> THERESA: They sang "Morena boloka sechaba saheso" ["Lord Save Our Nation"].
> JUDGE: What is that? No, I am asking the interpreter.
> (Interpreter: It means that the king must protect our nation.)
> JUDGE: The king must protect our nation? What king?
> THERESA: I don't know, that is how the song went.

If the name of that song had been given in Zulu, the judge would most certainly have recognized it for what it was, the black national anthem. "Morena boloka sechaba saheso" is to Sesotho-speakers what "Nkosi Sikelele iAfrika" ("Lord Save Africa") is to those who speak Zulu and Xhosa. The interpreter was asked what the Sesotho words meant and answered the question without elaborating. No one else was asked to explain, though every black in the courtroom could have done so, as could many of the whites. The anthem is heard at almost any gathering. It is emotive, like any national anthem, but it is not banned, and it is not subversive. Perhaps it makes no difference that in this trial it was not recognized by the judge and that although the prosecutor asked what the crowd was singing, the response he received clarified nothing.

> JUDGE: Did they not scream "Amandla Gawetu" [sic] ["Power to the people" – usually said by more than one speaker: "Amandla!"/"Awethu!"]?
> THERESA: I did not hear it.

Theresa continued, "The police came on shooting and throwing tear-gas." She was shot with a rubber bullet. "It reached me on my head. At the time I was just feeling a burn."

When she was shot, Theresa was in Zwane Street, opposite the "motor wrecks," on the right as the crowd moved eastwards towards the administrative offices. She described how she went into a nearby house and received attention for her wound. She had heard that hair around a wound could cause more damage, so she asked the people in the house to cut off her hair around the affected area. Neither before nor after her injury, Theresa said, did she wear a *doek* or any other form of head-covering. After receiving treatment, she went home. This meant that she was not part of the regrouping after the police had dispersed the original crowd.

Billy Gasapane, who lived in a little road the other side of Zwane Street from the Radebes', supported Theresa's evidence that she had come to his house, the fifth on the left from the Zwane Street corner, and his brother had shaved the hair around her wound. He said Theresa had told him she had been hit by a rubber bullet. Questioned by the prosecutor, Gasapane said he had not asked her where she was when she was injured.

During cross-examination about whether she could see Dlamini's house from the place where she was shot, the prosecutor said to Theresa, "The crowd was on its way to the deceased's house, not so?"

She answered, "No, the talk was that people must go to the office." And here there was an intervention, the same statement of assumption made to Reid.

> **JUDGE:** But we know they did not go to the office. Haven't you heard all the evidence here? They were not on the way to the office, they were on the way to the deceased's house in order to kill him.

Soon after this Dr. Hertzog, the assessor, asked whether the office the crowd was supposed to be going to was in the same direction as Dlamini's house, or in another direction. Theresa replied that one would pass Dlamini's house and then go on around the corner. Indeed, a short distance beyond Nhlapo Street, Zwane Street meets Dubula Drive, and a left turn takes one straight to the administration office by the most direct route.

It was Mabuti's evidence alone that implicated Theresa.

Christiaan and Gideon

"Was there something wrong with your eyes that day?"
MR. ACTING JUSTICE WESSEL JOHANNES HUMAN

The case against Motseki Christiaan Mokubung and Motsiri Gideon Mokone was very simple. The only evidence against them was that they were part of the crowd and among people who threw stones, and that they were in the front section of the group.

It was Mabuti alone that implicated them. In his evidence-in-chief, he attempted to convey that they were leaders of the group with stones, but in cross-examination he conceded that they were not, and that they gave no orders and threw no stones. Both admitted that they were unwilling members of the original crowd, and both denied that they were part of the regrouping.

Mabuti said Christiaan was in the front of the crowd as it stoned Dlamini's house. Yes, said Christiaan, that was so, he was near the front, but not at the very front. And he escaped when the police dispersed the crowd.

Christiaan testified that Billy Gasapane (the man who had received the injured Theresa in his house) had started a *stokvel* (a drinking party where the host charges an entrance fee) over the weekend of September 1–2. Christiaan knew the party would continue on the Monday. Soon after seven o'clock in the morning, he was on his way there when he met some people who asked him where Dlamini the councillor lived. He said he knew only the Dlamini who was a teacher. The people said they wanted the one with the silver-grey Cressida.

Then several of them grabbed Christiaan by his trouser-waist, turned him around, and forced him to go along with them to Dlamini's house. All but one relinquished their grip, but that one held him firmly. When he let go, Christiaan immediately ran away, back to Gasapane's, and stayed there until about 11:00 a.m., drinking.

In cross-examination, Christiaan said he didn't know why this unknown man dragged him along to Dlamini's place where people were throwing stones at the house and the car, which was in the garage.

While he was detained at Groenpunt Prison, he was taken on a "pointing-out" tour on December 18, 1984, by Lieutenant Roux, just as Reid was, and a photographer recorded the landmarks he allegedly indicated.

> **Roux:** When I got to Sharpeville, I noted – on – he said, "On 3 September 1984 at 7:30 in the morning a group confronted me in Zwane Street near house 7528 and asked me where Dlamini lived. I said I didn't know. . . . The group forced me to go along with them to Dlamini's house. I stood in front of house 7508 near a rock and saw how Dlamini's house was stoned. . . . They stoned Dlamini's car, a Cressida, silver-grey. I then got a chance to run away from this group, [to run away] home."

Christiaan contradicted Roux's claim that he had told him what happened at Dlamini's house, or described the stoning of the car. He denied telling Roux anything of these events.

❖

Gideon testified that he was on his way to his brother's house on the morning in question, when he met a group of people marching along Zwane Street in the direction of the offices of the Administration Board. They said everyone had to go with them, and surrounded him in a threatening manner. He was scared, and went along with them.

They passed the motor wrecks and then met the police head-on. Gideon said he turned tail and fled, wanting to run back to his house, but he did not manage more than a few steps. He heard a shot, and fell down, with a pain in his left thigh and the sensation of having no more strength in his body. It is common cause that Gideon was shot in the back of his left thigh by Dlamini, firing from inside his house.

> **DEFENCE COUNSEL:** . . . was this crowd behaving in such a way that if anyone was looking towards it from Mr. Dlamini's house, they might have thought that the crowd constituted a dangerous threat to the house or the people there?
>
> **GIDEON:** Yes.
>
> **DEFENCE COUNSEL:** And could – in those circumstances then – could one expect that if Mr. Dlamini was looking, he would have fired towards the crowd because of the threat?
>
> **GIDEON:** Yes.
>
> **JUDGE:** Are you suggesting, accused, that Mr. Zwane would have fired at them before they attacked his house?
>
> **GIDEON:** Zwane?
>
> **JUDGE:** Dlamini fired a shot at the people in Zwane Street before they attacked his house?
>
> **GIDEON:** Perhaps there were people who were attacking his house, but I did not see them.
>
> **JUDGE:** You did not see – there were people attacking his house, but you did not see them?
>
> **GIDEON:** I said perhaps.
>
> **JUDGE:** Pardon?
>
> **GIDEON:** I say perhaps.

After Gideon was shot he could not get up, and some people carried him to a nearby house – the Radebes'. From there he was driven to Sebokeng Hospital, where he was admitted. Thus he was put out of action definitively when he was shot, and could not have been present during the attack on Dlamini, nor could he be held to have had common purpose with the killers.

Mabuti had testified that Gideon was at the front of the crowd as it stoned Dlamini's house, and that was why he was shot. He insisted that when he was shot, Gideon was facing Dlamini. The medical evidence did not support Mabuti.

Mrs. Dlamini said she could hear from her house when Gideon shouted that he had been hit, but Mabuti, who said he was standing on the corner of Zwane and Nhlapo streets, at the very place where Gideon was shot, did not hear him shout.

Gideon, in cross-examination, said he did not see the house being stoned, he did not see who shot at him, he was not in front, he did not see Dlamini, he was running away when he was shot, and he did not know what Dlamini was shooting at.

The judge made use of heavy irony.

> **JUDGE:** We know from evidence that he [Dlamini] shot. Now what do you think he was shooting at? Was he shooting pigeons or what, that day? Or guinea-fowl, or ducks, what was he shooting?
> **GIDEON:** He was shooting people.
> **JUDGE:** Oh, I see now. Why? Where were the people he was shooting?
> **GIDEON:** People walking in Zwane Street.
> **JUDGE:** Oh, he just shot them in the street, in Zwane? People walking past in the street, past Nhlapo Street?
> **GIDEON:** No, I don't know why he shot.
> **JUDGE:** He was just practising a bit, that day, to see how many he could shoot?
> **GIDEON:** No, I don't know why he shot.

Gideon denied that he had shouted, "He got me!" or words to that effect.

He saw no placards; the crowd did not scream or yell, it only sang, and it sang in Zulu, and Gideon did not know that song.

He knew Theresa by sight, but he did not see her that day.

> **PROSECUTOR:** And No. 5, did you see him being dragged around by his belt?
> **GIDEON:** No, I did not see him at all, either.
> **JUDGE:** Was there something wrong with your eyes that day?
> **GIDEON:** No, there was nothing wrong with them.

> **PROSECUTOR:** Did you see that some of the people around
> you had stones in their hands?
> **GIDEON:** No, the people who were around me had nothing
> in their hands.

Gideon affirmed they had no weapons either.

Why was he so frightened then, the prosecutor asked. That
was because there were so many people in the crowd.

Did they threaten to do anything to him? Yes, he could see
that they could easily hit him.

Did they scare him? Yes.

At the end of the case for the prosecution, the defence made
application for the discharge of Christiaan and Gideon on the
first count, the murder charge, and the prosecutor opposed the
application. The ruling was delivered the same day: "The application for the discharge of Accused nos. 5 and 6 on the charge
of murder is refused at this stage as well as the application for
the discharge of Accused 1 to 6 on the alternative charges of
arson and malicious injury to property – [alternative] to the
charge of contravening Section 54(2) of the Internal Security
Act (count No. 2)."

The faces of the Sharpeville Six. Oupa Diniso, *left* (photo: IDAF: International Defence and Aid Fund); "Ja-ja" Sefatsa.

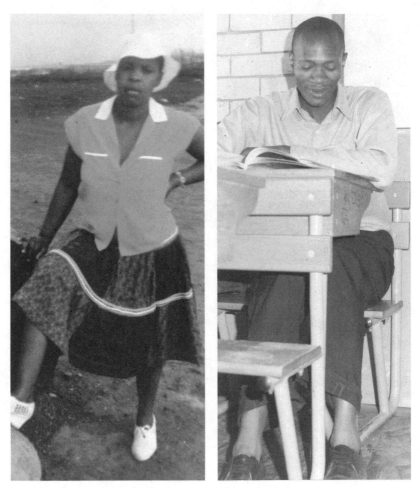

Theresa Ramashamola and Duma Khumalo

Francis Mokhesi, *left*; Reid Mokoena (photos: IDAF)

Top: Oupa Diniso's daughter, Lindiwe, *left,* and son, Thembile (photo: IDAF). *Below:* Reid Mokoena's sister, Martha, and his mother, Leah (photo: Ingrid Gavshon, IDAF).

In March 1988, family members came to London to ask the British Government to plead for their relatives in death row. *Top:* Francis Mokhesi's sister, Joyce, and Theresa Ramashamola's mother, Julia (photo: IDAF). *Below:* Women gather in front of the South African Embassy in London, March 3, 1988 to demonstrate their support for The Six (photo: Sandra Cumming, IDAF).

Half a world apart, people gather in support of the Sharpeville Six. *Top*: Norman Willis, General Secretary of the Trades Union Congress, addresses a protest outside No. 10 Downing Street (photo: IDAF). *Below*: South Africa waits outside the Supreme Court in Johannesburg (photo: Richard Nezar, *Pretoria News*).

Prakash Diar is hoisted to the shoulders of a jubilant crowd outside the Supreme Court. It is March 17, 1988: a stay of execution has just been granted The Six (photo: *Pretoria News*).

Francis Mokhesi's daughter, Mamodise Ruth, with Nelson Mandela in February 1990, shortly after his release from prison. Extending the definition of "political prisoners" to include those, such as The Six, convicted under the law of "common purpose" is central to the discussions between Nelson Mandela and the South African government.

Duma and Francis

> **"I am sure Mabuti did not know me. He used to call me by my full name, Joshua. Nobody has called me Joshua in the townships except when I was very young and at school."**
> DUMA JOSHUA KHUMALO

> **"What are you saying? What are you saying? You are talking rubbish."**
> MR. ACTING JUSTICE WESSEL JOHANNES HUMAN

Duma and Francis were implicated in the murder of Dlamini by the principal eyewitness, Jantjie Mabuti, with some corroboration and some contradiction from Joseph Manete.

Mabuti, giving evidence in English, described how the crowd approached along Zwane Street, singing as they came, and most of them gathered at the "motor wrecks." At this point the police appeared and dispersed the mob. The crowd regrouped, and started stoning Dlamini's house. Dlamini then fired into the crowd, and hit Gideon, who fell. Mabuti went on, "The people fled from there, they went back to the motor wrecks. After that I saw how they went to work opening the boots [*sic*] of the cars there, and tapping petrol."

Mabuti went to Dlamini, who was standing near his garage with his wife, and told them to flee because the crowd was coming to burn down their house. Dlamini asked him to take his wife and his car away, but he himself would not leave. Mabuti, so he said, declined to take the car, for he knew it would be dangerous to be seen in the township in that well-known vehicle, and anyway, Mrs. Dlamini refused to abandon her husband. As we have seen, Mrs. Dlamini had not mentioned this episode in her testimony.

Now, according to Mabuti, some of the crowd were busy making petrol bombs. There was petrol in large containers, and it was being poured into smaller bottles. He recognized two of the people involved in this process: No. 7 [Duma] and No. 8 [Francis].

> **JUDGE:** Were they the ones who made petrol bombs?
> **MABUTI:** Yes.
> **PROSECUTOR:** Now describe for me what they did.
> **MABUTI:** I saw that the petrol was poured into bottles and they were then handed over to others.

Mabuti continued to use the passive voice off and on: "They were handed over to others and they in their turn went and threw them into the deceased's house. . . . Some of those who received petrol bombs went onto the deceased's stand, some went and stood on the roof of his garage. There they used the bombs. Some went to the backyard of the deceased's house. From that point, in the backyard, these bombs were then thrown into the house. . . . The whole house was surrounded."

The prosecutor asked Mabuti whether anyone set the kitchen door alight.

"Yes," said Mabuti, "the kitchen door had petrol thrown at it, matches were struck and it was set on fire."

The petrol, he said, came out of a five-litre container.

Who threw the petrol onto the kitchen door and set fire to it? No. 7.

Moving on to Francis, Mabuti said, "Accused 8, he showed the people who were standing around with petrol bombs where and how to throw the petrol bombs. After that these people then threw the petrol bombs."

Then, he said, "those two at the end" (Duma and Francis) pushed the car out of the garage.

> **PROSECUTOR:** Was it Nos. 7 and 8 who pushed the car or were there others who helped them?
> **MABUTI:** No, there were many.

The pushing of the car is like a microcosm of the murder: two got named, so two got blamed, whether in truth they were present or not; and the "many," the others, melted anonymously away into the township and out of the story forever.

The car was pushed into the street, and Mabuti saw then that it was on fire. It was turned over onto its side. The house was also burning. People were still stoning it. Then Dlamini emerged through his kitchen door, gun in hand, and went around the back of his house, towards Maile's property.

The incident in which Mabuti implicated Ja-Ja – the struggle for the gun – occurred then. A stone hit Dlamini on the back of the head. He fell. He was dragged out to the street.

Mabuti produced a last allegation against Francis. As Dlamini lay burning, Francis said to the people assembled there, who were singing and giving black-power salutes, "Come, let's go now to the municipality's yard."

In cross-examination, counsel spent some time trying to elicit from Mabuti how long it took for the crowd to regroup after the police had left.

MABUTI: When the police arrived, it was early morning. The sun was up. I will accept that it could have been some eight o'clock.

DEFENCE COUNSEL: My question to you is, after the police had left and when you went out of your house and the crowd came back, what approximately was the time then?

MABUTI: That is why I said I am not certain of what the time was, but it did happen that way, but I could not care what the time was then.

DEFENCE COUNSEL: Yes, my question was, was it fifteen minutes after the police had left, half an hour after the police had left, three-quarters of an hour, any kind of guidance you can give us?

MABUTI: Fifteen minutes after the police had left, then the crowd regrouped and came back.

From Duma's point of view, this was the most important piece of Mabuti's evidence, for his defence would be an alibi.

The next chronological aspect of the incident took some time to thrash out.

> **DEFENCE COUNSEL:** Is it not correct that the shot was fired by Mr. Dlamini at the time that the police were coming along the road?
>
> **MABUTI:** No. Mr. Dlamini fired the shot while the police were not there.
>
> **JUDGE:** Fired the shot?
>
> **MABUTI:** The deceased fired the shot while the police were not there, or not coming.
>
> **JUDGE:** The police were not there when he fired the shot?
>
> **MABUTI:** Thank you.
>
> **DEFENCE COUNSEL:** By that are you suggesting that he fired the shot before the police came or after the police had left?
>
> **MABUTI:** He fired the shot after the police have left.
>
> **DEFENCE COUNSEL:** Are you absolutely sure about that, or is it possible that it happened while the police were coming along as you described what I have said is the first occasion, is that possible?
>
> **MABUTI:** I am sure that Mr. Dlamini fired the shot while the police were not there, before the police came.
>
> **DEFENCE COUNSEL:** Before the police came?
>
> **MABUTI:** After the police have left.
>
> **DEFENCE COUNSEL:** Oh, you just said before the police came. Are you confused? I do not want to confuse you. You just said before the police came and then you say, you corrected it and said after the police came. Now which is it?
>
> **MABUTI:** Before the police came, it so happened that Mr. Dlamini should fire a shot, before the police came.
>
> **JUDGE:** What is it now?
>
> **DEFENCE COUNSEL:** He says before the police came, Mr. Dlamini fired a shot.
>
> **JUDGE:** I understood your evidence to be that this shot was fired by Mr. Dlamini after the police had left. Is your evidence now that the shot was fired before the police came? The police were only there once, were they not?

MABUTI: Yes, they were there once.

JUDGE: Once. Now this shot was fired before the police came or after the police had gone, by the deceased?

MABUTI: The police went to the police station and so the crowd came back, come for Mr. Dlamini, that is why he shot them, that is why he shot his assailants.

JUDGE: Were the police there then?

MABUTI: The police have already left.

DEFENCE COUNSEL: You seem to be a little uncertain, because His Lordship just had to question you upon the different answers you made. I will come back to it in a moment . . .

MABUTI: Not – I am not uncertain. I am certain about the fact that Mr. Dlamini fired a shot a while after the police had left.

DEFENCE COUNSEL: Why did you tell His Lordship and all of us a little while ago that, in fact, as I understood you, this had happened before the police came or while the police were there? I did not understand your answer. Why did you say that?

MABUTI: I must have – my tongue must have slipped there . . .

Cross-examination was concerned for a long while with the exact place where the petrol bombs were made. Mabuti said it was in the yard of the corner house, Emily Moeketsi's, on the side facing Dlamini's kitchen door. Counsel asked whether one could see the backyard of the corner house from the windows of Dlamini's house.

Mabuti's reply to this was, "No, it is quite impossible, for only the kitchen door is facing the corner house where the petrol bombs had been prepared." Door or window, it made little difference, for Mabuti went on to assert that, when he was advising the Dlaminis to flee, as they all stood near Dlamini's garage, "That is where I saw the petrol bombs to be made for that is the very same corner, so I just shifted so that the mob could not see me."

DEFENCE COUNSEL: Were you standing on the *erf*, on the piece of land of Mr. Dlamini, when you saw these petrol bombs being made?

MABUTI: No, I was now at the corner house . . . in the yard.

DEFENCE COUNSEL: And you say that was in this yard that there were the large containers of petrol from which petrol was being put into the smaller bottles?

MABUTI: I was in that yard.

JUDGE: No, where did they fill up the containers with petrol?

MABUTI: The big containers?

JUDGE: Yes, the five-litre containers?

MABUTI: The five-litre containers? They came with it, the petrol bombs were being prepared at the corner house.

JUDGE: Yes, but listen, did you see at all when they were filling the big containers, the five-litre containers with petrol, did you see that yourself?

MABUTI: No, I did not see.

JUDGE: From the cars that were being repaired?

MABUTI: No, I did not see the petrol being taken into the big containers.

JUDGE: I was under the impression that you told me in your evidence-in-chief that you saw them filling up containers from the cars that had to be repaired, that is where all the wrecked cars were, and the cars that had to be repaired, you saw them tapping out petrol from the cars that had to be repaired into containers. Now, did you see that or did you not see that?

MABUTI: As I said, they were tapping the petrol – just by using the word "tap" – they were tapping the petrol from the cars there.

JUDGE: Now did you see that yourself?

MABUTI: I saw that myself.

At that stage, Mabuti said, he was outside the corner house, on the street. He stated further that he could not see, when the mob rushed from the Radebes' place to the corner house, whether they were carrying containers, for he was hiding then.

A discussion ensued about the pouring of petrol into bottles, and the carrying of bottles from one point to another. The judge gave the court a detailed account of how petrol bombs are made. Counsel asked how the petrol bombs – or bottles of petrol – reached the people in front of Dlamini's house. It turned out there was no fence between the corner house and Dlamini's property.

> **DEFENCE COUNSEL:** But the people who were to receive the bottles of petrol, where were they standing?
>
> **MABUTI:** They were among the groups, they were the people who were looking for something to throw at the house. Now, if he finds a bottle here, he could take a bottle, but now if he had the petrol, the distributor gave him the petrol – pardon, I should tell you the names of the people who gave out the petrol?
>
> **JUDGE:** Yes.
>
> **MABUTI:** Sure. As I said, Duma Khumalo and Don . . .
>
> **JUDGE:** Who is Khumalo?
>
> [This question went unanswered.]
>
> **JUDGE:** What did he do?
>
> **MABUTI:** When they were doing the petrol bombs, he made the – they made the bottles and go to give the people, like anybody come looking for a stone, then he gives the petrol bomb, then Don Mokhesi, by the other end, he carried also, he also carried bottles and gave them to other people and then show the people how to do that, to throw them.

Where did all this happen, counsel asked. Many inconclusive words later, the judge suggested the matter be settled once and for all with the help of Exhibit G, a photograph showing Dlamini's house and the corner one, taken from Nhlapo Street. A lot of pointing and asking followed, and eventually the judge felt he'd got it clear.

> **MABUTI:** . . . just between the deceased's garage and the house here, just by the garage.

> **JUDGE:** Are you referring to the area one can see here, where the petrol bombs were made? Here in front? Here? Here?
> **MABUTI:** Yes.
> **JUDGE:** This is where he points out.
> **MABUTI:** Yes.
> **DEFENCE COUNSEL:** Yes, in other words, where the grass is.
> **JUDGE:** Near the garage, near the garage, in front of the door of the garage.
> **MABUTI:** That is it. No.
> **JUDGE:** Not in front of the door?
> **MABUTI:** Not in front of the door of the garage.
> **JUDGE:** But to the right?
> **MABUTI:** Yes, to the right, but in this yard, in the corner house.

Finally the judge said, "Can you make a cross there where the petrol bombs were made?" This Mabuti did, or so the Court believed. Certainly he placed a mark on the photograph, in the corner stand but level with Dlamini's garage door.

On further questioning, however, he seemed to say that the place was elsewhere, in fact behind the corner house, near Emily's kitchen door, which faced east, away from Nhlapo Street. Confronted with the very mark he had made on the photograph, Mabuti said it was not a cross indicating a place, but an arrow marking a direction, because the actual position was invisible in the photo, being obscured by Emily's house.

The judge now perceived on the photo "a distinct arrow." Defence counsel got no satisfaction when he asked the witness why he had not told the Court he was making an arrow instead of the cross the judge had requested.

The next question was that of Mabuti's own whereabouts while Dlamini's house was being stoned, and after.

> **DEFENCE COUNSEL:** Very well, now you are at that point. Give us your movements after that. You were at the back of the corner house and you claim that you could see what was happening. Tell us what your next movement was.

MABUTI: From that point – as I have said earlier that there was somebody to put the fire off or to extinguish the fire.

DEFENCE COUNSEL: To extinguish the fire?

MABUTI: Yes, My Lord, at the kitchen door.

JUDGE: At the kitchen door? Who set light to the kitchen door?

MABUTI: No, I do not know who set light to the kitchen door, but it was poured with petrol and then it got light up.

JUDGE: It was light up. Who poured the petrol on the kitchen door?

MABUTI: At the kitchen door?

JUDGE: Yes.

MABUTI: As I pointed in my statement on Friday, it was Duma Khumalo.

Mabuti may not have known who set fire to Dlamini's kitchen door, but he had already implicated Duma in that act. He did not know who doused the flames, either, for this was done from inside the house. Surely, he said, it was the deceased.

DEFENCE COUNSEL: Did you see him or are you assuming that he did it?

MABUTI: I am assuming that as he was the only person inside the house at the time.

DEFENCE COUNSEL: How did you know he was the only person inside the house?

MABUTI: For the wife had already left with the kids.
[Where had the children gone? To Stoffel Maile's house, at the same time as their mother. This was a surprise, for Mrs. Dlamini had not said any such thing.]

DEFENCE COUNSEL: She does not say she accompanied the children. In fact she really does not know where they went. She just knows they were out of the house.

MABUTI: Oh.

The witness was, however, undaunted, and went on to claim that his account was correct, and Mrs. Dlamini's was probably wrong – though he wouldn't go so far as to say she was lying – because she was confused and scared and didn't know what was happening.

Cross-examination moved on to another vexed point: whether, from where Mabuti had stood with the Dlaminis, near their garage, it would have been possible to see the petrol bombs being made. The answer to this had originally been yes, and later it had been no. The judge felt that there was no contradiction here, but a misunderstanding because Mabuti had not realized that the question was purely geographical, and had thought he was being asked whether the petrol bombs were actually being made while he was standing with the Dlaminis near their garage, and whether they could see that going on.

At this point the Court adjourned, and the matter of the arrow on Exhibit G received a final word when proceedings resumed after tea.

JUDGE: Well, the witness said "error" in his evidence. What he was saying was "arrow," not "error." "Arrow."

At the end of his evidence-in-chief, Mabuti had been questioned by the judge as follows:

JUDGE: But tell me, who are those three men, do you know them, those who dragged him [Dlamini] away from Stoffel's yard to the street and put him across the motor car?
MABUTI: I did not recognize them.
JUDGE: And the person who poured petrol over him and set him alight?
MABUTI: I could not see him clearly from the point where I stood. The burning car obscured my vision.

After watching Ja-Ja's alleged attack on Dlamini from the yard next door to his own house, behind Maile's, Mabuti moved into Nhlapo Street, and stood opposite the fourth house, Maile's neighbour's, to see the burning of the car and of Dlamini's body.

And he was better placed to hear the woman scream, "Don't burn him!" – in the midst of all the uproar and singing – and to see Theresa slap her face, for by then, he said, he had moved along from the fourth house to the third, the one opposite Maile's. But in cross-examination, he contradicted himself.

DEFENCE COUNSEL: Mr. Mabuti, just so that I have got the picture quite clearly in my own mind, at the time that you saw the petrol being poured over the deceased, you were in Nhlapo Street?

MABUTI: Yes.

DEFENCE COUNSEL: It was either Stoffel's or the one farther away from Stoffel's. I am not saying that you said this, just correct me if I am wrong.

MABUTI: It is the house opposite Mr. Maile or Stoffel, the same street.

DEFENCE COUNSEL: The same street, and it is from there you watched the burning.

MABUTI: Yes.

JUDGE: Did anybody hit the burning body with sticks or anything like that?

MABUTI: No, that kind of thing I did not see, My Lord . . .

DEFENCE COUNSEL: Mr. Mabuti, I am asking you that question because it has been drawn to my attention that the evidence that you gave on Friday was to the effect that when petrol was thrown on the deceased you could not see clearly who was doing that because the burning car blocked your vision. That is the note that my learned junior has taken of your evidence.

MABUTI: That?

DEFENCE COUNSEL: The burning car blocked your vision.

MABUTI: No, My Lord, put that – I do remember saying that, but that was not to say the car was blocking my way, My Lord, not totally obscuring my vision to it for the car did not stand straight. It had a squinch, it stood squinch there . . .

DEFENCE COUNSEL: You see, I am going to show you Exhibit E2. Do you see that is a picture of a car on its side?

MABUTI: Yes . . .

DEFENCE COUNSEL: And being to the left of the picture, your view of the deceased could not possibly have been obscured by the vehicle.

MABUTI: Yes, sure, My Lord.

Near the end of cross-examination, counsel tried again to get some accuracy on Mabuti's whereabouts when the petrol bombs were being made.

DEFENCE COUNSEL: At one stage did you want to hide from the mob that were coming?

MABUTI: No.

His earlier evidence, counsel reminded him, was that he did hide.

DEFENCE COUNSEL: Why did you answer my question in the way you did, that you did not want to hide?

MABUTI: My Lord, I think your questions are so many that I do not know at which stage or before what or after what has happened, My Lord . . .

Afraid of being observed by the mob, and wanting or not wanting to hide, Mabuti said that he went into the very yard where the petrol bombs were being made, but that no one could see him there. Here's how:

DEFENCE COUNSEL: So where did you go?

MABUTI: I went in there. There was a shack, what we call "makuku," in the same corner yard [Emily Moeketsi's].

This was a startling revelation. He had not mentioned it at all in his evidence-in-chief, and it was appearing now for the first time near the end of his cross-examination. It seemed to be an afterthought. His choice of an English word to describe the structure was perhaps a trifle misleading too, though the name stuck throughout the trial. In Sharpeville, a shack is something people live in. This was more like a garden shed; it was low and windowless, and no adult could have stood up in it. One problem led to another for Mabuti, once he had said he was in there.

MABUTI: It was clear that the mob was now rushing in the street, then I took cover so that the mob should not see me, the mob, but not the crowd, the bystanders.

JUDGE: At what stage did you take cover? Before you talked to the deceased and his wife or after you had spoken to them?

MABUTI: After I had spoken to them, My Lord.

JUDGE: And then you took cover?

MABUTI: Yes, My Lord, for the oncoming mob not to see me.

JUDGE: And then you went into a shack where?

MABUTI: The very same house there at the corner house . . .

Mabuti was, he said, frightened of the crowd because they might have seen him talking to the Dlaminis.

DEFENCE COUNSEL: Now, Mr. Mabuti, if this is so, why didn't you then continue hidden in the shack until everything was over so that you could be safe?

MABUTI: No, My Lord, I could not stay there as the police were outside and everybody was outside. So, I found it easy for me to go out again.

But the police were not there. They arrived, and that is their evidence, only after Dlamini was killed. Mabuti could not escape the trap that he had set himself up in. He said himself that the shack had no windows. Could he see whether the police had arrived? Could he be certain that the mob was not still in the very yard where he was hiding? Wouldn't somebody notice if he emerged from the shack into the yard?

If it is accepted that Mabuti hid in the shack and came out when the police were present, he could not have seen the making and distribution of the petrol bombs, the burning of the house, the wrestling for possession of the gun, the stoning of Mr. Dlamini, the pushing and burning of his car . . .

After all these events, Mabuti said, he went with the crowd half-way to the municipal offices, where Francis had ordered them all to go.

An incomprehensible point he made here was that he went along for fear of the police. This seemed to change to fear of the crowd, but the matter was never elucidated.

❖

Joseph Manete stated in his evidence-in-chief that he was on his way home from his uncle's house on the morning of September 3, 1984, when he noticed a large crowd of people fleeing from the police, who were firing rubber bullets and tear-gas. People sought shelter, and then the police left. Manete was moving on in the direction of his house when Francis Mokhesi confronted him, saying, "Where are you going to? Why are you not with the people? Why don't you fight, why do you not take part, because we are fighting for the community?" Manete was frightened, and without answering, he joined the group.

At that time, Gideon was already injured, and people were carrying him away. Manete saw Gideon's wound, but he only knew by hearsay that it was Dlamini who had shot him.

Manete then heard Francis give orders that Dlamini's house should be surrounded and set alight. The people, he said, listened to Francis.

Manete gave his version of the incident, all the way to the placing of Dlamini's body in the boot of the car – an occurrence that no other witness observed or even imagined. When he saw this, he said, he got such a fright that he ran away home.

Right up to this point in his evidence, Manete had not mentioned Duma.

PROSECUTOR: Do you recognize any other person or do you know any other person that was on the scene, besides the persons you already mentioned, No. 6 [Gideon] and No. 8 [Francis]?

MANETE: Oh, *ja.*

PROSECUTOR: Who is it?

JUDGE: He is pointing at No. 7 [Duma]. Is that all?

MANETE: That is all.

JUDGE: Where did you see him?

MANETE: He was amongst the many people who stoned the deceased's house.

That is the sum-total of Manete's implication of Duma. Not a word of his throwing any stones himself, setting the kitchen door on fire, or pushing the car; nothing about the making of petrol bombs.

Concerning Francis, Manete was cross-examined about whether he could be mixing him up with someone else. Definitely not, he said. And when had Manete last seen Francis before this incident?

MANETE: I had seen Accused no. 8 on numerous occasions over the past week. . . . I saw him at the sports grounds going out for training, exercise.

JUDGE: Now tell me, when you met this crowd, and you were stopped by Accused no. 8, when this crowd marched to the deceased's house, did they have petrol bombs and petrol with them at that stage or where did they get the petrol?

MANETE: There were those carrying petrol in tin containers, others carried petrol in bottles.

This was one of those observations Manete made that no one corroborated.

DEFENCE COUNSEL: During the attack upon the house, where were Accused no. 7 and no. 8 standing? Can you tell us?

MANETE: They were moving around the house.

DEFENCE COUNSEL: They were – and that is all? That is the only movement, around Mr. Dlamini's house?

MANETE: Yes.

Mabuti, of course, had them in Emily Moeketsi's yard, making petrol bombs.

The judge asked Manete whether he ever saw people in Stoffel Maile's yard that day, and Manete said, yes, he saw Francis there.

JUDGE: At what stage was it? Can you say?

MANETE: It is at the stage that people threw stones at the deceased's house, before the deceased came out. That was still before he was killed.

> JUDGE: What did he do there? Can you tell me what he did in Stoffel's yard?
>
> MANETE: He had stones in his hands.

This was another contradiction of Mabuti's evidence. Manete had nothing else to add to his implication of Francis and Duma.

He was cross-examined, fairly briefly, on aspects of his story, and then proceedings took a new turn.

> DEFENCE COUNSEL: Do you remember where you were on the night of 9 April[1] of this year?
>
> MANETE: No.
>
> DEFENCE COUNSEL: My Lord, may the witness be asked at this stage to leave the court for a few moments . . .
>
> [After a short explanation, the judge acquiesced.]
>
> DEFENCE COUNSEL: My Lord, we wish to take the Court into our confidence by saying to Your Lordship and the Gentlemen Assessors that we have in our possession evidence as to a statement made by this witness . . .

Counsel explained that in May 1985 Manete had made a statement to Mr. Soman, a partner in the firm of attorneys instructing in the present case. Naturally the statement enjoyed the privilege ordinarily attaching to any communication between client and attorney. Soman had not known at the time that his firm was acting for the accused in this case, but when Manete wanted to see Soman again in September 1985, he was advised to find another attorney, which he did.

Any communication between client and attorney enjoys "privilege," which means that it is confidential unless the client waives that privilege. Counsel requested the judge to explain that to Manete and to ascertain whether he would consider, after consultation with his legal adviser, waiving the privilege and allowing himself to be questioned on the statement.

If Manete refused to waive his privilege, counsel argued, the judge could overrule the privilege in the interests of justice. There was no South African case in point, but an English decision[2] was quoted, with other argument concerning legal principles. The English judge had found no authority for a decision, but, working on what he conceived to be the rules of natural justice, he had found that if a document contained "evidence which will help the accused in resisting these accounts to which he has pleaded not guilty," the document should be disclosed.

> **JUDGE:** My difficulty is I do not know how this statement will assist, even if I adopt that principle, how will this statement assist the accused to prove their innocence? How can I make a ruling before I know that?
>
> **DEFENCE COUNSEL:** Well, My Lord, without going into the matter in any detail . . .
>
> **JUDGE:** Well, I must know.
>
> **DEFENCE COUNSEL:** Yes. Well, if I may, with Your Lordship's permission, do so, the contents of this statement are to the effect that the implication of Accused no. 7 and no. 8 is not a voluntary implication, but an implication that was dictated to this witness and because of that . . .
>
> **JUDGE:** I beg your pardon? It was not a voluntary what?
>
> **DEFENCE COUNSEL:** It was not a voluntary implication of Accused no. 7 and 8, but he was told to implicate them. In other words he is not giving the evidence absolutely untrammelled, he did it because he was told by the police to do it.

More argument was presented by counsel, after which Manete was recalled and his rights were explained to him.

> **JUDGE:** . . . I must enquire from you whether you claim privilege, in other words you refuse to answer questions about that statement.
>
> **MANETE:** Yes, I refuse.
>
> **JUDGE:** Pardon?
>
> **MANETE:** Yes, I do not want to answer questions about that statement.

Manete was sent out of the courtroom again, further argument was heard, other English cases cited.

Acting Judge Human's judgment on this matter concluded thus: "I am of the view that where the witness claims privilege in regard to a statement that he made to a professional person and he does not waive that privilege that I have no power to order him to be cross-examined about that statement. I therefore cannot accede to defence counsel's request that I should order him to be cross-examined on that statement which he admittedly made on 11 May 1985 to a Mr. Soman, an attorney, acting for the accused at the present stage."

So that was that, although this was a murder case with the death penalty mandatory unless extenuation could be proved. The vital document was wiped right out of the trial, and we shall see how the judiciary dealt with its existence when subsequently confronted with it.

Manete came back into the witness box.

> DEFENCE COUNSEL: Were you arrested following these events of 3 September 1984?
> MANETE: I was not.
> DEFENCE COUNSEL: And you were not questioned by the police then?
> MANETE: In what connection?
> DEFENCE COUNSEL: Well, in connection with the events of 3 September.
> MANETE: I was taken by the police in connection with Dlamini's killing.
> DEFENCE COUNSEL: When you say you were taken, do you mean that you were arrested in connection with the killing?
> MANETE: No.
> DEFENCE COUNSEL: Well, what do you mean by you were taken by the police?
> MANETE: I was taken by a policeman to the police station in Krugersdorp.
> DEFENCE COUNSEL: And were you questioned there?
> MANETE: Yes.

Dr. Hertzog, the assessor who seemed to be following closely, asked Manete whether he saw the petrol bombs being made. No. Whether he saw a woman with a blood-stained *doek*. No.

Whether he saw anyone tapping petrol from the cars at the Radebes'. No.

❖

Emily Moeketsi, who lived next door to the Dlaminis in the corner house, gave evidence for the defence. She contradicted Mabuti on material aspects, notably his fairy-tale about her shack, and the tapping of petrol at Radebes'.

From her house on the corner of Zwane Street, Emily could see nearly all the early part of the action, and it would have been curious indeed if she had not watched constantly, not least because of the potential danger to herself and her property. She was a friend of the Dlaminis, unlikely to give false evidence to absolve wrong-doers.

She told the Court what she could see of Dlamini's property and the rest of the scene from her various windows. No one, she said, came into her yard to make petrol bombs. If anyone had come into her yard, she would have seen them. Before she could go further, she was interrupted.

> **JUDGE:** So you, in fact, you were watching at three different windows that day? The first was looking at the cars of the Radebes to see that no petrol was taken, is that correct? You were looking into the yard to see that no petrol was poured in bottles; and thirdly, you would look through the side windows to make sure that no petrol bombs were made there, is that correct? Was that your duty that day?

"Yes, that is so," said Emily, most likely answering the factual questions.

But the judge insisted: "You had three functions that day?"

He spoke in a harsh, intimidating tone, but did not wait for an answer, instead firing some more questions at her about the time she had spent at each window. Not long, she replied.

> **JUDGE:** Well, you will readily agree with me, I take it, that if you were looking at the cars, you could not see what was happening in the backyard? Is that correct?

EMILY: Yes, that is correct, because there were no people on that side, the people were on the other side.

Emily testified that she had a shack in her yard in which she stored an old stove and her wood and coal. Because these were valuables, she always kept the shack locked with a padlock. In the evenings, she opened the shack to get wood and coal for her kitchen stove, and was always careful to lock it again for fear of theft. No one asked her for a key to get in there that day, and it was definitely locked.

JUDGE: Did you see Mabuti that day? Do you know him?
EMILY: No, I never saw Mabuti.

She was cross-examined at some length on what other events she observed that day, and gave an accurate description of the police speaking to Dlamini outside his house and taking his gun and then returning it to him. After that, she said, she never saw Dlamini again.

Thus she missed seeing him emerge through his kitchen door (which faced her house) and run around the back towards Maile's. The rest she could not have seen, for Dlamini's last moments occurred the other side of his house, and then on the other side of his burning car – invisible from Emily's house.

Emily could see clearly from inside her house down Zwane Street and into the Radebes' yard. She assured the Court no petrol was being tapped from the cars. Mabuti had placed himself at her house when he claimed he could see people tapping petrol from the cars. Two other independent witnesses supported this contradiction of Mabuti.

❖

Ezekiel Radebe testified that when Gideon was brought into his house after he was injured, he drove him to hospital. When he left for the hospital Dlamini's house had not been burnt, but when he came back it had, and Dlamini lay dead in the street. He went to check whether the cars had been interfered with, and found nothing amiss.

Two days after the incident, he noticed that one of the cars had a broken window, and when he investigated more closely, he found that two of the cars had broken petrol caps.

His father, Steven Radebe, aged seventy, was in the house throughout the incident, and was worried about possible damage to the cars.

> **JUDGE:** Did you specifically watch for that? Did you specifically watch the people, to see that they did not take the petrol?
>
> **STEVEN RADEBE:** Yes, I was inside the house, looking at the windows and I was also looking outside . . .
>
> **JUDGE:** When did you inspect the petrol caps of these cars on that day [September 3, 1984]?
>
> **STEVEN RADEBE:** I inspected them when the Europeans of high ranks arrived.

These police officers were at the Radebes' shortly after the murder. No broken petrol caps were produced at the trial as exhibits.

Steven Radebe had been consulted by the police and the prosecutor, and subpoenaed to give evidence on behalf of the State. The State failed to call him as a witness, and the defence called him. Perhaps it was because the version he gave them in consultation was the same as the one he gave in court that the State made no attempt to discredit Steven Radebe's evidence.

❖

Duma said he was coerced into joining the march, and witnessed the stoning of Dlamini's house. He was related to Dlamini and had no quarrel with him.

His defence was an alibi. After the police had dispersed the crowd, Duma noticed a friend, Ismail Moketsi, known as Mangu, lying helpless on the pavement in Zwane Street. He had been struck by a rubber bullet in the heel. Mangu had not arrived with the crowd: he had been out jogging, and had approached the Nhlapo Street corner from the opposite direction. Duma picked him up and carried him into a house second from the corner, in the street that runs off Zwane Street roughly opposite the Radebes'.[3] Here Mangu's wound was bathed and treated, which took approximately thirty minutes, and then Duma carried him home to his own house. This took ten to twelve minutes.

Thus Duma was away from the scene of the murder for at least forty-two minutes, and he was supported in this claim by Mangu and Mrs. Shabangu, who occupied the house where Mangu was treated. The prosecution accepted Mrs. Shabangu's evidence, and elected not to cross-examine her. Mangu testified that, after Duma took him home, he saw him cross over Zwane Street and turn left in the direction of his own house.

The regrouping – on Mabuti's uncontradicted evidence – took only fifteen minutes after the dispersal of the original crowd by the police. Duma's absence began, like the regrouping, just after the police left the scene.

❖

Francis testified that he was a professional footballer, and played for Vaal Professional Football Club. On Sunday, August 26, 1984, he had injured his right ankle playing soccer. He had to stay at home because he could only limp around with much pain and difficulty. His wife, Alinah, gave evidence in confirmation of this.

On September 3, 1984, he told the Court, while he was washing in the room where he lived, he heard people making a noise. He looked up towards Zwane Street from his house, which was in an adjoining road, but saw nothing unusual. He went back into his room, and stayed there for the rest of the day.

Counsel named the various pieces of evidence against Francis, that he had pushed the car into the street, and so on, and Francis said all these allegations were lies.

JUDGE: You see Motsumi [Joseph Motsumi Manete]. Do you know him? He says you are a soccer player. He knows you.

FRANCIS: I agree with him when he says that I am a soccer player, but I do not know him.

JUDGE: Well, he told the Court that he has known you for five years.

DEFENCE COUNSEL: It is Manete.

FRANCIS: He can say that, perhaps he has seen me play.

JUDGE: Pardon?

DEFENCE COUNSEL: The name is Manete.

JUDGE: Well, he has also got the name of Motsumi. Joseph Motsumi, that is the name he gave to this court.

FRANCIS: Yes, I can say that I know that name, because I heard from the police when they asked one of the witnesses here whether he knows that person, Joseph Motsumi.

JUDGE: Do you tell me you do not know him at all?

FRANCIS: No, I do not know him.

JUDGE: How would he know that you are a soccer player?

FRANCIS: We are playing for big soccer groups, the teams. When we go and play I do not know actually how many people do know me.

About Manete's evidence, that Francis had asked him why he did not join the people, why he did not fight, Francis said, "No, he is telling a blue lie."

JUDGE: A what kind of lie?

FRANCIS: A blue lie.

JUDGE: A blue lie? I have never heard that before.

Francis said all the other things Manete had said were also lies.

During his cross-examination, he said he could not say that the people of the Vaal Triangle knew everyone who played for Vaal Professionals.

The judge intervened, to say he must be well known, for he was surely a good player. Francis admitted this was true.

JUDGE: Did you score a lot of goals?

FRANCIS: Yes, it happens in a match.

The prosecutor argued that it was unlikely two people would make a mistake in identifying such a well-known soccer player. The other witness who had seen Francis on the day of the incident was Jantjie Mabuti.

Francis said he did not know Mabuti at all. He had seen him for the first time in his life in the witness box in this court.

Asked about the noise he had heard that morning, Francis said it was a noise of people singing. It had not made him curious. He had finished washing, and only then had he gone out to have a look what was going on.

> PROSECUTOR: And then you go, and when you see nothing, why don't you go further away to see what is going on?
> FRANCIS: No, I didn't attach any importance to it.
> PROSECUTOR: You could have gone looking if you wanted to, not so?
> FRANCIS: Yes, if I had wanted to.
> PROSECUTOR: Nothing prevented you?
> FRANCIS: Something did.
> PROSECUTOR: What prevented you?
> FRANCIS: The state of my life at that stage.
> PROSECUTOR: The state of your life?
> FRANCIS: Of my life.
> PROSECUTOR: What was the state of your life?
> FRANCIS: The injury I had suffered.
> JUDGE: The ankle injury?
> FRANCIS: Yes.
> JUDGE: You couldn't walk there at all, to Zwane Street?
> FRANCIS: I walked very slowly.
> JUDGE: But you could walk?
> FRANCIS: Yes.
> PROSECUTOR: So you could get to where you wanted to be?
> FRANCIS: No.
> PROSECUTOR: Did people carry you to where you wanted to be?
> FRANCIS: No, I couldn't go anywhere, because I have already told the Court that the injuries I had suffered to my ankle,

because of that I didn't attach any importance to going anywhere.

The judge asked if he walked on crutches, or if his ankle was in plaster of paris. No, it was merely bandaged. And who had treated it? Francis's uncle, one of the members of his team. Francis's uncle was a doctor? Yes. Where did he study?

Francis said he did not know where his uncle had qualified as a doctor.

The judge persisted. "What is his name? Is he a doctor there in Sharpeville?"

FRANCIS: He is a doctor in Sharpeville.

JUDGE: What is his name? Why are you having so much trouble? Looks to me as if you don't know what his name is.

FRANCIS: He is Dr. Mokhesi.

The prosecutor asked Francis how far he lived from Dlamini's house, and Francis said it was a long way.

JUDGE: Do you know Dlamini, the deceased?

FRANCIS: Very well.

PROSECUTOR: Where from?

FRANCIS: I knew him when he was a school-teacher. He was also a manager of a football team in Sharpeville and also he was a block man.

PROSECUTOR: A block man and a member of the town council, a councillor?

FRANCIS: I only heard now, recently, that word "councillor."

Did he know Dlamini was involved in the rent increase? No, he only knew the increase came from the office.

PROSECUTOR: And were you [Afrikaans *julle*: "you" plural] satisfied with the rent that was increased?

FRANCIS: I would like to know whether the question is put to me, "Were you [plural] satisfied with the rent that was increased?" I want to understand, because I live alone where I live.

JUDGE: Alone in a house? No, I am just asking you the question, do you live alone in a house?

FRANCIS: I don't say I live alone where I live, I mean I am alone where I stand now.

JUDGE: Where you stand now? What are you saying? What are you saying? You are talking rubbish. You just said you live alone.

FRANCIS: No, where I live, I do not live alone.

JUDGE: Are you married?

FRANCIS: I am married, yes.

JUDGE: Your wife lives with you?

FRANCIS: That is true. We have a child.

PROSECUTOR: Were you in your solitude satisfied with the raising of the rent or not?

FRANCIS: I say I was satisfied with it, because I had not been paying rent for very long.

PROSECUTOR: And the rest of the people who lived around you, were they all satisfied with it?

FRANCIS: I don't know.

The judge found out from Francis that he did not live alone with his wife and child in the house, but that his father and his younger brother lived there too.

PROSECUTOR: You say you have no knowledge of the people being angry with the councillors or the block men because the rent had been increased?

FRANCIS: I was asked about my neighbours, whether they were satisfied, and to that I replied that I do not know.

In support of Francis's defence, his uncle, Dr. Mokhesi, manager and medical adviser of Vaal Professionals, was called to testify. He said that Francis was an above-average player and injury-prone. On Sunday, September 2, 1984, Francis had not accompanied the team to a match at Alexandra Township, because he had a sprained ligament of the ankle.

> DEFENCE COUNSEL: Having regard to that injury, would he
> have been able to walk long distances at that time?
> DR. MOKHESI: I very much doubt, because he had a painful
> injury, but he was able to move around.

With an ankle so badly hurt that it had kept him out of a match the day before, and at home for a whole week, Francis, according to evidence against him, had marched from his house to Nhlapo Street, made and distributed petrol bombs and demonstrated their use, helped push Dlamini's car into the street, and exhorted the crowd to march with him to the municipality yard, another two kilometres away.

In summary, Ja-Ja was implicated by Mrs. Alice Dlamini, who said he threw a stone, and by Jantjie Mabuti, who said he wrestled with Dlamini for possession of the gun; both allegations concerned the same moment in time. Reid was implicated by his own confession, that he threw a single stone at the back of Dlamini. Oupa was found in possession of the gun sixty-seven days after the incident. Theresa, Christiaan, and Gideon were implicated by Mabuti only. Duma and Francis were implicated by Mabuti and Manete, contradicting each other on many points.

CHAPTER 13

The Verdict

"She had the impression he was going to blow his nose."

MR. ACTING JUSTICE WESSEL JOHANNES HUMAN

On December 5, 1985, judgment in the trial-within-a-trial was delivered, and the reasons were explained for the admission of Reid's statement as evidence against him.

The judge recapitulated that Reid, Accused no. 2, had to establish on a balance of probability that he was assaulted in this case, and that as a result of that assault he made the confession to the magistrate, Mr. Muller, on November 21, 1984.

The Court found various discrepancies between Reid's statement of November 19, 1984, his confession to the magistrate on November 21, 1984, his letter to the Minister of Law and Order, and the actual evidence he had given in court. These discrepancies were cited in detail, and the judge described Reid as a mendacious witness who evaded questions. Citing minor discrepancies, he found that the evidence of Reid's mother and siblings was mutually contradictory and not in accord with Reid's own evidence.

Not for the accused and their families the attitude the judge would display three days later in his main trial judgment concerning two vitally important and mutually contradictory State witnesses: "it cannot be expected that their testimony should be absolutely harmonious. . . . "

Serious improbabilities were found in Reid's testimony that Detective-Sergeant Gillmer had told him what to say in his confession to the magistrate. "If Gillmer had told him what he had to tell the magistrate it would be sheer stupidity on his part if Gillmer did not tell Accused no. 2 that he must inform the magistrate that he had killed the deceased, that he and the others there present doused the body of the deceased with petrol and set him alight and that they seriously injured him by throwing stones at him. Gillmer is an intelligent witness and cannot be described as a stupid person by any means. No. 2 also stated in his evidence that Gillmer did not shout at him nor did he lose his temper, in contrast to what was put to Gillmer during cross-examination."

If Ja-Ja and Theresa were assaulted by the same investigating team on the same day and the *modus operandi* was allegedly the same, the Court found there would be a sufficient *nexus* in respect of time, of method, and of circumstances to add weight to Reid's evidence that he was assaulted.

However, correlating Theresa's evidence with the sketch plan of the rooms where people were questioned at Sebokeng, the judge had this to say: "Any person, including other police officers, could enter the room at any stage. The curtains were not drawn and people outside could also see through the windows what was happening inside. The probability that Warrant Officer Schoeman would have not done what No. 4 alleges he did are [sic] so overwhelmingly in his favour that the Court cannot credit her evidence for one moment unless Warrant Officer Schoeman was bereft of his senses."

An interpreter named Sergeant Fred had confirmed that Theresa spoke Sesotho. "It is obvious therefore that Warrant Officer Schoeman must have made use of an interpreter because he does not speak the native language," the judge reasoned. Therefore, he concluded, Schoeman was never alone with Theresa.

Theresa speaks Afrikaans in addition to Sesotho. The question was never at issue during the trial. She certainly understood enough Afrikaans the day she was brought to court at Oberholzer to follow the little slanging-match between the police and the lawyers – the Boers and the coolies. She would not have needed much more to participate in the dialogue with Schoeman that she described.

Ja-Ja's statement of November 19, 1984, was found to conflict with the evidence he had given in court, and with Regina's evidence, which was also judged to be self-contradictory.

A detailed analysis followed of Ja-Ja's alleged assault injuries and Dr. van der Westhuizen's report dated November 13, 1984. The doctor examined Ja-Ja again on November 30, 1984, and the only complaint then was in regard to his hearing.

The manner in which Judge Human dealt with this aspect of Ja-Ja's injuries should perhaps be singled out. The doctor had noted at the first examination a fresh perforation of the left eardrum. This, he said, could have been caused in several ways: by a fist blow on the ear, blowing of the nose, diving, or infection. No infection was found. Diving was implicitly excluded. That left a blow on the ear, or a blown nose. The judge permitted himself the following comment: "It is to be noted that Accused no. 4 stated in her evidence that on 9 November she saw No. 1 accused at the Sebokeng police station. He had in his possession a piece of white paper and she had the impression he was going to blow his nose."

There was nothing improbable, the judge found, in the evidence or cross-examination of Schoeman and Matunzi:

> The Court was at all times aware that they could possibly have had a motive to assault Accused nos. 1, 2 and 4 in order to obtain incriminating evidence against them or to manoeuvre No. 2 accused in a position where he would be willing to make a statement to the magistrate.
>
> The evidence of the three accused, as well as that of their witnesses testifying as eyewitnesses to these alleged assaults, was untruthful and unreliable for the reasons I have already stated. Their evidence is riddled with improbabilities and their evidence is unworthy of credence.

Improbabilities were what the judge found. But what were the probabilities? Was Johannes Mongaule, the discredited State eyewitness, in fact assaulted by the police and told to lie in court? If so, was it unreasonable to imagine that these assault allegations brought by Ja-Ja, Reid, and Theresa were not fabrications? Could their versions of events be true? Was Theresa asked to testify on behalf of the prosecution? If so, and if she had agreed, would she have been charged?

If there was any truth in these allegations against the police, what about Manete, who went voluntarily to an attorney and stated that he had been assaulted?

Finally, one cannot avoid asking whether Mabuti, the star witness for the prosecution, was himself assaulted or threatened or induced by the police to implicate six people. Mabuti's motivation is hard to fathom. It is not easy to believe that he loved truth and justice so much that he was ready to send old friends and close neighbours to the gallows; and that he was prepared to risk being called an informer – knowing what was happening to "informers" all over the country – for no reward but a pat on the back from the judge.

❖

On December 10, 1984, the Court resumed to hear the full trial judgment. It filled 114 pages of court record.

Starting with Accused no. 1, the Court found that Ja-Ja told the police that Oupa had the gun, and led them to him. The necessary corollary, that Sergeant Wessels had no idea where Oupa lived, was accepted. Ja-Ja could not have known Oupa had the gun unless he had been at the scene on September 3, 1984, when the deceased was disarmed. The judge's reasoning moved forward to this remarkable conclusion: "The fact that No. 3 was found in possession of the weapon proves incontrovertibly that both No. 1 and No. 3 were on the scene when the deceased was disarmed.

"The alibi of No. 1 that he was not there can therefore not stand and is rejected as being false beyond all reasonable doubt."

Ja-Ja, of course, had claimed that he was busy rescuing Warrant Officer Malachia during the morning of September 3, 1984. Although Malachia denied in evidence that he had received any help, the Court did accept a statement dated September 21, 1984, in which Malachia said of the crowd that had attacked him: "the group divided into two. One part still wanted to kill me, and the other group not, and people from this group helped me to my house where I lay down on the grass."

Judgment went on: "It is also clear to the Court that through the passage of time since these events took place, Malachia possibly forgot that he was indeed helped by certain people, but who offered him help is another problem which must be resolved according to the available evidence."

Dlamini was killed before 9:00 a.m., and the judge reasoned that the attack on Malachia was later in the morning, so Ja-Ja could well have gone to his assistance, but that constituted no alibi.

Mrs. Dlamini claimed to recognize Ja-Ja because they had frequently travelled to work in the same taxi. Ja-Ja said he never took taxis. Discussing this, the judge said, "The Court has a very favourable impression of Mrs. Dlamini. She is a neatly dressed person and her honesty cannot be questioned. Mr. Unterhalter threw no doubt on her honesty as a witness but he claims that she was mistaken when she recognized No. 1 on the scene that day and testified that he threw a stone at the deceased."

Mrs. Dlamini's evidence that Ja-Ja threw a stone at her husband and did not wrestle with him, and Mabuti's that Ja-Ja wrestled with Dlamini for the gun and threw no stone at him, were found to be in no way contradictory. "It is clear that if No. 1 was the person who wrestled with the deceased and that No. 3 finally got possession of the pistol, as the Court has already found, No. 1 had the opportunity after that to stand back and then throw a stone at the deceased. The events occurred rapidly and the two witnesses took note of different episodes. They observed the events from different directions and it cannot be expected that their testimony should be absolutely harmonious concerning all the events. That it was indeed No. 1 who was on the scene and wrestled with the deceased for possession of the pistol, is, as I have already indicated, support in the material respect that No. 1 knew that No. 3 was in possession [of the gun] and took Sergeant Wessels to No. 3. It proves in point of fact that Mabuti's evidence is not disputable insofar as No. 1's identity is concerned.

"Mabuti," said the judge, "was an impressive witness. During a lengthy and testing cross-examination he did not contradict himself. He answered questions clearly and gave a logical exposition of the events of that day. . . . He is an intelligent person and was purposefully occupied at taking note of what happened that day because he intended to inform the police, as he did, what happened there."

The defence impression had been that Mabuti contradicted himself throughout. To cite a few examples: in his evidence-in-chief, he said he saw some people standing on Dlamini's garage roof; but, in cross-examination, he said he saw only one person. He said he saw Duma burn Dlamini's kitchen door, but later on he did not know who set fire to the kitchen door. He said that he did not want to hide from the mob, but almost immediately after that he agreed that he had previously said he wanted to hide from the mob. Mabuti testified that when the mob was approaching, he was standing at the back of the corner house, but later he claimed that he had hidden in a shack so that the people would not be able to see him.

Mabuti's evidence was supported in very important measure, the judge found, by the fact that Ja-Ja knew who had the deceased's weapon. "Mabuti is in the opinion of the Court an outstandingly able, intelligent, honest and trustworthy witness and the Court has no doubt that he saw No. 1 when he attacked the deceased with the object of disarming him. Mabuti, in addition, has known Accused no. 1 for years. There is no possibility he could be making a mistake in identifying him in his evidence."

Ja-Ja however, the judge found, often contradicted himself. For example he admitted, after first denying it, that he did occasionally take a taxi.

The intelligent and compassionate allowance made by the judge to Warrant Officer Malachia – that time had passed and he could have forgotten important facts – was never extended to any of the accused or the defence witnesses. Whatever they might have forgotten or become uncertain about was evidence of their unreliability or dishonesty.

❖

Reid was found to have lied in his claim that Schoeman had told him to admit he threw a stone at Dlamini's back, and to have lied again when he said he never reached Dlamini's house on the fatal day. After citing Reid's letter to the Minister, and Lieutenant Roux's record of his pointing-out tour, the judge said, "That the accused was at the deceased's house is beyond doubt, because he confirms it in this letter as well as in the statement made before Magistrate Muller, and also to Lieutenant Roux.

"Accused no. 2 identified himself with the murderous attack on the deceased and took part in it himself. There can be no doubt that at the stage when the house was set alight, the crowd had the intention to kill the deceased, because everyone there realized then that the deceased would either burn to death or he would flee from the house, and if he fled he would be attacked."

Reid had said he had told his advocate that during the pointing-out tour with Roux, he had his hands tied behind his back and he never left the car. Counsel had never taxed Roux with this information, and this proved, the judge said, how Accused no. 2 improvised as he went along in his evidence.

We had heard the finding, five days before, that Reid's self-incrimination was not made under duress, but voluntarily.

Reid confessed that he threw a single stone on the back of Dlamini. That is all. There was no mention of the size of the stone, or the time or stage in the proceedings when Reid allegedly threw it. Nothing to show it was before Dlamini was dealt the fatal blow, or indeed before his death. A stone thrown after the fatal blow could have led to a charge only of attempted murder. It is the prosecution's responsibility to prove guilt beyond all reasonable doubt. Where was the proof?

Let us assume for a moment that Reid did throw a stone at Dlamini's back while he was still alive. Did it cause any injury? None was proved. The district surgeon who performed the autopsy could find no injury on Dlamini's back. In any event, the cause of death was brain injury and/or burning. Reid had not performed the act (*actus reus*) of murder. Could it be said without any doubt that by throwing a single stone, he demonstrated the necessary intention (*dolus*) to kill? If he had had that intention, would he not have done something more effective than throwing one stone, which resulted in no injury?

❖

Concerning Oupa's case, the essence of the finding was this: "The fact that Exhibit 1 was found in Accused 3's possession links him directly with the events that took place at the deceased's house on 3 September 1984. There is no doubt that the deceased was deprived of his firearm that morning. Later, on 9 November 1984, it [the gun] was found in the possession of Accused no. 3. The only inference is that No. 3 was one of the persons who seized the fleeing deceased near the fence of his house on that morning with the intention of disarming him so that the deceased was rendered harmless and the way paved for the other rioters present there to pelt him with stones with the intention to kill him."

South African criminal law states quite clearly that, where another inference may be drawn, the accused cannot be convicted and should be given the benefit of the doubt. This "only inference" is one of the hardest lumps to swallow in the whole judgment. So many other possible inferences spring to mind. Oupa could have bought the gun unlawfully and had no licence to possess it. He could have been keeping it for someone, perhaps even Ja-Ja. He could have stolen it. Any number of other circumstances could have intervened between September 3 (or 4) and November 9.

On the difference between the evidence of Oupa and that of Sergeant Wessels about how Oupa came to have the gun in his possession, the judge found that the conflict provided further proof that Oupa was an untrustworthy and untruthful witness, and that if he did have an innocent explanation for his possession of the gun, he had not made it available to the Court. The defence argument that Exhibit 1, the firearm, was not the same colour as the one found in Oupa's possession was rejected as "transparently false."

Oupa was found by the trial judge to have lied, and if he did lie – and Wessels told the truth – about what he said on November 9, 1984, about how and when he had acquired the firearm, what then? There is an appeal court judgment[1] in which caution is specifically advocated about attaching excessive importance to untruthfulness, and emphasizing that false evidence does not always justify the worst conclusion. It urges the Court to be vigilant not to conclude that, because an accused is a liar, he is therefore probably guilty. Important are the nature, extent, and materiality of the lies; the accused's own circumstances insofar as they may explain the lies; the possible reasons why people may resort to falsehood, such as the fear that they could be implicated in a crime, and that admitting their involvement, no matter how slight, holds the danger of an inference of participation and guilt out of proportion to the truth.

Oupa, caught completely off guard by Wessels and his colleagues, produced the gun without a moment's hesitation. It is overwhelmingly probable that if he had obtained it in the course of a murderous assault he would have shown some hesitation or reluctance to produce it; or he would have taken more effective steps by hiding it and denying all knowledge of it, or disposing of it long before November 9.

Moreover if, as the trial court found, Ja-Ja and Oupa had acted in concert in depriving the murder victim of his weapon, the presence of Ja-Ja in the company of the police could only have warned Oupa that the police were on a trail that might lead him to the gallows. Perhaps his ready response to Wessels's demand suggests in very strong terms that he did not participate in the murder.

❖

Theresa was implicated and convicted by a single witness, Mabuti, corroborated by no one.

Judgment ran: "if Mabuti's evidence is to be accepted, it places Accused no. 4 on the scene and her defence therefore falls away. Mabuti identifies her as the person who slapped the black woman in the face. . . . If this is correct it proves irrefutably the disposition of Accused no. 4, namely that she had identified herself with the purpose of the persons who burned the deceased, and her purpose to kill him is then proved. But she also incites the crowd to kill the deceased and as a result of that she should be guilty as inciter of the crime of murder."

No evidence was ever placed before the Court that the people who actually killed Dlamini heard Theresa – or anyone – shout those words and, as a direct result of hearing them, killed him. The State would have needed to prove beyond all reasonable doubt that the words were Theresa's and that they had that effect.

The judge added: "Mabuti knows her well and she admits it. It was broad daylight and there is no possibility that he is making a mistake when he identifies her on the scene. According to her evidence, she was a part of the crowd at a stage before the regrouping. She testifies that she was hit by a rubber bullet and that she bled. Mabuti sees that she has a blood-stained *doek* around her head. In her evidence she testified that she went to a certain house where her hair around the wound was shaved off."

It was significant, the judge found, that Theresa had said she went to "a certain[2] house" for help, not saying it was Gasapane's house. And then, Gasapane had been unable to say what time it was when Theresa was at his house. His evidence made it clear that Theresa's own house was not far from his. Why she could not go home to her own house was therefore inexplicable. Conclusion: "The Court finds it false beyond reasonable doubt that she ever went to Gasapane's house that day."

Did anyone ever ask Theresa whether she could have gone home for attention to her head injury, and if she could, why she didn't? Perhaps it was just a bit too far? Perhaps she knew there was no one there? Perhaps she did not want to attract any more unwelcome attention to her mother's house that day?

What are the probabilities? A woman has been forced to join a crowd; she has just been shot at by the police and wounded in the head. Does she go in search of treatment?

If she does, and receives it, is it probable that she returns to the danger zone, knowing that the police are in the area and she may possibly be injured again, or even killed?

"The Court accepts Mabuti's evidence that No. 4 was indeed on the scene when the deceased's house was attacked for the second time, and that she uttered the words ascribed to her after the deceased had shot No. 6."

The killers may not have heard those words, but Mabuti, from where he said he was, not only heard them but could also swear with certainty that they were uttered by Theresa and no one else. If the woman who was allegedly slapped in the face had been identified and called to testify, the story might have been more convincing.

In terms of South African criminal law, a Court may convict on the evidence of a single witness, but great care should be taken to make certain that the single witness's evidence is satisfactory in every material respect. Was Mabuti's evidence satisfactory in all material respects? Many portions of it require scrutiny, because it was so important, and on it the conviction and lives of so many depended.

We have seen how Mabuti contradicted himself on various points.

He also contradicted other State witnesses. A very important instance was his claim that it was Ja-Ja who wrestled with Dlamini for the firearm, against Mrs. Dlamini's certainty that it was not Ja-Ja who did this.

He made assertions that no other witnesses corroborated, and examples abound in the record of the trial. He said that Mrs. Dlamini went to Stoffel Maile's house with her children. Three witnesses could have confirmed this: Mrs. Dlamini, Mr. Lekone, or Maile. None did. Mabuti said that Ja-Ja grabbed hold of Dlamini at the fence when they wrestled for possession of the gun and then "he jacked his leg and the deceased went over the fence. This is what I meant by throwing him over the fence." None of the other eyewitnesses said they saw Dlamini being thrown or heaved over the fence. Mabuti asserted that Maile's house was also attacked – the TV aerial wires were cut and the windows broken – but none of the people who were actually in that house on the morning of the incident – neither Mr. Maile nor Mr. Lekone nor Mrs. Dlamini – supported that evidence.

The points where Mabuti's evidence contradicted Manete's, or his, Mabuti's, have been noted, and seem barely worth adding to this catalogue, for Manete's evidence was suspect, to say the least.

On at least three important occasions, Mabuti also contradicted reason, common sense, and/or established fact.

He said Gideon was shot (by Dlamini) as he advanced (towards Dlamini), yet Gideon had a wound in the back of his thigh.

He stood to the left of the burning body of Mr. Dlamini, and his view was obscured by the burning car, which was to the right of the body.

He hid in a windowless[3] shack. Yet he observed everything that happened. He came out when the police were there. The police were not there until everything was over.

❖

During the trial Emily Moeketsi, Dlamini's next-door neighbour on the Zwane Street side, had come in for some scathing criticism from the judge for moving around in her house from one window to another to observe what was happening.

The judge persisted in his misunderstanding of Emily's motives in looking out in all directions during the attack on the Dlaminis' house. "She admitted that on that day she had three functions to fulfil, namely to see whether petrol was tapped out of the cars at Radebe's house, secondly to see whether people in her back yard were pouring petrol into bottles, and thirdly to see whether petrol bombs were being made at point X on Exhibit G.

"This evidence of hers is totally absurd and untruthful. How can she have known at that time that she would have to fulfil these functions with the object of giving evidence later unless she had had a prophetic glimpse of the future."

Emily said she was watching everything happening all around her, as well she might, from different windows in her house. The result was that she did in fact observe the Radebes' place, her own yard, and the Dlamini property, but at no time did she say or agree – although this was suggested to her – that she was watching *in order to give evidence later.*

Mabuti also moved around as he watched the scene – and changed his position time after time, when trapped in cross-examination. The judge tolerated this without the slightest criticism.

The problem was that Emily did not see things the way Mabuti saw them. If his evidence was to stand, hers had to be discredited.

The judge also found she was "thoroughly untrustworthy because although she knows Accused no. 6, she did not see him that day. It is generally accepted that No. 6 was shot that day by the deceased." (The defence could have done with an equivalent comment about Mabuti, such as: "He is thoroughly untrustworthy because, although he knows Accused no. 2, he did not see him that day." Mabuti did know Reid, and he did not see him that day. Yet Reid was found to be there.)

Finally, the judge made a comment that seemed to imply that he believed in Mabuti's fairy-tale about being inside Emily's garden shack. "Concerning the locked door of her *pondokkie*, her evidence is that it was her habit to lock it and therefore she claims that it was indeed locked that Monday morning. How she can remember such a triviality fourteen months later it is self-evident it is impossible to accept."

Obviously this kind of remark cannot sustain much analysis. Does one often forget to close a padlock, and leave it hanging open? If Emily was in the habit of locking the shack, locking it would hardly be a triviality to remember. Omitting to lock it would be an aberration, especially that Sunday evening when a mob was around, stoning her next-door neighbour's house.

Does it matter whether Mabuti could or could not gain entry to the shed? He said he could.

❖

Coming to the case against Christiaan and Gideon, the judgment ran: "Concerning 5 and 6, the only evidence is Mabuti's that they were among the people who threw stones at the deceased's house, that is to say, after the regrouping. The State has argued that their presence there is sufficient for them to be found guilty of murder. It must also be remembered that No. 6 was shot in the back of the thigh and it is possibly true that he was fleeing at the point when the deceased shot at him.

"[Christiaan] admitted Mabuti could have seen him but that was when he was on the corner of Zwane and Nhlapo streets. He was not forced as far as Dlamini's house. He didn't throw any stones that day. He did see the police on the scene, and when the people ran away, so did he. The police shot tear-gas and rubber bullets. The people who held him let go when the crowd started stoning.

"In cross-examination he claimed he did not know the man who held him. He could see the back of Dlamini's car. He denies that he said to Lieutenant Roux that the people had stoned the car, though he had admitted just before that the crowd threw stones at the car and perhaps hit it with their stones.

"He admits that he knows Mabuti well and that Mabuti is right when he says he saw him at the front of the crowd, but the man who was dragging him along was in front of him, he was not right in the front with No. 6. He didn't see any of the other accused because he was so scared that he didn't look who was there. He admitted he was among those who threw stones.

"This proves once more the accuracy of Mabuti's observation. . . . Mabuti's evidence does not go so far as to say that Accused nos. 5 and 6 threw stones, and even if they had, then in our opinion it was not yet clear what the intention of the crowd was. That only became evident with the setting of the house on fire and what followed that. There is no evidence that No. 5 did anything and concerning No. 6, it is clear that he was removed from the scene after he was injured, and that was at the stage when stones were being thrown at the house."

The judge found that, if Christiaan had been at Gasapane's, surely they would have talked about what happened to him on the way there, and that the fact they did not discuss this proved beyond all doubt that Christiaan did not go to Gasapane's that day.

"The Court is of the opinion that in the case of Accused nos. 5 and 6 it is not proved beyond reasonable doubt that they had the intention to kill the deceased. They are therefore found not guilty of murder."

The judge defined public violence, and concluded, "There can subsist no doubt in our opinion that they are guilty of the crime of public violence."

This is a competent verdict on a charge of murder. But in terms of the South African case law, an accused should not be found guilty of the crime of public violence merely because some acts of violence have been committed by some members of a crowd of which he is also a member. It must be shown that he was a party to those acts.

❖

Nothing that Duma said appeared to have been believed. The Court accepted the evidence of Ismail Moketsi (Mangu) and Anna Shabangu that Duma took Mangu to Mrs. Shabangu's house, "but that does not exclude that Accused no. 7 went back to the house of the deceased after the regrouping. Mabuti and Manete saw him there and they support each other that No. 7 was indeed there and actively busy with the process of burning the deceased's house."

In his evidence, Manete had reached the point where he got such a fright that he ran away home before the prosecutor asked him if there was anyone else he knew on the scene. Only then did he name Duma, to say he was among the many people who stoned the house. That was Manete's entire implication of Duma.

Here we had two witnesses testifying that Duma was part of the crowd when it re-formed, and this was seen as mutual corroboration, although they had him doing different things in different places at the same time.

Mabuti, the judge said, had known Duma for many years. Manete had known him for three years and knew that he peddled clothes. "That No. 7 was at the scene is confirmed by Manete, who noticed him at a stage when he was in the mob that was stoning the deceased's house."

The forty-two minutes of Duma's absence from the scene were not taken into account. The crowd regrouped within a period of only fifteen minutes.

"The Court rejects No. 7's defence that he did not participate actively in the burning of the deceased's house as false beyond reasonable doubt. His intention at that stage was to kill the deceased. About that there can also be no doubt."

❖

Francis, despite his wife's evidence and that of his cousin Dr. Mokhesi, manager and doctor of his football team, was found to have been well able to move around on September 3, 1984, although he had not been able to play in the match on September 2. His ankle injury, the judge emphasized, was already a week old.

"No. 8 accused was responsible with No. 7 for the making and distributing of petrol bombs which were thrown into the deceased's house. According to Mabuti he showed the others present where to throw the petrol bombs, and this was indeed then done. Manete supports the evidence of Mabuti in an essential aspect. According to Manete No. 8 screamed that the crowd must surround the house and set fire to it. The people obeyed. According to Mabuti he and No. 7 together with others pushed the deceased's car into the street, where it was set alight. That the house was surrounded is also supported by Mabuti. After the deceased had been set alight, he [No. 8] said to the people there that they must go to the municipal offices. Manete also testified that No. 8 asked him where he was going and why he was not together with the crowd. Manete also says Accused no. 8 said to him, "Why aren't you fighting, why aren't you taking part, because we are fighting for the community?" As a result Manete accompanied the crowd to the house of the deceased. He was involved in a direct conversation with No. 8 and can hardly be mistaken about No. 8's identity.

"While we accept the evidence of Dr. Mokhesi it seems clear that No. 8's ankle injury did not prevent his going along with the mob. No. 8's evidence and that of his wife Lena [her name is Alinah] is rejected as false beyond all reasonable doubt."

Nearing the end of his judgment, Mr. Acting Justice Human cited cases involving complicity, notably a 1920 judgment in the Appellate Division[4] concerning accessories and accomplices.

" 'All persons who knowingly aid and assist in the commission of a crime are punishable just as if they had committed it.'

" 'But if a person assists in or facilitates the commission of a crime, if he stands by ready to assist although he does no physical act as where a man stands outside a house while his fellow-burglar breaks into the house . . . if he gives counsel or encouragement . . . then he aids the latter to commit the crime.'

"According to general principles there must be a causal connection between the accessory's help and the commission of the crime by the culprit or co-culprits. Because an accessory identifies himself consciously with the commission of a crime or consciously helps in the commission of the crime, he has the purpose of helping the doer or accomplices to commit the crime. The disposition of an accessory to murder consists in that he has the aim to help the doer or accomplices to kill the victim. His own deed consists in the help or furtherance of the commission of the murder . . .

"Accused nos. 1 [Ja-Ja] and 3 [Oupa] disarmed the deceased and took his pistol from him. This had to be done because the deceased represented a threat to the crowd. Their deed facilitated the task of the crowd, to throw stones at him and to kill him. No. 1 himself threw a stone at the deceased, which hit the deceased at the back of the head. He is therefore not only an accessory, but also an accomplice. No. 2 [Reid], as already indicated, also furthered the crime by throwing a stone at the deceased. No. 4 [Theresa] incited the crowd to kill the deceased and she associated herself with the burning of the deceased. Nos. 7 [Duma] and 8 [Francis] furthered the commission of the crime and gave support to the crowd whose purpose seemed clearly to kill the deceased through taking part actively in the burning of the deceased's house.

"The result is therefore that Accused nos. 1, 2, 3, 4, 7 and 8 are found guilty of the crime of murder . . . "

I could not believe it.

None of the accused was found to have directly caused the death of Dlamini. A conviction of assault for some of them, or even assault with intent to do grievous bodily harm, would not have surprised the defence. But not murder. And it was impossible to see evidence that any of them had had the necessary intention to kill Dlamini.

The judge ploughed on, confirming what he had said earlier: "Accused nos. 5 and 6 are found guilty of the crime of public violence."

Dealing with the subversion charge, the judge said that according to evidence the intended raising of the service charges was one of the causes of the unrest.

"According to Dr. Mokhesi, 'this triggered off the riots'. According to Mr. Louw it was also a cause, although not the basic cause. The evidence of Maile, Mabuti and Manete, as well as that of Col. Viljoen is also that they [the riots] were consequences. By burning down a councillor's house and property and by killing him, it was clearly the intention of all the accused, as well as that of the crowd that was with them, to influence the Lekoa council not to raise the service charges.

"The acts of the accused also had the effect that the inhabitants of the Sharpeville area were frightened and that was also another objective of the accused. There is overwhelming evidence even from the defence evidence, that they were frightened by the accused and the other rioters that day."

At that moment this piece of sophistry was especially jarring: (some of) the accused were frightened into joining the crowd; they became part of the crowd, which by their own admission was a frightening crowd; therefore, they were engaged in frightening the inhabitants of Sharpeville.

"They committed the acts of violence set out in the charge sheet with the intention of dissuading the Lekoa council from implementing the intended higher service charges. They also had the intention of making the people in the area afraid. There can subsist no doubt about that. The accused denied in their evidence that they had the intention of achieving any of the aims listed. . . . "

All the accused, 1 to 8, were found guilty of subversion.

Intention is an essential aspect of subversion. Several of the eight had given uncontradicted evidence that they were forced against their will to join the crowd. The crowd itself, at the outset, was engaged in a rent protest. The implication of this finding seemed to be that any protest could be construed as an attempt to subvert the government. It was difficult to see proof that any of the eight had had the necessary subversive intention.

❖

Yes, the Sharpeville Six were convicted of murder on the basis of common purpose – a concept not unique to South Africa, and known in some countries as complicity. It applies to parties who have agreed on a certain enterprise, have reached consensus to achieve a common goal, and have given the enterprise their prior consent and approval.

Take a simple example: you and a friend meet and plan a bank robbery. It is agreed that your friend will go into the bank and hold up a teller with a firearm loaded with live ammunition. You will sit in the driver's seat of the get-away car, with the engine idling. You both know or you must foresee that, if someone puts up resistance during the robbery, your friend may be called upon to use his or her firearm. In fact, this is what happens, and he or she pulls the trigger and a teller is killed. You are both arrested and charged with murder. Now, although you were outside sitting in the car, you are equally responsible and liable for the killing of the teller, for you and your friend had a common purpose and you must have foreseen, since you knew he might use the firearm, that someone might get killed. So, on this basis, both of you could be convicted of murder.

No one quibbles with that kind of usage for the concept of common purpose. But the Sharpeville Six case was unprecedented. This was the first time in South Africa that common purpose had been used to convict members of a mob. There were not two or three conspirators, but a random crowd of more than a hundred. Meetings were indeed held to organize the protest against the rent increase, but no meeting was held to plan the killing of Dlamini. It was not possible to conclude that each of the accused had the direct intention to kill Dlamini, or even that they could have and must have foreseen his death.

On the fateful day of September 3, 1984, more than thirty people lost their lives. But only four murder charges[5] arose, each of them out of the killing of a community councillor. As the instructing defence attorney in two of these other cases, I was in a position to make close comparisons, and the facts in all the cases were very similar. So were the legal principles.

Of the three Vaal Triangle cases in which I was involved, the first to reach conclusion was the Sharpeville one. There was no escaping the question: would these indictments based on common purpose in a mob situation lead to many more convictions of murder?

Or was the Sharpeville case different? We would find out in due course. My clients told me they felt they were not getting a fair hearing. Meanwhile, I felt a great deal of doubt subsisted on the merits of the case.

Violence had spread since September 3, 1984, all over the country. The thought was perhaps legitimate that Judge Human might be on a crusade to set an example, and to show that if any local government officials came to grief, it would cost their communities dearly. Someone would have to pay the price.

CHAPTER 14

The Sentence

"Well, it is a matter of life or death?"
MR. ACTING JUSTICE WESSEL JOHANNES HUMAN

It is important to distinguish between conviction, which establishes legal guilt, and sentence, which concerns moral blameworthiness. Once the Court had found the Six legally guilty of murder, argument on that subject was closed.

It often shocks the lay person that defence counsel argues the presence of extenuating circumstances as if he accepts, all of a sudden, the entire prosecution case and judgment against his clients. There is no alternative to this in our system. The degree of moral guilt is determined after legal guilt has been established, and argument must be within the context of the verdict of the Court, however unacceptable that verdict may be to the defence.

Sentence deals with three main considerations: the crime, the interests of society, and the interests of the individual convicted. The judge has discretion; he has to weigh up all the factors, including the personal circumstances of the individual and his degree of participation in the crime.

In South African criminal law, the death sentence is mandatory for murder unless extenuating circumstances are found to exist.[1] Generally, where a convicted murderer is very young or has acted under severe emotional stress, or under the influence of alcohol, or in a "passionate" or "love triangle" context, it is very unlikely the death sentence will be imposed. It is up to the convicted person to prove, on a balance of probabilities, that extenuating circumstances are present and that he or she should therefore not be sentenced to death.

Friday, December 13, 1985, Reid's twenty-third birthday, was the day of sentencing. I am not superstitious, but I was very anxious.

❖

The defence called Professor Graham Allison Tyson of the Department of Psychology in the University of the Witwatersrand to give expert evidence on crowd behaviour and what happens to individuals in a mob situation. He had prepared a memorandum, and was asked to read it to the Court. It dealt with the factors that may turn a crowd into a mob: a focus on an event, loss of normal inhibitions, a sense of cohesion; a common objective; arousal, with highly aggressive impulses directed onto the common objective.

"In some situations," the professor told the Court, "the likelihood of mob behaviour is greatly increased by socio-political conditions. It is particularly likely when there is structural strain. This means that there are perceived inequalities or conflicts in the social system and no perceived legal or acceptable ways of changing this." The professor discussed the effects on the less privileged of their beliefs concerning the causes of their oppression, and the production of "a large reservoir of frustration which sets the stage for mob behaviour." He went on, "Research indicates that frustration is most likely to increase aggression when it is intense [hence increasing arousal] and when the cause of the frustration is seen as being arbitrary or illegitimate action. NB: It is the individual's perception which is important, not the actual situation."

Individuals learn as they grow up that certain impulses are unacceptable in their particular culture. They adopt restraint mechanisms, but in a crowd situation the effectiveness of these restraints is diminished. Anonymity within a crowd, excitement or arousal, a sense of group unity and diffused responsibility, with a focus on external goals – all these lead to a loss of self-awareness.

The opposite of objective self-awareness, the professor said, is deindividuation. This leads to behaviour that is "emotional, impulsive, irrational or atypical for the person in a given situation". He gave precise examples – "increased aggression, increased risk-taking, non-conformity, increased expression of obscenities, theft and cheating" – and stressed that it can occur in all types and groups of people, and no one is immune.

Aggression, Professor Tyson said, is often associated with mobs and deindividuation. He cited factors that contribute to aggression, for example, frustration, direct verbal or physical provocation, the presence of aggressive models, and heightened arousal.

"Physiological arousal dissipates slowly, so if an individual moves from a situation which has led to arousal to another situation, some of the arousal may persist. If in this new situation the individual experiences some provocation, the residual arousal may intensify any feelings of anger experienced by the individual and hence increase the likelihood of an overt aggressive reaction. This process has been called excitation transfer."

The professor concluded, "I consider, on the basis of my assessment of the psychological literature, that it is highly probable that an individual in a mob situation will experience deindividuation and that this deindividuation will lead to diminished responsibility in much the same way as do the consumption of too much alcohol or great emotional stress."

Defence counsel established from Professor Tyson that he was acquainted with the details of the case, and that he had sat in the court when judgment was delivered.

Counsel asked whether, within the crowd in question, the noise and the singing would have increased arousal. Professor Tyson said he had no doubt that it would.

> DEFENCE COUNSEL: Now still dealing with arousal, would the arrival of the police have any bearing on the matter, what would have happened if the police were trying to disperse the crowd?
>
> TYSON: Certainly it would increase arousal in the sense that people might become more scared, which would increase arousal, yes.

JUDGE: Increase arousal?

TYSON: It would increase arousal.

JUDGE: But if they dispersed – say, for instance, they were attacking a person's house and they were dispersed by the police – doesn't that break the strain of arousal?

TYSON (after a pause): My Lord, it would depend on for how long they were dispersed. If it was for a relatively short time in fact I would say it would increase arousal . . .

JUDGE: But doesn't it clearly show their determination to carry out their objectives? Isn't that true also?

TYSON: I would suggest that at that stage the people are so aroused, that they are actually not necessarily thinking in what we would call a rational way and that in these situations it is like any situation of excitement, people tend to gravitate back towards that situation. If the police ask them to move back they will tend to move forward again. I do not think it necessarily indicates that they have malintentions. It might simply be that in that heightened arousal state they want to be with others, they want to know what is going on, they want to find out what is happening, and hence people will gather together again.

JUDGE: Yes, but if they not only want to find out what is happening but they actively take part, for instance, in the killing of a human being, setting his house alight and setting his car alight, doesn't that show that they intended to harm this man? This regrouping is to obtain the object?

TYSON: I do not think it necessarily does. I would say certainly if it was a very calm situation . . .

JUDGE: But do you say that people in such a situation, they have no intent to kill?

TYSON: No.

JUDGE: In law?

TYSON: I can only speak as a psychologist. I do not know in law. I would say that in this sort of situation people are not able to make rational decisions, much as in the case when they are under the influence of alcohol, and that they are not able to weigh up the implications of their actions to the same extent as if they were totally by themselves in a relatively calm situation. I think when they are in the crowd there is such a level of excitation that people may well act in very violent ways without realizing the implications of their behaviour.

DEFENCE COUNSEL: Professor, there was evidence that the deceased at a certain stage discharged a firearm. There is clear evidence that Accused no. 6 was struck . . . as far as the crowd is concerned there was this firing by the deceased, can you express any view as to what effect this would have on arousal, or any other relevant factor?

TYSON: Certainly the research on aggression shows that when there is provocation from either side, people will tend to react and over-react and that this quickly leads to an escalation, so . . .

JUDGE: Will you call the firing by the deceased as acts of provocation?

TYSON: In a sense, My Lord, I . . .

JUDGE: The poor unfortunate deceased, was he not entitled to defend himself?

TYSON: Oh, indeed, My Lord, I would say that . . .

JUDGE: If he does fire at this crowd, who was threatening his life, are you suggesting that is a form of provocation which justifies their behaviour?

TYSON: Perhaps "provocation" has a different meaning in *law* to the way I am using it. All I am saying is that it would have served as a stimulus to increase the aggressive reactions of the crowd.

JUDGE: Stimulate the aggression, the aggressiveness?

TYSON: That is correct. Certainly I would say that his reaction is also a response to what he perceives as provocation.

Speaking of Theresa, the professor considered that the pain and fear she would have experienced when she was shot with a rubber bullet could have increased her level of arousal, and with it the possibility of aggression. "I should perhaps stress that arousal is a physiological state, the way we interpret it depends on situational cues, so we can determine or we can interpret it as fear or anger or whatever, depending on the situation."

JUDGE: But if people themselves are the cause of that by marching with a mob and now the police come along and disperse them and shoot off rubber bullets and she is struck, do you say that she is to be regarded in the same position because of her pain and fear and anger as a person under the influence of intoxicating liquor or drugs?

TYSON: In terms of behaviour, yes, but because of the situation, I would say that a person in that situation would be less able to think rationally to evaluate their behaviour, to evaluate the consequences of their behaviour. And essentially I believe that this could happen to anyone, any of us, given the right situation and the right circumstances . . .

In cross-examination, the prosecutor asked whether the impairment of rational thinking in such a situation would differ from person to person, and the professor agreed it would.

PROSECUTOR: And I take it that you did not have any interview whatsoever with any of the accused before Court?

TYSON: No, I did not.

PROSECUTOR: Yes, so you are not able to say whether they in fact were influenced by the crowd or by the police or by the shooting of the deceased whatsoever? All you are saying is that in general that is the position?

TYSON: In general that is the position, and probabilities on which we work suggest that the majority, the vast majority of people would be influenced by these factors.

PROSECUTOR: Yes, but you cannot say, for instance Accused no. 3, that he was influenced by any of these factors?

TYSON: What I feel I could say with certainty is that all of them would have been influenced to some extent. I cannot say which would be influenced more or less, but I certainly believe that all of them would have been.

PROSECUTOR: Yes, but as you said, you did not interview them at all?

TYSON: No, I did not interview them at all and I do not believe that that would have served any purpose, because outside the actual situation it would be very difficult to assess who would be more susceptible to the event.

Dr. Hertzog the assessor asked whether the people in this mob would have any consciousness of acting against the law.

TYSON: I believe that in fact it would not even have crossed their minds.

The judge referred to Colonel Viljoen's evidence that the riots had been well planned and executed, that specific people had specific targets on that day. "If this was a pre-planned thing," he asked, "would that have any influence on your evidence?"

TYSON: I do not believe so, because . . .

JUDGE: You mean people can predetermine to go in a mob and they can then lay claim to the fact that that influences their behaviour?

TYSON: No, My Lord, what I was about to say is I think people who plan the riots certainly do not fall into this category, but I think what happens is that you only need a few people to start it off and then a lot of perhaps should I say innocent – fairly innocent – people get caught up in the process and get involved in it. I would suspect that if it was planned, that in fact the planners were probably not even present. That once a mob gets started, it does not need any direction and very often it can be people who had no idea about what the aims or the goals were that get caught up in it . . .

JUDGE: You say the influence that this arousal and possible provocation has on their – has it got any bearing on their intentions?

TYSON: I really am not sure how to answer that. I would say that once there is this high level of arousal and deindividuation that people do not necessarily think in terms of intentions. They think in terms of very basic almost primitive urges that we all have, which is why aggressive behaviour comes out so frequently. Our aggressive behaviour is usually controlled by social mechanisms and fear of disapproval by other people, or fear of being caught, whereas in this situation that mechanism drops, so that people will release more primitive types of behaviour, whether they are aware of the intentions and the consequences, I think that is unlikely.

Defence counsel, in his address, cited judgments delivered in South African courts concerning the lack of control resulting from intoxication, and equated this with the loss of inhibition occurring among people caught in a crowd situation.

JUDGE: Well, he says the effect on their behaviour is to be judged as if – as a diminished responsibility.
DEFENCE COUNSEL: Yes, that is so.
JUDGE: In the same way as consumption of too much alcohol is concerned.

Defence counsel then quoted the recent case of S *v.* Smith 1984 (1) S.A. 583, concerning a woman who procured the murder of her husband. "The first appellant had planned the murder, the second appellant had assisted her by finding a person who was willing to kill the deceased, and by luring the deceased outside his home to where the killer was waiting. . . . "

So, the second appellant, who also switched off the lights (so that the victim could not see) not only associated himself with the crime but actively assisted in carrying out the murder.

Yet the appeal court judge, Mr. Justice Wessels, found: "In my opinion it is open to this Court to reconsider the issue of extenuating circumstances. In my opinion second appellant discharged the onus resting upon him on this issue. Quite apart from the circumstances relied upon by the court *a quo* [the trial court] in concluding that second appellant's moral blameworthiness had been reduced to a certain extent, it is a further extenuating circumstance that second appellant's participation in the commission of the murder was of a far lesser order than that of both third and first appellants."

Likewise, counsel contended, the moral blameworthiness of the accused in this case was in no way equivalent to that of the people (never identified) who dragged the body of Mr. Dlamini into the street, poured petrol on it, and set it alight.

Still on comparative moral blameworthiness, the address continued:

> **DEFENCE COUNSEL:** . . . and let me take the worst example that we know in the Criminal Law – the calculated premeditated poisoning of one person by another – I mentioned during the course of the trial at a certain stage what Mrs. De Melcker did to her husband – then one says in a case like that, there can be no excuse whatsoever in respect of there having been lack of restraint, whereas in a case like this, if there was lack of restraint because of the influences that the crowd scene and the crowd environment brought to bear upon the accused, it is something that will serve as an extenuation. And –
>
> [At this point, the judge intervened.]
>
> **JUDGE:** The Professor's evidence goes a bit further. He says that it actually led to diminished responsibility. . . . He considered: "on the basis of my assessment of the psychological literature, it is highly probable that an individual in a mob situation will experience deindividuation and that this deindividuation will lead to diminished responsibility, in much the same way as the consumption of too much alcohol, or great emotional stress."
>
> **DEFENCE COUNSEL:** Yes, that is so, My Lord . . .
>
> **JUDGE:** Well, if that is so, of course; if it is the case of diminished responsibility, that would be an extenuating circumstance?
>
> **DEFENCE COUNSEL:** Yes, and that is our submission.

The Court was asked to consider Professor Tyson's evidence and its relevance to background factors prevailing in the black communities: lack of understanding of local government, resentment as explained by the Town Clerk of Lekoa (that decisions were always made by others), fundamental dissatisfaction with the total situation, and a strong sense of grievance over the rent increases.

> **JUDGE:** Assuming for the moment that there were grievances, can this Court put its stamp of approval on the way they aired their grievances by killing councillors?
> **DEFENCE COUNSEL:** No, My Lord.
> **JUDGE:** Chosen councillors?
> **DEFENCE COUNSEL:** No, My Lord . . . it will not be an approval by the Court of whatever behaviour took place, it will be a distinction by the Court between certain of the behaviour that took place and other forms of behaviour that took place . . .

The prosecutor cited, in reply, authorities to the effect that the Court must ascertain whether circumstances exist that could have affected the judgment or the emotional state of the accused; if so, whether such circumstances did influence the accused subjectively; and whether the subjective influence on the accused's judgment or emotional state was such that it made the accused's behaviour less punishable or blameworthy from the point of view of the death of the deceased, according to the objective verdict of the Court.

> **PROSECUTOR:** My Learned Friend mentioned the evidence of Professor Tyson . . .
> **JUDGE:** Have you any evidence to refute it?

The prosecutor had no quarrel with the professor's claim that a person in a group might behave in a certain way.
The judge interrupted: "He says it is highly likely?"

> **PROSECUTOR:** It is highly likely but . . .
> **JUDGE:** Any person, generally, who moves around with such a group suffers from a certain "diminished responsibility."
> **PROSECUTOR:** "Diminished responsibility," but now Your Lordship will remember . . .

JUDGE: Now, if it is so, is it not an extenuating circumstance?

PROSECUTOR: It could be, I submit, if the accused had gone into the witness box and said, "Normally I would not do such a thing, but the crowd so aroused me that I could not help myself and they dragged me along with them, as a river carries someone. . . . "

JUDGE: Yes, but Professor Tyson says . . .

PROSECUTOR: But not one of them gave that evidence. . . . All the accuseds' evidence was that they knew nothing of the situation – the political situation in Sharpeville – they didn't even know there were councillors; most of the time they were not there or they were forced to be there. They did not take the Court into their confidence and say these aspects are aspects that influenced me. . . .

Here the prosecutor quoted again from the judgment in the recent Smith case "the fact that an accused person acted in anger is not in itself extenuating. That depends on the circumstances which influenced his mental capacity or his emotional condition."

JUDGE: Is your argument that because there was no evidence from the accused how this mass of people influenced them, we cannot find Professor Tyson's findings are relevant to them?

PROSECUTOR: That is my submission.

The prosecutor argued that, in the same way, none of the accused came forward to say he or she was dissatisfied about the rent increase, or about anything else. Could the Court then speculate in their favour where they had not taken the Court into their confidence?

Now argument came to the crucial question.

JUDGE: Now each person who contributed to the death of the deceased is just as guilty as the persons who burned him.

PROSECUTOR: That is correct, and then one cannot argue that Accused no. 2 [Reid] for example participated to a limited extent because he threw only one stone onto the man's back. One holds him accountable for the whole action that occurred because he had identified himself – he was not an individual who threw a stone *in vacuo*, he was one of a crowd that threw. I take him now as an example. And therefore one cannot say that because there is an individual who participated to a lesser extent, that can serve as an extenuating circumstance.

Defence counsel's argument – that the people who had dragged the deceased to the car and thrown petrol over him were more blameworthy than the others – was faulty, the prosecutor submitted "with respect," because Dr. Church had testified that the cause of death was not only burning but also brain injuries. These three unidentified people who had doused the deceased with petrol had merely put the final seal on the death. Furthermore, the argument would not serve the interests of Theresa very well, for she had definitely identified herself with the burning.

JUDGE: Are there cases to the effect that even where extenuating circumstances are found, the Court can look at the seriousness of the crime? At the aggravating circumstances, and then nevertheless impose the death penalty?

The prosecutor assured the judge that there were such cases and ended his argument by saying: "I submit that this Court cannot under any circumstances place any stamp of approval on the actions of the accused."

In reply, defence counsel asked the Court not to take away its own discretion: if extenuating circumstances were found, the Court could yet impose the death sentence if it saw fit. If none were found, the Court had no choice but to impose the death sentence. "But to close the door at this stage . . . cannot be consistent with a judgment of moral guilt, and I am saying that . . . with emphasis, because the whole tradition in the courts on this matter is to that effect."

Taking Reid again as an example, counsel went on, "to sentence [him] to death because he happened to be in a crowd and he threw a stone which hit the deceased while he was lying on the ground does not require legal submissions. One looks at it from the point of view of the ordinary man making an ordinary moral judgment . . . " [Judge intervenes.]

JUDGE: If there was a concerted attack, throwing stones at the deceased, and he joins in, with the intent to kill?

DEFENCE COUNSEL: Yes, he has . . . [Judge intervenes.]

JUDGE: You say he is less morally blameworthy?

DEFENCE COUNSEL: I say he is less blameworthy, My Lord, and I say it with emphasis . . . [Judge intervenes.]

JUDGE: But then not one of them throwing stones would be guilty of – there would be extenuating circumstances?
[Counsel, agreeing, was interrupted a fourth time.]

JUDGE: In the case of each one that threw stones?
[Counsel cited Tyson, and was again interrupted.]

JUDGE: So, even if there is a murderous attack on a deceased person, then one must look at the individual act of each and every accused to determine whether there are extenuating circumstances?

DEFENCE COUNSEL: Oh yes, My Lord, that must be so.

Counsel sketched "what was probably the situation: . . . there was this heightened excitement, there was the aggression of which the professor speaks. There was the whole background which I have . . . " [Judge intervenes.]

JUDGE: Well, it seems to me they associated the person of the deceased with the increased rentals and therefore he had to be eliminated.

DEFENCE COUNSEL: That may well be and . . . [Judge intervenes.]

JUDGE: And therefore he had to be eliminated because he was the sell-out, according to them?

DEFENCE COUNSEL: That is background, My Lord, but looking at it . . . [Judge intervenes.]

JUDGE: Well, it will be a sad day for South Africa if that would constitute an extenuating circumstance.

DEFENCE COUNSEL: No, no, My Lord, if it had been done . . . [Judge intervenes.]

JUDGE: Well, then all the people who have grievances in this country cannot go the legal way about airing their grievances but they can kill and maim people.

DEFENCE COUNSEL: But, My Lord, please contrast the situation of a man who sets out sober and alone and he is inspired by some kind of misguided social zeal and he says, "I am going to kill this man because he has been responsible for increasing the rentals" and he kills him. . . . But . . . our case is that this was done by these people in respect of their particular contributory acts in a crowd scene where there was diminished responsibility.

JUDGE: You are relying on diminished responsibility as a result of mob psychology?

Yes. And taking Reid's case again, counsel said, "There is legal guilt because Your Lordships have found there were accessories and accomplices. But on moral guilt he cannot be punished, in our submission, with the extreme penalty because he threw a stone at the back of the deceased when he was lying on the ground."

JUDGE: But then that argument – if that argument is correct then none of the accused can be sentenced to death?

DEFENCE COUNSEL: Well, My Lord, that is . . . [Judge intervenes.]

JUDGE: Because their moral guilt was affected?

DEFENCE COUNSEL: Well, that is what we are urging upon Your Lordship and Gentlemen . . .

Argument continued about diminished responsibility and crowd psychology.

JUDGE: But who created that situation?

DEFENCE COUNSEL: The crowd.

JUDGE: Well, then, everybody in this country intent upon

killing a person can just assemble a crowd and say we are now subject to crowd psychology, and therefore we can murder and kill.

Counsel asked the Court to distinguish between the cynical organizers who manipulate a crowd and the people in the crowd.

The judge said there were no leaders in this case, and the people took part voluntarily because when the crowd was dispersed by the police they reassembled "with the object no doubt of doing what they intended to do."

Again counsel invoked crowd psychology.

JUDGE: Now, how do I know that when they reassembled they were under crowd – they were suffering from the impact of crowd psychology?

DEFENCE COUNSEL: Because Professor Tyson has told Your Lordship that a very good period of time is required to dissipate the effects of crowd psychology. Unfortunately what happened in this particular case was that the police, because of pressure upon them, dispersed the crowd and went elsewhere. Even Colonel Viljoen himself found that he had to go elsewhere although he was on the scene.

JUDGE: Well, evidence was there, within what time did they regroup?

DEFENCE COUNSEL: Well, Your Lordship has the following times, that the colonel came there at twenty minutes past seven and he was talking to the deceased and his wife. There was an adjustment to the firearm. He went off to see what he could find by way of injured people and then Lieutenant Bezuidenhout said that he received a message at eight o'clock, the effect of which was that he had to come at once, although it is not said explicitly, but obviously he came there because of the attack. . . .

JUDGE: Well, we will take it in favour of the accused, they reassembled almost immediately after the police disappeared?

DEFENCE COUNSEL: That is so. . . . Our submission is it is similar to the influence of liquor upon them, it is an extenuating circumstance, and, My Lord, I do not want to dwell on it any more, I . . .

JUDGE: This is certainly the first time that this has been urged as an extenuating circumstance in our courts. There are no precedents for this.

Counsel was rounding off his address with the words, "debate the moral blameworthiness and our submission is that on the . . . " when the last interruption came.

JUDGE: Well, it is a matter of life or death?
DEFENCE COUNSEL: Yes, and I leave it in the hands of the Court.

The judge adjourned proceedings until three o'clock.

❖

When the Court resumed in the afternoon, there was not even standing room. In the absolute quiet, the judge sat down with an assessor each side of him. "Six of the accused, namely numbers 1, 2, 3, 4, 7 and 8, were found guilty on a charge of murder," he began, and launched straight into his finding on extenuating circumstances.

He made a few points that had not been raised during the morning's argument. No evidence had been placed before the Court, he said, that the accused were pressed or forced to join the crowd. Among the people who regrouped, each of the accused was seen and identified. The accused wanted to murder not only a person, but society itself.

Professor Tyson's evidence on what happens generally to an individual in a mob situation was accepted, but the defence had failed to show that each of the Six had been affected individually by mob psychology.

Responding apparently to the prosecutor's main thrust, that none of the accused came forward to give evidence and confirm that yes, he or she was there and was influenced by the crowd to the point of deindividuation, and did not realize the consequences of their actions, the judge criticized the six for failing to discharge their onus.

His conclusion ran, "The spirit of the crowd including the accused was one of violence and disregard for the law and for the rights of others. They linked the deceased, an elected member of the Lekoa Town Council, with the increased service charges, and killed him in a gruesome, mediaeval and barbaric way. Such action cannot be permitted in a modern State. The Court is unanimously of the opinion that no extenuating circumstances, on a balance of probabilities, have been proved here."

In the bitter disappointment, we realized a couple of things about this finding. One was that the judge seemed to have chosen to regard "the crowd" as only that crowd that regrouped after the police dispersed the people. That was how it was possible to claim that no one was coerced into joining the mob. Tyson's important evidence about residual arousal and new provocation was ignored.

And then, on the prosecution's pivotal point, there is Supreme Court case authority that states quite clearly that if a convicted person fails to testify in extenuation it is not necessarily fatal. Furthermore, it is elementary law that the judge is duty-bound to look at the case in its entirety for the purposes of sentence.

How could the Six give evidence? They were denying that they had anything to do with the killing. Taking the witness stand now, after their conviction, would be admitting that they had done exactly what the Court had found them to have done, and that would be the end of their appeal against their conviction. So they chose not to testify.

Counsel was then allowed to plead in mitigation of sentence for Christiaan and Gideon on the charge of public violence, which he did. And the prosecutor supported his request that their sentences for that offence (public violence) and for subversion should run concurrently.

❖

Sentencing began with the personal particulars of all eight accused. The sad litany of broken homes, financial pressure, interrupted schooling, and many dependants was delivered in fairly sympathetic terms.

Then the judge said, "What counts above all in favour of the accused is the fact that although some of them had minor (previous) convictions, I shall regard them as first offenders, in particular Accused nos. 5 and 6 [Christiaan and Gideon]."

All eight accused were sentenced to eight years' imprisonment on the count of subversion. Christiaan and Gideon were sentenced to five years' imprisonment on the count of public violence, to run concurrently with the eight years.

Then, each one of the Six was sentenced for murder.

> **JUDGE:** Ask Accused no. 1 if he has anything to say before the sentence of death is passed upon him.
>
> **JA-JA SEFATSA:** My Lord, yes. I wish to ask this Court to show me mercy and I beg this Court to see if it is not possible to see its way clear that although you have found me guilty of this charge you will, nevertheless, consider to rather send me to a prison for very long or to give me a suspended sentence. I will not do it again. That is all.
>
> **JUDGE:** Tell Accused no. 1 that he will be go back to a place in custody and there he shall hang by the neck until he is dead. He must stand down.

Ja-Ja looked shocked. The judge showed no emotion. One could hear people crying in the public gallery.

> **JUDGE:** Ask Accused no. 2 if he has anything to say before the sentence of death is passed upon him.
>
> **REID MOKOENA:** My Lord, I cannot completely understand how you found me guilty because throughout the trial I informed the Court that I did not at all take part in this crime. I was not there. You have my personal particulars

and I ask you to take that into consideration and give me a suspended prison term. That is all.

JUDGE: Tell the accused that he will be taken back to a place in custody where he will hang by the neck until he is dead. He must stand down. Ask Accused no. 3 if he has anything to say before the sentence of death is passed upon him.

OUPA DINISO: My Lord, I want to ask you to consider and take into account my personal circumstances. This is the first time that I have had a brush with the law. I was never previously in any court, not even involved at any time in crime. I am a married man. There are my minor children who are dependent on me. I wonder if you cannot see your way open in these circumstances to consider giving me a long jail term instead of the sentence you have in mind. Then I give you the assurance that what has happened here will never happen again. I ask you to show me mercy. I have family dependants. I am married and if you give me a chance, I will give you the assurance that I will look after these people and again I ask you for mercy. I just wish to repeat and I hope that my request, my plea, does not fall on deaf ears. That is all.

JUDGE: Tell Accused no. 3 that he will be taken back to a place of custody where he shall hang by the neck until he is dead. Ask Accused no. 4 if she has anything to say before the sentence of death is passed upon her.

THERESA RAMASHAMOLA: My Lord, I wish to ask for mercy. I am certain that the conclusion you have come to is the wisdom of God, and that it is God's will and I believe that it is God that has told you to come to this decision. In the circumstances I wonder if you can, with the Holy Spirit in mind, not see your way clear that you can think otherwise and not impose this sentence on me. That is all.

JUDGE: Tell the accused that she will be taken back to a place in custody where she shall hang by the neck until she is dead. Ask Accused no. 7 if he has anything to say before the sentence of death is passed upon him.

DUMA KHUMALO: My Lord, I laid my case before you. You heard much evidence that, according to me, was lies. Notwithstanding that, you have decided to accept that type of evidence against me. I have nothing further to say. Let the law take its course. That is all.

JUDGE: Tell Accused no. 7 that he will be taken back to a place in custody where he shall hang by the neck until he is dead. Ask Accused no. 8 if he has anything to say before sentence of death is passed upon him.

FRANCIS MOKHESI: My Lord, my colleagues have already pleaded with you. You have accepted the evidence of all the people who laid [lied] against us in their testimony. I have attempted throughout to persuade you not to accept that evidence. Yet, in your wisdom, you have accepted it. What else can I say?

JUDGE: Now tell him he must stand up.

FRANCIS MOKHESI: Let the law then take its course.

JUDGE: Yes, tell the accused that he will be taken back into custody where he shall hang by the neck until he is dead.

The judge had said it counted above all in their favour that he would regard them all as first offenders. What if they had had a string of previous convictions?

The judge adjourned the Court and left. The family members, and many other spectators, were weeping. The wives, mothers, all those closest to the Six, wanted to hold them and speak to them, but the police became very impatient, and one young white constable literally pushed Reid down the steps that led to the court cells. When counsel protested, the young policeman was too arrogant or insensitive to relent – or perhaps he was afraid of the powerful emotions of the crowd.

I went down to the cells with counsel, and we spoke to the Six there. We told them about the possibility of an appeal; but they were on their way to death row, and none of them seemed to be paying any attention.

Outside, we tried to comfort their families with hope. Some felt Mr. Acting Justice Human had been biased against the Six;

we told them the appeal court would be impartial. At the very least it would find that the death sentence was too severe. The six could even be acquitted on the merits of the case. But the families were very angry in their distress, and as far as they were concerned, one court was no more likely to be fair than any other, and there was no hope in the law.

P A R T   T H R E E

The Consequences

❖

CHAPTER 15

Death Row

"Like birds and animals in a cage."
FRANCIS

From the Supreme Court cells, the Six were taken to Pretoria Central Prison, only two kilometres away, where the five men went straight to Maximum Security, which houses what is technically the only death row in South Africa.[1] Theresa was entirely separated from them now, in the women's section of the prison.

Warrant Officer Schoeman, who had presided over their case from the start, was there when the Six were brought in, and they had the impression he was laughing at them. He was talking to a colleague, a tall, thin man who also seemed to find their plight amusing. It was as if Schoeman was handing over what was left of their future to this prison official, whose name, they soon learned, was Warrant Officer Arlow.

Arlow's duties necessitated his presence at every important encounter between the condemned and officialdom. For the Six, he personified all that was cruellest and hardest in death row.

The sheriff informed the Six as they arrived that they could appeal against the death sentence.

"He said our defence was strong and our case was good. He was a good man," Reid said.

And then they were hustled and pushed along, as they climbed the steps to the room where they would take off their own clothes for the last time. As they put on the regulation garments, some of them thought of the previous wearers, dead men, men who had been hanged.

The first real surprise was the noise. Everyone going into Maximum Security for the first time remarks on it. "I could hear so many noises. It was like birds and animals in a cage," said Francis.

In death row the general rule is silence, in the showers, in the exercise hall, and also in the cells, except at certain times, notably between 4:00 p.m. and 8:00 p.m.

Yet the noise permeates the prison. Ordinary prisoners hear it, the condemned in death row hear it, even visitors sometimes hear it.

The special cells where the condemned spend their last seven days and nights are part of Maximum Security, and there is no attempt to control the noise those prisoners make. That is where the shouting comes from, the banging on the walls, the calling out, and especially the singing, rising and falling, all day and often all night, especially the night before an execution.

It was Arlow who took the men to their cells. Reid said, "He was walking behind me fast and he was hurrying me up. The cell was already open, waiting just for me. I passed the cell because we were walking so fast. He screamed, 'Come in here!' and pushed me into the cell and said I must sleep nice."

Ja-Ja understood the motivation behind the command, "Maak jouself toe!" ("Shut yourself in!") – "It is an automatic door. When you close it, it locks from the outside. It was not nice doing this, you do not want to close that door, you know you do not belong here, but you must do it. You think about what you are facing.

"I felt bad for the first time when I get in and then I was always thinking about my family and to be away from them for a crime that I did not commit. I did not know how to explain my feelings to my wife when she paid a visit for the first time on the Saturday."

Death row in Pretoria has three sections, each with about fifty-five cells in it, only a few of them communal. The five men, who had been together since April 1985, were now separated: Francis and Oupa in one section, Ja-Ja and Duma in another, and Reid alone in a third.

Each of them was put in a single cell, about two metres by three, with a very high ceiling. Straight opposite the door, in the back corner, is the toilet. In the other far corner, a small wooden flap attached to the wall serves as a table. The bed is also a plank fixed to the wall. A radio speaker completes the furniture. There is no chair, nothing movable except the toilet bucket. High up above the occupant, too high for him ever to see the sun, is a small window, and a walkway from which the warders can look down into each cell as they do their rounds.

Dirt is a constant feature, apparently. Smelly blankets, absence of sheets or pillow cases, and filthy toilets have been specifically mentioned by several death-row occupants who have lived to describe the place.

❖

Since December 1985, when the five Sharpeville men arrived, until the end of 1988,[2] this has been a typical day in death row.

A bell rings at 6:00 a.m. to announce the start of a new day. The prisoners must get up, tidy their beds, take off their pyjamas, and put on their day clothes, green cotton shirt and trousers.

At 7:00 a.m. the warders do a round to count the cell occupants, who must stand at their doors until they have been inspected; thereafter they may sit down if they like.

Then, when the toilet buckets have been collected, eleven cells in each section are opened. Their occupants go to the communal showers, where there is hot water and soap, but the men have to share the six taps. Five minutes is the maximum time allowed, sometimes less, and those who delay under the water are generally dragged out. No one may talk during the showering, not even to ask someone to pass the soap.

All meals are served in the cells. Breakfast, at 8:00 a.m., is soft porridge and cold coffee, "like dirty water, with not enough milk and sugar." Around this time, a man comes by with medicines, asking if anyone wants tablets for aches and pains. After breakfast the dishes are collected – they are all plastic, for it is a serious concern of the authorities to prevent the condemned from pre-empting justice and committing suicide.

Every second day the prisoners shave, under careful supervision, in the ablution area, and once a week, on Mondays, the clothes are changed, and each prisoner receives a clean shirt and trousers and a pair of socks.

Visits from family and friends are permitted between 9:00 and 11:00 a.m. daily, and again between 2:00 and 3:00 p.m.

At 10:00 there is exercise for those who want it. They are taken to a hall where they spend 20 to 30 minutes walking round and round in a circle, forbidden to talk. No jogging or other exercises are allowed. These can just as well be done in the cells, some prisoners have been told.

Then, every day, the head of the prison does a round, to inspect the prisoners and take complaints.

Lunch, served between 11:00 and 11:30, is five thin slices of brown bread, sparsely smeared with white margarine and jam, and either a "soup" consisting of water, raw cabbage, crushed oats, and sometimes raw carrots, or a fruit drink so diluted that it colours the water but does not flavour it.

At midday most of the warders go for their lunch.

Two o'clock is the time reserved for items not on the daily program, such as haircuts.

And 3:00 p.m. is supper-time. Sometimes this is boiled fish, sometimes chicken – carefully deboned – or boiled pork, mutton, beef, or soya mince, with vegetables, and rice or samp. There is little or no salt, pepper, or spice in the food, or on the plain raw cabbage they call salad. After supper, hot water is given to those who ask for it, to make tea or coffee or to mix with milk powder.

At 4:00 p.m. the day warders knock off. From then until 8:00 p.m., the condemned may write, read, or talk to each other from cell to cell, and this is when they sing, preach, and even conduct entire church services.

At 8:00 p.m., when the bell rings, the men have to be in bed, and silence is the rule. But it is not "lights out," for the lights are never switched off.

That is the time structure, unvarying, day after day, and within it, of course, the special features: clean clothes on Mondays, a haircut, and most important of all, the visitors from outside.

The condemned are allowed to be up and dressed only between 6:00 a.m. and 8:00 p.m., and that leaves ten hours out of twenty-four for insomnia. "I could not sleep" is the commonest of all descriptions of death-row experiences documented. Perhaps the cramming of all three meals into seven hours makes its own contribution to the long wakeful nights?

Those who ask for them are given tranquillizers or sleeping tablets, but they do not suit everyone and there is a limit to the number of hours one can sleep, drugged or not.

Any consultation with a doctor must be approved by the authorities, and a warder is always present throughout every medical examination.

Medical attention in death row is a stop-gap to keep the prisoners alive until they meet the hangman, and to prevent epidemics in the jail. But unless a condition is life-threatening, there is no point in spending public money on it. The contributions medicine can make to well-being and health, from vitamins to false teeth or hearing aids, would be wasted on people who are going to be hanged anyway. So when Duma, Francis, and Theresa had trouble with their eyes, and it was discovered that all three needed glasses, the defence paid for them because the prisons department would not.

In line with official dedication to the prevention of suicide, visitors may not bring in any food. But the condemned can supplement their meals from the prison tuck shop, and are allowed to spend up to R100 a month there, if any of their families, friends, or well-wishers supply them with money. The tuck shop sells things such as biscuits, peanuts, powdered milk, sweets, processed cheese, tomato sauce, cereals, and dried fruit. Approved magazines and newspapers may also be obtained from the shop.

In the communal cells in the men's death row, the occupants can play cards or chess or draughts. But the main resource for the prisoners, especially those who land – by apparently random selection – in the single cells, is reading – reading the Bible, the newspapers, the James Bonds and other novels from the prison library. Prisoners awaiting death are not allowed study books.

There are many South Africans who cannot read, and according to studies,[3] most of the people who end up in death row are from deprived backgrounds and poorly educated, and some are indeed illiterate.

Another occupation that takes on great importance, for those equipped to pursue it, is letter-writing. Prisoners may write and receive unlimited letters, though both incoming and outgoing mail is censored.

The same censorship governs all contact with family members and legal advisers. A warder is always present in the visiting room, well within hearing, and certain topics of conversation – notably prison conditions – are forbidden. No "contact visits" are allowed to death-row prisoners.

Greater "privileges" are afforded those who are going to die than long-term prisoners. These include the daily visits from family and friends, "unrestricted" in the sense that anyone[4] may come and applications do not have to be made in advance; the tuck shop and the correspondence facilities; the "prescribed diet" indicated above; this and a couple of other concessions suggest basic institutional care of the terminally ill: the availability of tranquillizers prescribed by a doctor on request, and the freedom from any obligation to take exercise or perform labour; there are regular visits from the head of the prison and a response to "reasonable requests"; spiritual books are provided, and visits from spiritual leaders; and women may use "hair solutions," make-up, and deodorants.

❖

Theresa was not in Maximum Security itself, but within the same prison complex, in the women's section. She said she was among white "ordinary" prisoners (those not sentenced to hang), though, of course, in a separate cell. The condemned white women were in another section of the prison.

Apartheid is expensive, cumbersome, and curious. The prisons, like the public health service, keep whites apart from others. But it seems there is, or was then, no black female death row at Maximum Security, and expediency prevailed.

Theresa said, "The white prisoners were all right. They were never nasty to me. They gave me food. They prayed for me. Two were found guilty of murder but were not sentenced to death. We would often pray together.

"The only fighting that I heard between the women prisoners was between the black prisoners. . . . They got a serious punishment – they are not allowed to fight."

Theresa had heard that some people lived in death row for a month, a few months, or even a few years before they were executed. "But for us I felt maybe it will even happen tomorrow."

Her day was less rigidly structured than the men's, but the program and meals were similar. The other prisoners cooked the food, and sometimes, she said, it was nice, but sometimes it was raw, or dirty, with cigarettes or hair or matchsticks in it.

At night, when she could not sleep, a warder would call the major, the head of the women's section, who would give her tablets and tell her to sleep and to pray. "All around you feel is death. I would wake up at any time. I did not eat much. . . . I was feeling there was no hope." One of the women sergeants, who was very good to Theresa, told her she must not lose hope, and advised her to pray. Everyone who wished her well said, "Keep praying!"

While the men in death row received no psychological or rehabilitative help apart from clergymen's visits, Theresa's wardresses were generally far more sympathetic than their male counterparts, and they used their own discretion.

"They keep you busy. You got knitting, video, exercise for an hour, and sometimes I would be allowed to stay for the whole day in the courtyard. Sometimes when they see I am very sad and my heart is not all right, they would let me watch the white prisoners fixing flowers in a room and they showed me how to knit jerseys. They always said to me that they must keep me busy so I did not get my heart broken."

Theresa had her kind warders and very soon she had the company of someone in the same boat as herself, Elizabeth Witbooi, who came in in January 1986. She had been sentenced to death, but this was later commuted to fifteen years. The two women, both Roman Catholics, talked about their problems and prayed and sang together.

"She was an old lady. She was forty-nine. She killed her husband."

Another condemned woman came in, Ruth de Vos, "a coloured woman, who apparently killed a relation of P.W.'s [P.W. Botha, State President at that time] family. We also used to pray together and we spoke about our case."

❖

Francis and Oupa received a warm welcome when they arrived in their section. Their cell neighbours had heard about the Sharpeville Six on the radio, and some of them had seen Francis playing football in the courtyard of Pretoria Prison during the trial.

Oupa was put next door to a man called Boysie Masiyane, who gave him sugar and tea on the very first day, and spoke to him encouragingly. From that moment, and for the six months they were together, the two were firm friends.

Reid was with no one he knew. But it was not only his isolation and the lights that shone all night that prevented his sleeping or eating the whole of that first weekend.

The day he arrived, Friday, the prisoners in the neighbouring cells told him that the executioners were short one man for the Monday hangings, and they would come and fetch Reid at six o'clock on Monday morning. Meanwhile, they said, he must be careful, because a rope would come down from the window, and seek his neck, so he should look out for it and move out of the way when it came down.

Although "Mr. Jack" (Unterhalter) had told his clients that there was still a long way to go, Reid believed what the other condemned were telling him. He tried not to show them how frightened he was.

On the Monday[5] morning, the man in the next-door cell knocked on the wall and said the people were coming and Reid must wait at his door to greet them. If anyone should ask him what he was doing, he must say he was waiting for the hangman.

Reid stood at his door. He declared to the other prisoners that he was ready to die, he was innocent, he did not kill Dlamini. He stood there waiting from seven o'clock until nine, expecting to be fetched and taken to the gallows. He would have stood there all day, if a black warrant officer had not come and asked him what he was doing.

He explained that he was waiting to be executed and the rope was going to come down from the window.

The policeman told him not to worry, the rope was far away from him and he would not be executed for a long time.

Afterwards, Reid laughed with his tormentors over their elaborate joke. He insisted he was not angry with them, for he had also played tricks on others. Then, he said, "I told them how clever I was, because I was going to appeal to Bloemfontein."

❖

Two conflicting realities accompanied the Six through the first two years of their stay in death row. One was reasonable, legitimate hope and the other the close, daily presence of death.

It was almost five months after their arrival that leave to appeal was granted. Then it was eighteen months until the appeal court heard their case, and another month before it delivered its decision. Disillusioned after the trial, and lacking confidence in justice, the Six had good reason for despondency. But at the back of their minds, there was first the hope and then the certainty that their case would be considered by five judges of the Appellate Division, and the expectation that whatever had gone awry during the trial would be rectified in Bloemfontein.

Meanwhile they were right there, as Duma said, "among the death" – the previous occupant of his cell had been executed that very week. They were wearing clothes that the dead had worn, eating from their plastic dishes, using their dirty blankets. Soon "the dead" would no longer be shadows, unknown victims, but people they knew well, cell-neighbours, even close friends.

Thanks to the Christian calendar, the Six were spared an immediate introduction to the physical realities of hanging, for they arrived in mid-December, just as the holiday period began. It seems executions are suspended over Christmas and resume only in the New Year.

For a fortnight, it was possible to be in death row without being confronted by an actual death. Duma chatted with his young cell-neighbour Shongwe, who told him all about his case, and explained why he felt he was innocent. The two became quite friendly, and Duma was convinced that Shongwe – like himself – had been wrongly sentenced.

And then, at the end of December, Shongwe was taken away to the "bottom cells." "Stay in peace, my brother," the young man said as he left. He died at the opening of the 1986 hanging season, on Monday, January 6.

The shock filled Duma with fear. It was his first encounter, though far from his last, with this kind of death. And because he did not believe Shongwe was a killer, he had identified with him.

❖

Holding onto hope despite the evidence of their senses was not easy for the condemned as they waited through the days and nights in their cells.

First among their resources and common to all six was their Christian faith. Methodists, Catholics, whatever their denomination, they all believed in one God who had sent His Son to earth to save their souls, and in a new and better life to come. The prison administration gave its full support to its Christian prisoners, allowing them ready access to their priests and pastors, providing Bibles and spiritual literature, and permitting – after 4:00 p.m., when the day warders had left – the spontaneous communal worship that Oupa described.

"The whole place would keep quiet, actually, so that they must give us a chance, the people who are holding the church at the time. When we preaching, somebody is shouting to one another, so that is how we managed to hold the church together for a certain time, for maybe two hours.

"If somebody has got a scripture for us to preach then he is the one who open with a prayer, and after the prayer he would give us a text where to read, then after we had read the text, then he would reveal it, make some revelations . . . give an interpretation what has been in the scripture. When he is finished and if there is anyone who wants to continue or to add to what he had said, then he can do that too.

"Then until we are all finished or we are all content with the scripture, well, now we sing two songs before we end, and then we close up with a prayer. That is where we are free to talk whatever we like with our neighbours or to comment on what the scripture was about."

These services, conducted by men who were nearly all isolated in single cells, brought everyone together as if the separating walls were not there. And they were generated and entirely controlled by the prisoners themselves, an assertion of autonomy in a world of subjection.

The Christian belief that suicide is sin kept many of the condemned from considering it seriously, except in moments of overwhelming despair.

Francis made both these statements:

"If it was not a sin to commit suicide, I would have killed myself while I was still on death row. The pain a person felt on death row, oh the pain I cannot compare with other pains of people living freely or meeting accidents of any sort that people can encounter. On death row you are tortured mentally and physically because you are without energy and have no appetite. You are full of despair. Any things you want to do, you don't have the power to do them properly."

And "I never thought of killing myself. I was afraid to do so. It was a lesson I learned from my family . . . that you put yourself more in danger by taking your life because it is not your life, it is God's life."

After God, people. Two groups were vital for the preservation of the prisoners' sanity: their families and their mates in the death cells, who were sharing their destiny. Both were also sources of great pain: the families because of the constant reproach they never uttered, "we need you, you have deserted us"; and the friends inside, because of the inevitable parting to come.

Five of the Six had someone outside the prison who provided steady, undeviating support, and in each case this was a woman. Ja-Ja, Francis, and Oupa had their devoted wives, who visited them constantly and brought news of their children. Reid and Theresa had their mothers, strong, loving women whose belief in their children's innocence never flagged. These two also had their betrothed: Dorothy, the mother of Reid's child, who came regularly to the prison, and Andrew who never stopped visiting Theresa and continued to want to marry her. Brothers and sisters were very important, and other relations and loyal friends contributed to the emotional survival of the condemned.

Duma was the only one of the Six whose outside support seemed to crumble away. It was never very strong, because he himself was the core of his family. Betty, the mother of his child, had been faithful the whole year, throughout his detention, his imprisonment at Potchefstroom, and the trial itself.

But when Duma went to death row, things changed.

"My girlfriend started disappearing. She never paid a visit to me. But after thinking about it, I think it would be wrong if I can blame her, because we never discussed some of these things if they might happen, what are we going to do. Because actually we were not interested in politics. I know that she loves me but what happened is very easy to separate us, and she was still too young and her parents expect her to get married."

Then his younger brother Ishmael,[6] who had been very close to him, died in 1986. This was more painful than anything else, according to Duma. Because he could not see his brother's face or pay his last respects, he found it impossible to accept that his brother was dead or to come to terms with his loss.

The friendships made in death row were intense and dramatic.

The condemned were permitted to receive visits from other prisoners. Security [political] prisoners – the Six were in this category – had to put in an application, and this had to be approved before the prisoner they wanted to see might visit them. Nevertheless, the visits were usually granted and provided the only friendly contacts with anyone other than clergymen that were not through a glass partition. The prisoners were allowed to give things to each other; these gifts, sometimes practical, more often symbolic, were very important to both parties involved, especially when the giver was on his way to the gallows.

For the first three months Francis was there, he had no appetite and he could not sleep properly. But he got to know the man in the cell opposite his. Eric Ndlovu gave him huge encouragement because he was clearly coping very well. "He tried to show me that he was like myself when he first came here," Francis said. Eric urged him not to despair about the way the warders handled the prisoners and not to believe this was the end of his life. He also had practical tips to offer against depression. He himself did a lot of exercises in his cell, and on his advice Francis started doing push-ups and running on the spot three times a day.

Francis had another friend, Mtshali. They shared whatever they had, they prayed together, they encouraged others to pray with them. "We said that we were in the same road. We will all die. We will see each other again. We will meet in a place where most believers are together."

And then one day Mtshali banged the walls and shouted, "It is now my time."

"Keep strong, I will not lose hope for you," Francis replied, and promised to pray for his friend while he was on the gallows. Seven days later, knowing exactly when Mtshali's time would be, he did.

He bore the separation by reminding himself that it was God's will, and anyway his friend was not dead. "Only his body remained on earth, and where he is, he is alive."

Francis did not write to Mtshali's family, because, he said, he did not want to remind them of their beloved son. But he was determined to go and see them as soon as he was free.

Oupa had Boysie, whose warmth and kindness had made his arrival in death row bearable. Boysie was an artist, and taught Oupa as much as he could about drawing and painting. He was not much older than Oupa, and they found they could talk to each other about everything that mattered to them.

Boysie was one of four condemned for a bank robbery during which someone was murdered. He had already been in death row for three years. For himself, he never had the slightest hope, but he was sincerely optimistic about Oupa's chances of being pardoned. To prove it, he gave Oupa his parents' address, so that he could go and see them when he got out, and they would realize their son had had somebody who was close to him.

Oupa was always trying to find out how people were executed. "That was something that Prakash would not discuss with us." But Oupa felt he needed to know. "I must not be surprised, I must know exactly what is going to happen with me, because all of us were in a death row, all in the death row we were expecting one thing."

Because he truly believed Oupa would escape the gallows or because he understood that fear of the unknown can be worse than any other, Boysie told Oupa what he had managed to glean. Most of it is corroborated by other sources.[7]

"When you leave the church on the morning of your execution," Boysie told Oupa, "they take away all your clothes. Then they lead you to the place.

"There are some twenty-two stairs to that place. When you arrive there, there are some ropes hanging, I think seven of them and then they would put that black bag on the head and after that they would put the rope. After they put the rope, he told me that there is a table, and when they press a certain button, I don't know where, it falls down. . . . When the table has fallen some have not yet passed away, so then they pull them up again. I don't know whether there is a machine.

"When they open the door, the rope is still on your neck and you are hanging. If one or two have not died, to make sure they have to put these ropes in order it must get more and more into the neck until all the necks are broken. . . . If your family wanted to see you they would only show your photo.

"Even the place where you are going to be buried, well, he was not sure but actually he told me that it might happen that they ditch all the bodies in one grave because the coffins in which they carry the people to the graveyard, they bring them back again in order that they should be used again for other executions.

"Boysie told me that I won't be executed before I ever had that hope that I won't be executed."

The last time Oupa saw him, Boysie said, "*Mfowethu* [my brother], my friend, I am leaving now. I will be grateful if you can keep firm on your faith. I have enjoyed your friendship very much." And he gave him an Afrikaans Bible, a small dictionary, and his writing pad where he had made some drawings; also some pens, and his photos and his old letters from his parents. He said he would send Oupa some other things on the last day – which he did.

At 7:00 a.m. on a Wednesday in June 1986, Boysie and his three co-condemned were executed.

Oupa said, "Well, because I have stayed a long time on death row – I don't know about other people – but with me if somebody was going to be executed, really I don't feel anything, because I knew the same thing was going to happen with me. Even if I can feel pity for him, there is nothing that I can do, because I am expecting the same thing. But he was my close friend."

Oupa made friends with another prisoner, Sibusiso Tindane, and tried to help him as he had been helped by Boysie.

"Firstly, when I got to know Sibusiso, when he arrived he was placed next to me. Well, he was a shy somebody, being embarrassed for being on the death row. But anyway because he was close to me I encouraged him a lot to forget about the past."

Oupa was not a typical death-row prisoner. Some of his black warders realized this and took an interest in him. Here was a relatively well-educated man, quiet, courteous, respectable, who seemed a far cry from any stone-throwing mob, and at the same time utterly removed from radical politics.

Late in the evening, some of them would come and talk to him for an hour or two. They would discuss what he should study if his death sentence was commuted to a long prison term. He thought he would like to be a businessman, and they advised him to study commerce and basic accountancy.

"Some they got suprised when I told them that I've got a family, I've got a house. To them I look like somebody who is still young. But I tell them no, I got my own family house. Then they would ask me how my family was coping and I would say through the mercy of God.

"You know, I used to tell them about my golf, so that was something they did not expect. Another point again, like for instance I was working as a quality-control inspector." Oupa knew exactly why they were surprised – these were such staid occupations.

One of the warders said to him, "I don't take you as a prisoner; I only take you as my friend." He shared some of his things with Oupa, though it was illegal, "but now he risked that I must share these things with him. Like when he brought food, sweets and everything."

When Oupa asked him for a pen, or stamps, or other things he needed, he would get them. "If by luck he is going to be on duty on that session, then he would make his full means that I must get all these things. Well, it was something that we kept secretly, nobody knew about it."

Of the white warders, Oupa said none were nice to him. "All of them were one and the same."

Theresa also had friends among her wardresses, and became exceptionally close to one in particular. And she had more than one prisoner friend. There was Elizabeth, whose death sentence was commuted. Then Ruth de Vos, the woman convicted of murdering a relation of the then State President. The separation from her was traumatic.

"On a Friday morning, at 6:00 a.m., they came and opened the door. They say she must go and bath. After they gave her trousers, they said that she must wear a dress over the trousers and socks. Then she came back to the cell, she prayed and then she asked to smoke. She told me not to cry. She was not afraid. After she smoked, they took her.

"The prison warders when they came to fetch her were crying. They were both black and white prison warders. She said to them they must not cry, they must pray. The last thing she said to me was 'You will not be hanged, but you must pray.'

"All of us, white and black prisoners that day, none of us would eat. Everyone was very sad."

Theresa's closest friend was Sandra. "At night I would talk with my friend, Sandra Smith, who was a coloured condemned prisoner. We would eat together. We would joke together about when we were outside and how she was with her boyfriend."

The two of them chatted away as if they had a future like anyone else. "We planned to do many things when we were released. We thought that we would soon start a business together. That we would teach people to crochet and make flowers and we would teach people all the things that we saw here. She said to me she would teach me to swim, but I told her that I did not like the beach. She said she did not want to live in Cape Town any more and that she would rather live with me."

The third resource, of different value to the different prisoners, was reading material. The Bible was what they knew best, and all the Six and most of the other condemned read it constantly. Then there were books from the library, and newspapers.

Duma had enough education to make full use of the available books. They even helped him sleep, which does not necessarily mean they bored him.

"Well there were periods where I could sleep because they used to give us library books and the light is on for twenty-four hours, and so reading, my mind become tired, actually I fall asleep."

The prisoners could get library books any time they liked. Duma read an Ian Fleming, *Moonraker*, and a couple of best-sellers made a special impression on him: *Indecent Obsession* by Colleen McCullough, and *The Bourne Identity* by Robert Ludlum. This last brought him comfort, "Because those people were people who were in more difficulties and at the end they survived. And as I told you that reading books in that place assisted me very much."

Oupa and Francis, in their section, seem to have had kinder black warders than the others, and, being together, they could share newspapers, which meant a lot to both of them.

Oupa was, as he said, "somebody who does not like food so much," which was just as well for him, as he literally could not stomach the ordinary rations. As a vegetarian – and for ulcer treatment – he was given eggs instead of meat or fish, and they were the only prison food he ate. He fed himself on cereals and other items from the tuck shop.

Everyone else handed in their dirty clothes on Mondays in exchange for clean ones, but Oupa's skin was sensitive to the chemicals used in the prison laundry, so he kept his two sets of clothes and washed them himself. At first he was allowed to wash them in the shower, until there was an instruction to wash them in the cell. Since there was no basin there, a plastic bucket was provided. Then there was another official decision, and Oupa could wash his clothes in the shower again.

Oupa and Francis had one strong bond apart from their common misfortune. Both were deeply and very thoughtfully religious.

Francis believed that nobody could save him but God, and that if he showed faith, love, and respect, and committed no sin, God would indeed save him. He asked no favours.

"From when I was young I was taught not to pray to God for things I fear or I want. For me to ask God to spare my life I would be commanding what He already knows, that in my inner self I am afraid to die."

He hoped fervently that God would give him strength in the final moments, "when I may want to turn back against Him and say there is no God."

Ja-Ja and Duma had bad luck with their black warders, who seem to have been especially hard on Duma. The shoes he had were for some reason not a pair; worse still, they were both left shoes. And he wore a jersey that was miles too big. The warders called him "Umgodoyi" [pariah dog].

Duma suffered agonies of humiliation over this until he finally reported it to the major, who ordered the warders to stop insulting him, and said Duma must report them to him if they persisted. They did stop, but they instructed the people who dished up the food that "the dog" should always get a smaller ration than the other prisoners.

As time went on, Duma understood some of the things being done to him and his colleagues, and his insights gave him strength. He felt he could no longer be pushed around.

Duma thought about the fact that the five men from Sharpeville were in three different sections: "Now, why are we separated? The authority, as far as I think, they want one of you to confess, because when you are together it is difficult to confess." Other prisoners – ordinary, not "security" condemned – were always advising him to confess.

There had been friction between Duma and Francis at Potchefstroom, until the Further Particulars made it clear that it was not Duma who had implicated Francis. But in death row, mistrust flared again.

This time Oupa Diniso was the object of suspicion. Duma said, "Let me explain it this way. There was a time when Diniso was called by the Reverend to come and confess. He refused to confess to the Reverend." But Ja-Ja, Francis, and Duma himself wanted to know what Oupa could have said to the authorities to cause them to send for him to confess, because he had always maintained he was innocent.

❖

Who would imagine there are degrees of horror in death row? Ja-Ja and Duma were in the section nearest the cells where the condemned spent their last seven days, and for the first two weeks they did not realize what this meant. Then, at the end of December, "the bottom cells" started filling up with men who had seven days to live.

Ja-Ja was the closest of the five to those men.

"I was in that cell for three years. I saw between one hundred and two hundred people in those cells before they were executed."

He was underestimating. His second year there, 1987, was the all-time record, with 164 executions; in 1988, there were 117. From 1980 to 1986 the total was 789, so 1986 probably accounted for another 100.

The equipment allows for a maximum of seven hangings in one session, and as Ja-Ja said, "Sometimes they can kill twenty-one people in a week. They kill on Monday, they skip Tuesday, they kill on a Wednesday, they skip Thursday, and then they kill on Friday."

Most of the year the execution days are far less frequent, but in almost all cases the condemned spend seven days in the "bottom cells."

"I heard them screaming. Some would say they deserved to die because they committed a crime. Others said they were not guilty because they never committed any crime. They just make a noise, they hit doors. Some they pray.

"Others would be crying. One is singing hymns. One is hitting the doors. You cannot sleep, there is too much noise. You are also then thinking about yourself. You are also facing this punishment at some time.

"I thought that when I get there I won't sing or scream because I know the pain of other prisoners. I don't want them to know the pain of what I had . . .

"The day before an execution, Arlow would get the pillow-cases from the storeroom, the cases they put around your head when you are hanged.

"That day, the men who were going to die would see their family for thirty to forty minutes in the morning and again in the afternoon.

"All night, they would be singing hymns.

"At 6:55 on the day of execution, they would come and collect you. They open the door. They do not say anything. You know where you are going. They take you by the collar. They then take you to a room, a small church, where you make a prayer with the Reverend. After that, they would lead them away.

"In my three years I never saw anyone put up a fight when they were led away.

"Then they would bring back the 'copper-heads,' and the death-row prisoners who are assigned to be cleaners had to wash the pillowcases filled with blood. They washed this in the shower.

"When the warders get back from the gallows or the 'machine,' they discuss the death amongst themselves. They stay and talk about which one did not die quickly and which one's heart was still pumping after he died.

"There were also three times when people got lost. They executed them but a few days later they were still calling out their names in roll-call."

❖

The administrative personnel at Maximum Security seem to have believed that the Six had arrived in death row for political crimes. They were technically, in fact, "security" prisoners, some of them the only ones in their section. They had been convicted of a revolting, brutal murder involving stone-throwing and burning, and it was natural enough for the uncritical to believe they had actually committed the deed. Furthermore, the murder had arisen out of politically inspired unrest, and they had also been convicted of subversion. Thus they were, in the eyes of their keepers, political activists, even terrorists. From there it was only another short step for imaginations already fired along these lines to make them members of the African National Congress. In Duma's succinct words, "The most senior members believed that we had done what brought us to Maximum, and they usually hate politicians."

Oupa also knew they were thought to be members of the ANC, constantly plotting to escape. White warders coming to the section for the first time would ask, "Who are the Sharpeville Six?" – their hostility already evident.

The assumption that they had been activists showed in small things. Oupa spoke English to the doctor one day, and then switched to Afrikaans. The warder said (in Afrikaans), "You can speak Afrikaans now. You're not a *harde gat* [hard-arse] any more."

In general, white warders are harder on politicals than on other prisoners. A neighbour of Oupa's, Mthetheleli Mncube, really was a member of the ANC, and had been convicted in the "Messina Trial." He arrived in death row before the Six, and told Oupa that he and his colleague Mzondeleli Nondula had been very badly treated, and had been given filthy clothes to wear and had their hair cut by force.

Arlow was always around. Many of the condemned wanted to beat him up, but some made themselves his henchmen.

Oupa and Francis spoke of a "coloured" prisoner by the name of Isaac Polsen, "a big shot with a big mouth," who was trying to placate the powers in the prison, in the hope of escaping the hangman. To this end he was informing on other prisoners, and bullying those whom Arlow especially disliked. This man had decided – or been told – that Francis and Oupa, the only "political" prisoners in their section, were terrorists.

Polsen was a big man, and Francis said Arlow always seemed to favour him, which made everyone afraid of him, "even the white warders, because they knew he was a pimp [probably from Zulu *impimpi* – an informer] of Arlow."

Polsen lost no opportunity to deride and mock Francis and Oupa whenever the radio reported anything about the ANC, and when Francis was talking to his friend Mtshali, from cell to cell,

Polsen and his mates would bang loudly on the walls, trying to drown out the conversation.

Francis reported him several times to Arlow, and threatened to fight him in the showers if nothing was done. After a while, Polsen was moved to another section, where he turned his taunts about the ANC on Duma and Ja-Ja.

Not long after that, a white sergeant came to Francis's cell, wishing to investigate it. None of the other cells in the section were to be investigated, and Francis objected and demanded to speak to Major Cronje, the officer in charge of death row. Arlow appeared during this discussion, heard what was going on, and made a point of accompanying the major on his next round. This manoeuvre did not silence Francis, who complained to the major in spite of Arlow's presence. The major said he would hear the details in his office. There he told Francis that he had been informed he was planning to escape – hence the cell-check. Evidently Polsen had made the report, in revenge for being moved away.

These incidents upset Francis greatly, and increased his general sadness.

Predictably, currying favour with Arlow did not help Polsen in the end; he was executed in November 1987.

Major Cronje, as Francis's story shows, was not an unreasonable man, though if he was aware of Arlow's attitude and behaviour, he appears to have done nothing about it. He was accessible to the prisoners, and it seems they respected him.

In my experience as an attorney consulting with prison inmates, many officials in these institutions are pleasant enough with people outside their control, and completely different when dealing with their prisoners. I do not think this was the case with the major, and my clients never complained about him. Certainly in all my own dealings with him I found him courteous and approachable. He showed an interest in the Six's case, and whenever he saw me at the prison he asked about the progress of the appeal and its chances of success. My impression was that his interest was sincere, and he was not merely making conversation with me.

I always behaved very correctly towards him, telephoning to make arrangements to see my clients, doing everything through the proper channels, and he reciprocated with unusual flexibility. Once or twice I pitched up at the prison without having made an appointment, because I had not known I would be in the area, and he was quite willing to let me go in and see my clients.

❖

An enormous irony lurks behind the story of the Sharpeville Six. For all the international limelight that has fallen on them, and therefore on hangings in South Africa, white judges trying black accused, township violence, mob murder, and common purpose, none of the Six was politically active, or even politically aware, before they were arrested.

Theresa liked cooking, gardening, social life. Ja-Ja's emotional focus was on Regina and his practical concern was his business. Reid was struggling to save, struggling to support his child, and spending most of his free time at home helping his mother. Francis had his family and his football. Duma was trying to study, and looking after his father and brothers. Oupa had his golf, his good job, and his ambition to provide more and better for his little nuclear family. All of them were practising Christians.

They were ordinary black South Africans, coping in their various ways with a bleak and difficult existence; not exceptional, certainly not heroic. They were caught up in events of much broader importance than the horrible murder of Mr. Dlamini, and much bigger than themselves. And so they became tragic figures, in a sense that would not apply to political activists constantly pitting their strength against the enemy in a heroic battle they know they will lose many times before they win.

Evidence during the trial showed how unconscious – even unconcerned – all the accused were about matters outside their day-to-day lives. They had personal attitudes towards Dlamini and other councillors, but no views about the black local authorities, or the tricameral parliament, or the causes of their own poverty. They seemed hardly to have taken note of the imminent rent increase, though it would have affected some of them quite severely in terms of what their families had to eat. They were "silent majority" people.

The "political" nature of their alleged crimes changed all that. They were forced to learn about Section 29 of the Internal Security Act. Accused of subversion, they had to find out what it was. And, in jail, they met and formed friendships with members of the banned organizations.

Even then, there was no sudden "awakening" to the political realities of South Africa. During the trial, they received a great deal of support from members of progressive organizations in Johannesburg, Pretoria, and the Vaal Triangle. They were grateful for it, for the personal warmth and the knowledge that they were not alone.

Nevertheless, after the appeal failed and the campaign to save their lives took off, the three best-educated of them, Francis, Duma, and Oupa, raised the question with me, whether the support of certain political groups inside and outside the country was in their best interest – whether it might not in fact jeopardize their petition. We discussed this at length, and finally they made not a legal decision but a political one, that all possible support should be canvassed, and all possible pressures used for their benefit. They were beginning to realize that the root-causes of their plight were political, whatever their own attitudes had been.

As they became more famous, and their case was featured on television around the world, it was reported that some organizations were claiming them as members. Whether in fact any of the liberation organizations officially made this claim we do not know. What we do know is that none of the Six belonged at that time to any of them.

But life was forcing a broader awareness on them. Their trial led to opinions on the judicial system, on the laws, on fairness and justice. The support they received from people they didn't know, inside South Africa and across the sea, raised questions they would never have dreamed of. It made sense of the news they read and heard, and the battered maps some of them had seen at school.

Prison taught them what rights one could demand, what rights one could not; what power was about.

Oupa gained strength in a small campaign in Maximum Security. His literacy skills were in demand among the condemned, and he was able to help some of them to read their case records, or to write to their advocates. Sometimes, the authorities would not allow prisoners to come to those who could read and write for help, but Oupa and others insisted they had the right, and in the end they managed to establish it.

In his capacity as scribe, Oupa observed what happened in death row, drew his conclusions, and gave tactical advice to other, more naive prisoners, among them his friend Sibusiso. Some wanted to write to the State President to ask for clemency, and Oupa urged them to refrain, because it would not help them; on the contrary, he told them, it could seal their fate.

"Don't write. . . . Ask your attorney how is the case going on, have you ever got the appeal in the Appellate Division, all those things, don't write anything that is going to contradict with your statement nor don't confess like some other prisoners . . . because I am seeing that some of the prisoners doing that, usually they all die, all of them. In court they talk another story and when they are on death row they start now confessing what they didn't say in court. . . . Such things will put you in trouble. Don't ever do that. All these things, they are in the hands of your attorney. He is the one who knows. Stick to what you have said in court. . . ."

Francis knew who was tricking people into hastening their own downfall. "Polsen," he said, "used to make people confess when they ask him to write letters. These people were semi-literate and he convinced them to write to the State President."

Of a little campaign launched around the time of the dismissal of the application to reopen the trial (June 1988), Francis said, "After three months after the stay of execution, we complained why we don't get privileges that other prisoners, who are not political and not prison murderers get, that is, they are allowed to visit other prisoners' cells [without asking special permission]. They then allowed us to do this."

Francis felt that as long as the case was kept alive by this or that legal endeavour, somehow in the end the truth would prevail. And at each new failure, as he said, "These thoughts made me less depressed and less despaired."

Theresa's way of coping with the third refusal was complete resignation. "I felt after the 13 June [1988] that there is nothing I can do. I will accept it if they say this, I will accept it if they say that."

For Oupa, that occasion was quite different. "Now I was angry really, when the application to reopen was dismissed by the judge in Pretoria."

He had pinned his hopes on a re-examination of Manete, and on a fair reassessment of the value of Mabuti's evidence in the light of the total discrediting of Manete's and Mongaule's.

The enormity of the injustice made him so angry that he had to force himself not to think about it. He made this penetrating comment, so strange at first glance: "If I can let myself think about how the appeal [this application to reopen the trial] was dismissed by the judge, really, my life won't be the same like what it used to be." (Oupa had been in death row then for two and a half years!)

The Six began to see their own situation in another light. Duma was perhaps the most articulate about the effects of his new understanding. He said it made him more and more secure in himself, ready for anything that might happen.

"What made me feel stronger is that when I become aware of apartheid, how evil it is, I start telling myself that I am not the first victim or the last. . . . Even if I had to lose my life I was happy because I will be counted among the warriors of apartheid."

Somewhere he had read, "A struggle without casualties is not a struggle." "So I take myself as a casualty in the struggle. Those things they mould you, they give you power."

CHAPTER 16

The Appeal

"These accused shared a common purpose with the crowd to kill the deceased. . . . "
Mr. Justice Botha of the Appeal Court

The very judge who had found the six guilty beyond all reasonable doubt of the murder of Mr. Dlamini now had to be persuaded that he could have been wrong and that another Court might come to a different conclusion. Even when an individual has been sentenced to death, he has no automatic right of appeal.

On December 13, 1985, six of my Sharpeville clients went straight to death row, and the other two began serving their eight-year sentences at Pretoria Local Prison.

On December 27, 1985, the defence lodged Notice of Application for Leave to Appeal with the Registrar of the Supreme Court, Pretoria, and with the Attorney-General.

The twenty-two grounds on which the accused appealed clarify the entire trial court hearing, and the defence's discontent with the judgment.[1] Briefly:

There was no evidence that the throwing of a stone by Ja-Ja or Reid, or any act of the other four, caused the death of the deceased. Nor was there evidence that any of the Six intended or must have foreseen that death, or that common purpose existed between any of the accused to commit any of the acts alleged in the indictment, or that Christiaan and Gideon were guilty of public violence.

Concerning Oupa, the judge had erred in finding that his explanation of his possession of the gun could not be true, and that the fact that the gun was in his possession meant he had disarmed Dlamini and was therefore guilty of his murder.

Because of the conflict between the evidence of Mrs. Dlamini and that of Mabuti, the finding that Ja-Ja had participated in the attack on Dlamini was unjustified.

The judge had erred in finding Theresa guilty of murder on the basis of words spoken by her and her attack on the woman who protested when Dlamini was being burnt.

The judge had erred in finding that Duma had participated in the attack on Dlamini's house, although he accepted the evidence of Mrs. Shabangu and Ismail Moketsi; and similarly in finding that Francis had participated in the attack, while accepting the evidence of Dr. Mokhesi.

The Court erred in allowing Mabuti to testify *in camera*, and in accepting his evidence and rejecting that of Emily Moeketsi and the two Radebes. Mabuti's uncorroborated evidence on petrol bombs and on the actions of Ja-Ja and Theresa should not have been accepted. And none of his evidence should have been found to be confirmed by Manete's, in view of the suspicion attaching to Manete.

The judge had erred in law in disallowing cross-examination of Manete on his statement.

The Court had erred on the subversion finding, and also in holding that public interest was relevant when extenuating circumstances were under consideration; it had erred in finding no extenuation for any of the Six and passing the death sentence on them.

The sentences of five years' imprisonment passed on Christiaan and Gideon for public violence, and of eight years on all the accused for subversion, were excessive.

❖

On May 6, 1986, in the Supreme Court in Pretoria, Mr. Acting Justice Human discussed possible grounds for the granting of leave to appeal.

On the twenty-two grounds advanced for leave to appeal, the judge said, "I am of the view that there is no reasonable prospect of success insofar as the facts found proved by this Court are concerned. However, on three other grounds, being points of law, I am satisfied that I should grant leave to appeal to the Appellate Division."

The first was causal connection between the acts of the accused and the death of the deceased. The defence had contended none was proved.

The judge quoted an appeal court judgment of Mr. Justice Corbett:[2] "Murder is the unlawful and intentional causing of the death of another human being. One of the essential ingredients of murder is, therefore, a causal connection between the conduct of the accused and the death of the deceased."

Mr. Acting Justice Human then cited other decisions concerning the guilt of accomplices, whether their action must be found to have taken place before the act which caused the death, or not. He also quoted Hoexter JA:[3] "In my view the law in regard to the present problem [causality] cannot be regarded as well settled." And finally he cited Botha JA, who considered that where more than one accused were involved, there did not have to be a causal relationship between the accused and the death, especially where liability was founded upon a common purpose.

> In view of these conflicting opinions, it seems to me that the question of causality is in the melting-pot and should once and for all be decided authoritatively by the Appellate Division. On that ground I am, therefore, of the opinion that leave should be granted.
>
> But there is a second ground in law why I should grant leave to appeal and that is that I disallowed the cross-examination of the witness Manete in regard to a privileged statement that he had made. Another Court may come to the conclusion in that respect that I erred in law and that may have been to the prejudice of the accused generally, especially Accused nos. 7 [Duma] and 8 [Francis]. . . .

I must point out that I gave a separate judgment in this respect and I did not agree with the judgment of an English judge which was quoted to me by Mr. Unterhalter for the defence. However I am still of the view that another Court may come to a different conclusion. . . .

The third ground on which I grant leave to appeal is the question of my interpretation of Section 54(2) as well as the provisions of Section 69 of the Internal Security Act No. 74 of 1982.

This section concerned the subversion charge. The judge added that it affected the conviction of Theresa on the charge of incitement to commit a crime, as the defence contended there was no evidence that others had overheard and acted upon her words. And it also concerned the conviction of Christiaan and Gideon on the public-violence charge.

"Another Court may come to a conclusion that my interpretation was not altogether correct in law. I am therefore disposed to grant leave to appeal to all the accused for leave to appeal [sic] to the Appellate Division.

"I am also disposed to grant leave to Accused nos. 5 and 6 to appeal on the charge of public violence."

The defence applied for bail on behalf of all the accused, and the judge refused.

The Six had been in death row for 144 days. We all waited now for the date to be set for the appeal, upon which we pinned very high hopes.

It was a long wait.

❖

In the meantime, the other three Vaal Triangle cases where a councillor had been murdered on September 3, 1984, reached their final stages.

In none of those other cases was any of the accused – some of whom were found to be members of a crowd – found to be the actual perpetrator of the murder. Some were found to have associated themselves with the murderous crowd, yet they were acquitted of murder.

In the case of Councillor Diphoko, in which I was the instructing attorney, there were six accused. One of them was convicted of attempted theft. Another was found to have sprayed Diphoko with fire-extinguisher foam while the councillor was being attacked by the mob. But he was not convicted of murder. He had not dealt the fatal blow and it could not be said with any certainty that he had had the intention to kill. He was convicted of assault.

In the other case I was involved in, that of Councillor Chakane, there were originally six accused, but charges against one were withdrawn. The remaining five were all acquitted on the main count of murder. Two admitted assault and were convicted of assault and given suspended sentences: Oupa Elias Molefe and Johannes Radebe, the man also known as Zulu, who had shared a cell with Johannes Mongaule. Zulu admitted having trodden on Chakane's hand because he was holding a gun, and as a result Chakane was disarmed. Yet Ja-Ja, found to have disarmed Dlamini, was convicted of murder.

I cannot see fundamental differences among the four murder cases. In each, the accused were found to be members of a crowd, and the crowd murdered a councillor. The accused could not be linked causally with the murder, neither could they be shown to have had the intention to murder.

❖

Eighteen months after the granting of leave to appeal, the defence team and members of the families of the appellants went down to Bloemfontein, the judicial capital of South Africa, about four hundred kilometres from Johannesburg. The appellants remained in Pretoria.

Mr. Unterhalter appeared in the appeal court on November 2, 1987, before five appeal judges: Botha JA, Hefer JA, Smallberger JA, Boshoff AJA, and Steyn AJA.[4]

Briefly, the appeal court was asked to consider the fact that none of the appellants had caused the death of Dlamini; that there was no evidence that they had the intention to kill or that they should have foreseen the killing; that there was no evidence of a common purpose between them; that the state witnesses' evidence should not have been accepted and defence evidence rejected; that the trial court should have allowed the cross-examination of Manete on the statement made under privilege to Attorney Soman; and finally that the trial court's had failed to find extenuation for any or all of the appellants.

Proceedings began at 9:45 a.m. with Mr. Unterhalter arguing on behalf of all the appellants. The appeal judges listened to defence counsel's argument until at least 4:30 that afternoon.

Prosecution counsel followed, and had been arguing for just over an hour when the judge presiding, Botha JA, informed him that he need not argue the facts of the case, and should concentrate on the law point. This was a deeply ominous indication that senior counsel's argument for the appellants had made no impression on the Court; we knew then that we had lost the appeal.

The court adjourned at about 6:00 p.m. Judgment was reserved, and there was no indication when it would be pronounced.

Another month went by. Judgment was delivered on December 1, 1987. The Six had been in death row for 718 days.

The appeal court could find no fault with the trial court's findings of fact, nor with the reasoning of the judge. The trial judge had not misdirected himself, and the appeal judges did not want to interfere with the findings of fact, that is, the acceptance of the evidence of state witnesses and the rejection of that of the defence witnesses.

The trial judge had refused to allow Manete to be cross-examined on his statement, because he found that in *law* he had no discretion, in other words, no legal power to do so.

However the appeal court found, for the first time in South African legal history, that a judge does in fact have discretion to order a witness to answer questions put to him in connection with a privileged statement.

But this new finding did not help the appellants, for the appeal court also found that the defence had failed to place sufficient information before the trial judge to enable him to exercise that discretion. So the trial judge was vindicated, and defence counsel was criticized for this "failure" by the appeal judge.

The defence had made available to the trial judge all the facts in its possession as to how, when, and why Manete had made the statement. And counsel had informed the Court explicitly: "The contents of this statement are to the effect that the implication of Accused no. 7 [Duma] and no. 8 [Francis] is not a voluntary implication, but an implication that was dictated to this witness [Manete]. . . . In other words, he is not giving the evidence absolutely untrammelled, he did it because he was told by the police to do it."

The trial judge had not seen fit to call for the statement to examine it himself–a request the defence would have welcomed –but had embarked on a lengthy consideration of the law point, making it perfectly evident that he believed what counsel had said and would take his word for it.

The appeal Court's finding meant that if the trial judge had had sufficient information placed before him by the defence, he could have exercised a discretion that he himself found he did not have.

One may speculate on the reasonings and motives behind the appeal court's decision, but the inescapable fact remains that people's lives were at stake, and the trial judge appears to have been protected.

An eminent judge, Curlewis JA,[5] once had cause to say: "A criminal trial is not a game . . . and a Judge's position . . . is not merely that of an umpire to see that the rules of the game are observed by both sides. A Judge is an administrator of justice, he is not merely a figure-head, he has not only to direct and control the proceedings according to recognized rules of procedure, but to see that justice is done."

To this end, the judge's role is an active one. If Mr. Acting Justice Human was not satisfied with counsel's indication of the contents of Manete's statement, he had only to read it himself.

As far as causation was concerned, Botha JA, appeal judge presiding, said:

The question that must be faced squarely is this: in cases of the kind commonly referred to in our practice as cases of "common purpose," in relation to murder, is it competent for a participant in the common purpose to be found guilty of murder in the absence of proof that his conduct individually caused or contributed causally to the death of the deceased? In recent years, much uncertainty seems to have arisen around this question. This is regrettable, since cases involving a common purpose, as understood in our practice, are of such frequent occurrence that it would probably not be an overstatement to say that they arise practically daily in the criminal courts of our country. There ought not to be uncertainty in this area of the criminal law, and it seems to me to be imperative that a clear answer be given to the question that I have posed. Unfortunately, the uncertainty has been created by a number of decisions of this Court.

Mr. Justice Botha discussed a number of decisions of the appeal court on the vexed subject, concluding: "it would constitute a drastic departure from a firmly established practice to hold now that a party to a common purpose cannot be convicted of murder unless a causal connection is proved between his conduct and the death of the deceased. . . . "

It was only five years since Mr. Justice Hoexter had commented that the law was not "well settled" concerning causality, and less than two years since Mr. Acting Justice Human had quoted widely differing opinions from the Appellate Division (including Mr. Justice Botha) to show that the question was "in the melting-pot." So the "firmly established practice" to which the appeal judge referred was not of very great age.

In the present case, on the facts outlined earlier, there can be no doubt, in my judgment, that the individual acts of each of the six accused convicted of murder manifested an active association with the acts of the mob which caused the death of the deceased. These accused shared a common purpose with the crowd to kill the deceased and each of them had the requisite *dolus* in respect of his death. Consequently the acts of the mob which caused the deceased's death must be imputed to each of these accused.

I should mention that counsel for the accused argued that the final act of setting the deceased alight fell outside the purview of any common purpose to which the accused were parties and that they could therefore not be held responsible for the deceased's death. There is no substance in this argument. On the particular facts of this case the precise manner in which and the precise means by which the deceased was to be killed were irrelevant to the achievement of the common purpose.

For these reasons the first ground of appeal fails.

Turning to the third ground of appeal, against the convictions of subversion, the judge referred to the Schedule annexed to the indictment. This document, he said, "contained a statement of the acts performed by the mob at or in the vicinity of the deceased's house, with which the accused made common cause. . . . "

Botha JA went on to say that the acts of the mob were aimed at inducing the town council of Lekoa to desist from enforcing the service-levy increases, and that as a result of the riots, the council did abandon the increases. Furthermore the inhabitants of Sharpeville had been "put in fear by the rioting mob."

The defence had challenged the trial court finding on this aspect with the argument that the denials of the accused should have been accepted. This, the judge said, "was doomed to fail. Not only were the denials of the accused contrary to the probabilities emerging from the evidence, but the trial court also found that all the accused were untruthful witnesses. The record shows that the trial court had good and sufficient grounds for rejecting the evidence of each of the accused."

The appeal by Christiaan and Gideon against their convictions of public violence was upheld, because the acts of these two, the causing of "general dislocation of law and order" (covered under the charge of subversion) simultaneously involved the forceful disturbance of the public peace and security and invasion of the rights of others (public violence). Therefore only the broader conviction (subversion) should subsist against the two appellants, for "in substance the punishable offence was the same."

On the question of extenuating circumstances, the appeal judges found that the evidence of Professor Tyson was "of a wholly generalised nature, and unrelated to the individual accused."

The appeals of the Six against the conviction of murder and the sentence of death were dismissed, as well as the appeals of all eight against their conviction and sentence for subversion.

The decision of the five appeal judges was unanimous.

Henceforth in South Africa members of a crowd who were present at and associated themselves with the perpetrators' purpose but were otherwise not directly involved in a murder may be found guilty of that murder. To illustrate this, the following is possible in terms of the Sharpeville Six appeal judgment:

If you are near the back of a crowd numbering hundreds or even thousands, and the gathering is a protest of one sort or another, for example a political protest, and the crowd is singing freedom songs, and you sing with the crowd and raise your fist in a black-power salute – and if the crowd in front, in the heightened emotion, grabs hold of a police informer or any other person, and murders him or her, you will have associated yourself with the crowd by singing and raising your fist. You may therefore be convicted of murder and sentenced to death.

❖

The trial judge had been critical of the Six for not testifying before they were sentenced. That was at the end of 1985. During 1987, however, three of the same five appeal judges who heard our appeal had found, in a case concerning prison gangs, that a convicted person need not necessarily give evidence when extenuating circumstances are being considered, and that the facts as a whole must be looked at.

It is elementary law that an appeal court has the right and power to consider the question of sentence, and to set aside any sentence it may consider inappropriate. Yet the judges who sat in Bloemfontein to consider the case of the Six failed to intervene, and thus gave their nod of approval to the trial judge and indeed, to the rest of the courts of the land, for appeal court decisions are binding on all the courts.

Since the Sharpeville appeal judgment, judicial officers all over South Africa have invoked the "common purpose" in mob situations to secure convictions without evidence of direct causality. Judges have found themselves bound by the finding of the so-called common purpose in deciding a murder charge in a mob situation, and people such as the "Upington 14"[6] have been convicted of murder on this basis.

The very distinguished British judge Lord Scarman had this to say about the Sharpeville Six: "I don't understand how the Court of Appeal could have blandly said that all these accused had the intention to kill. There was no evidence on which a safe and satisfactory conviction could be obtained because murder is a very specific offence. It requires conduct which played some part in the enterprise of killing, and the intention to be part in the enterprise of killing."

CHAPTER 17

A Petition

**"Probably I will be knocking at the door
this evening."**
OUPA

Susan Diniso visited Oupa in death row on the morning of December 1, 1987, and told him she had heard on the radio that the Appeal Court's judgment on the Sharpeville Six would be announced that day.

"So, because I knew that I am still standing a good chance of being pardoned or to be acquitted from the trial, I told her that now, well, I don't know, probably I will be knocking at the door this evening."

But after his wife left, Oupa saw a co-prisoner called Mukaswa, whose case had also gone to appeal. He had been acquitted and was going home. "I only saw him when he was wearing this suit and they were giving him his tie and a white shirt."

He wondered if Susan had been mistaken. It seemed the appeal court had given its decision on Mukaswa, no one else. But when Major Cronje appeared in his section, and "looked like his eyes were piercing us – me and Mokhesi," Oupa realized that there was also news about the Six. The major must have heard that their appeal had failed.

Oupa prayed, but did not read his Bible, and sat down in his cell. And on the one o'clock news, he heard that the appeal had been dismissed.

"Prakash and Ismail Hussain, they arrived to tell us. Well, my hope was shattered. I had hoped that Bloemfontein might give a better judgment."

Reid had put all his confidence in the appeal court, and was sure the judges in Bloemfontein were fair and reasonable and would throw the whole case out. It seems he barely entertained any doubts. So the smashing of this hope was a very severe blow for him.

At once, a new hope was proposed, when Hussain and I arrived and told him we would appeal to the State President. And in Reid's mind the old hope had to be discredited, to make the new one valid. Other condemned men contributed to that.

"Many prisoners told us that Bloemfontein is rubbish," Reid said. "They never help people. The only one who takes people out of death row is the State President."

The Six were left, in fact, with one sole recourse: to petition the State President.

In terms of Section 327 of the Criminal Procedure Act, the Head of State may – in certain circumstances – direct the Minister of Justice to order the reopening of a trial. And in terms of the same act, as well as the Constitution Act, he has the power to extend clemency.

But these are executive remedies. What about justice and the courts? Were we totally at the mercy of the State President?

My own problem was that each time I tried to explain to my clients what was happening to them and why, I felt I was participating in a charade. All my training had taught me to respect this legal system on which my professional career was founded. Yet I was unable to defend it, because I knew that a gross injustice was being perpetrated.

My other difficulty was that I had no illusions about fairness or equal treatment in our courts. The State President and the Minister of Justice appoint our judges, so that senior advocates whose political attitude diverges from the official line are unlikely to reach the bench. I am aware that appointments to the bench are political in many civilized countries, but in most of them the party in power represents the majority of the people.

The failure of the appeal was even harder to explain to the Six than the trial judgment. Now there were five more judges, very senior ones at that, who had found that although the Six had not actually caused the death of Dlamini, they had to be executed. "Common purpose" was still, after all this time, a mouthful of legal jargon to those it concerned most. Their attitude was rational: why should we hang when the courts know that we didn't kill Dlamini?

❖

Manete's statement to Mr. Soman was the obvious key to a reassessment of the whole case. The defence team considered the possibility of compelling his attorney to produce it, in terms of the British case of R v. Barton.[1] We consulted the Law Society about this and were advised to approach Manete through his attorney and find out whether at this stage he might be prepared to waive his attorney/client privilege.

It was good advice. Mr. Bham duly saw Manete and explained to him the possible consequences of his waiving his privilege; apparently, without hesitation, Manete agreed.

The Petition was carefully drawn up by counsel, Mr. Unterhalter and Mr. Hussain, and presented to the State President at the end of January 1988. It addressed three fundamental issues: the defence of each of the Six; the statement made by Manete to the attorney, Mr. Soman; and third, the death sentence, considering the facts of the case, and the appeal court's admission that it had not been proved that the conduct of any of the Six had contributed causally to the death of Dlamini.

A comprehensive analysis was presented of the defence of each of the petitioners, and the contradictions and improbabilities of the prosecution witnesses' evidence were thoroughly documented.

The history of the Manete affair was traced step by step: how counsel had advised the trial judge of the contents of the statement; how the trial judge had ruled as a matter of law, and not on grounds of insufficient information, that he had no power to order the cross-examination of Manete on that statement; then the appeal court finding that the trial judge did, after all, have a discretion to order that Manete be cross-examined on the statement, but that he had not erred in refusing to do so, because insufficient evidence had been placed before him and he could not therefore exercise this discretion.

The appeal court's judgment was specifically quoted: "In these circumstances it was clear that if this Court were to decide that the trial judge had erred in disallowing Manete's cross-examination, a re-appraisal of the entire case would be called for, leaving aside the evidence of Manete."

Attached to the petition were all the records and judgments pertaining to the case,[2] Manete's statement to Soman,[3] his waiver of privilege,[4] and an affidavit from Soman to the effect that the notes he had taken during Manete's consultation with him on May 11, 1985, were a true record of what the client had said, and that this client was the same person who had testified in the supreme court during the trial of the present petitioners, for he himself had attended court to identify him.

The affidavit dealt with a couple of other points: that he and Manete had spoken English together and understood each other very well; that at the time of the consultation Manete was not a State witness and Soman was not aware that "my partner, Mr. Prakash Diar, was then acting on behalf of Don Mokgesi and Duma Khumalo who, according to Manete, were still in detention"; and that he had corrected the last sentence of Manete's statement, where the word "me" had been inadvertently omitted: "These names were given to [me] by the police and I was forced to write these names in the statement."

A point raised in the petition was that if indeed the names of Duma and Francis had been suggested to Manete by the police, it was possible that suggestions had also been made to Mabuti, who had appeared to be a willing and co-operative prosecution witness.

Of particular interest was counsel's analysis of trial and appeal judgments in the matter of Oupa as victim of inference:

The gun found at Oupa's house was licensed in Dlamini's name; it was similar to the one Dlamini had on him on the day he was killed; *therefore*, the gun that Oupa had was the gun Dlamini carried the day he died.

And: Ja-Ja, who was found to have wrestled with Dlamini for his gun, brought the police to Oupa's house; the gun was there; *therefore*, Oupa was one of those who disarmed Dlamini on September 3, 1984.

Attention was also drawn to the fact that it took the police two months to begin – and seven months to complete – the arrests of the people Mabuti claimed to have identified in a statement to the police on September 4, 1984.

Finally, it was stressed that both courts had held that the association of the Six with the acts of the crowd was sufficient basis for finding them guilty of the murder of Dlamini.

The petition for clemency had to be addressed on the facts as the courts had found, and not on the defence case.

The plea for Reid ran: "The Second Petitioner threw a stone that struck the back of the deceased. It is quite clear that the throwing of that stone, which reached the back of the deceased while he was prone, has no causal connection with the death of the deceased. Must he pay with his life for such act which ordinarily would be either a common assault or an assault with intent to do grievous bodily harm?"

Oupa's: "The Third Petitioner had possession of a pistol. Inferences have been drawn from such possession, and these have been discussed above. Quite apart from these, can it be said that he should pay for such possession with his life?"

And Theresa's: "The Fourth Petitioner uttered certain words and slapped the face of a woman. Is she to pay with her life for such acts?"

The Petition for mercy ended, "And if His Excellency, the State President, is desirous of obviating such startling results in respect of the Second, Third and Fourth Petitioners, it is respectfully submitted that in regard to the First, Fifth and Sixth Petitioners, for all the reasons stated above, they too should have mercy extended to them."

❖

I had to decide on the best tactics to follow, within the very limited range open to us. It was obvious that a political campaign would be the only hope if the petition failed. But the State President, Mr. Botha, was so averse to pressure from outside the country that it could have been counter-productive while his decision was still pending.

Since the dismissal of the appeal, local and international support for the Six had been growing. The world was appalled at the fact that six young people were going to be hanged for a murder that both trial court and appeal court freely admitted they did not commit.

During the preparation of the petition and after we had lodged it, I gave as much information as possible to various organizations and foreign embassies, and was encouraged by their sympathy and support. But at that stage there was no high-profile campaign.

We all waited for the State President to exercise his independent rights.

CHAPTER 18

In the Pot

"We used to laugh about the measurements, which one has a bigger neck."
DUMA

At Maximum Security, it was prison routine as usual on Monday, March 14, 1988. For the Six, day 823 began just like all the others they had spent in death row.

But, for Oupa, it had an auspicious feel about it. "In the morning when I woke up," he says, "really I was happy. After we had done all the daily work, then I went for exercise. Whilst I was exercising I came back because I had intended to change a trouser of mine. After I had changed that trouser I did not go back to exercise, because my neighbour, he was there. So, I was standing at the door showing him how beautiful I am. He even said, 'Ai, you are so beautiful, you look like you are a driver.' Because you know we are not allowed to iron our clothing, we put them under the mattress. So that was the day now I was taking out the clothing which I kept under the mattress.

"Warrant Officer Arlow – I was surprised when he came to me. I was still reading the newspaper and he said, 'Oupa,' and when I come he said, 'Nou, jy weet man ek het sleg gedroom van jou.' ["You know, man, I had a bad dream about you."] Then I started getting frightened, because usually he knows me but I never talk to him. Why is he telling me that now he had a bad dream of me?"

"It was on Monday, at 9:45," says Francis. "I was with Father Patrick. After my visit with him when I was going back to my cell, one of the sergeants ask me to take my toiletries to go and shave. I went there with him. While I was still shaving, he told me, 'Leave it, you will shave later,' because other prisoners were coming to shower.

"Arlow came to me and said, 'Pack your things.' And he took my card. The sergeant escorted us. I knew we were going to the pot. I was shocked. I was a little bit afraid. I felt like I was being punch drunk."

"The pot." The prisoners call it that. They say it is the place where they will stew before they die. Or else the name comes from "gone to pot" – ruined – alluding to the pot into which refuse metal is cast to be remelted, or to be discarded as waste. It is that row of single cells where the condemned spend their last few days on their way to the gallows. They are the cells called "the bottom," though they are no lower than the ordinary death-row cells.

Ja-Ja, it will be remembered, was in the section nearest the pre-execution cells. So he was familiar with a procedure he had overheard many times:

"When they come to fetch you before you go to the pot, they say, 'Kom kom, baadjie en adres.' ["Come on, come on, jacket and address."][1] You know when they say this, there is no chance. You will be executed. I do not know what they mean by 'adres.' When they fetch you they bring your photo with them to see if they are collecting the correct person. Then you go to the office with a guard to meet the messenger, the sheriff who tells you that the State President has reviewed your case and you must be executed, and they take you with underpants, socks and shoes and you are led to the point. . . .

"I felt very weak when they came to fetch me. They rush you. They say, 'Pack all your things.' If you do not finish, they pack it in for you and they give it to you later.

"When I saw Duma Khumalo, then I thought about what the messenger will tell me at the office. I thought maybe I will get a reprieve. Then I saw all the accused [the other four Sharpeville men]. When the messenger said I was to be executed, I was very cross. My heart was very painful, and when he gave the date he said Friday, but we were only there on Monday."

Duma, who was in the same section as Ja-Ja, says, "The painful moment is the moment when they come to take you . . . the manner in which they put the lock in the door. You feel a beat inside your heart and he start saying, 'Pack your things,' and my neighbour was also told to pack his things. So I become crazy and afraid thinking what is happening, because this man is not my co-accused. But when I went down is when I started realizing that all the co-accused were there. I started becoming aware of what was happening. So they informed us that we will be executed on the eighteenth of the month. So we wanted to know why we were not given seven days like any other prisoners. He says, no they cannot answer that, it is a matter concerning the Department of Justice. So we went to the bottom cells. So we become as one. A unit, a strong one."

Oupa's lucky day had turned to ashes. "Well," he says, "when we arrived [at the office], we were showed some certificates. . . . That messenger he told us that the State President he is not prepared to grant us any mercy so we are to be executed on the eighteenth. Actually we did not want mercy from the State President, we only needed justice. So after he had told all of us, we asked him why does he give us five[2] days only, usually people are given seven days.

"Well, after that now we were told to take off all our clothes. Because I was angry, I did not care. All I said now was let them do what they think is right for them. After they had taken all our clothing, we went for the measurements. We went for the measurements of the neck."

Reid says, "It was done immediately after the sheriff told us that the State President refuse to pardon us. I felt there is no way. I will die, I will be hanged. When such things happen, my body becomes hot. I become stubborn. I do not see what is happening, I do not hear what others say and what is happening.

"I did not say anything to the sheriff. I just signed the paper which was my warrant of death.

"It was done by Arlow. . . . We stood up and had to look upwards and he then measured our neck. He then tells the sheriff what my measurement is. It was fifteen. Then the sheriff writes down. Then Arlow checks my weight, then he checks my height, how long I am. I cannot remember how much I weighed or what my length was. From there I put my thumb on some ink. From there we took our clothes to the pot, but we had to leave our underpants with Arlow."

Because it was Arlow who carried out the measurements, the experience was exacerbated for Francis, too. He says, "I was still shivering. They do things so quickly, you cannot have faith that things will work out. They always rush you. When he put the tape around my neck, because it was done by somebody with whom there was bad feelings, I could see inside he was happy we were going to die."

Over in the women's section, Theresa was also brought downstairs and informed by the sheriff that all the procedures instituted by her had failed, and that she was to hang on the Friday. She says, "I was shocked when I heard this. A sister gave me some tablets which calmed me."

Then she was taken to be measured. "They put an elastic with a numbering around my neck to measure me. It was very tight around my neck. I thought maybe they will hang me there. I was shivering when they put it around my neck. Arlow did the measuring. He was cheeky. He was happy when someone was going to hang, and he then smiled. He weighed me but I did not have to take off my clothes. I only had to take off my shoes."

Theresa had met Arlow before. "Once, when my hand was hurt and I needed plaster for it, Arlow said to another prison warder that the pole is ready for her hanging. He also said to the doctor he must not give me a plaster, it is a waste of money because I am going to hang."

Once out of Arlow's hands, Theresa received kinder treatment than the men. "Many warders came to me. They said even the last day I can be pardoned. They told me of others who had been pardoned. I was very afraid, but I took my Bible and it gave me courage."

For Ja-Ja, speaking nearly a year later, another painful memory was fresh and sharp: "We stayed in the pot for a day without meeting anyone from outside. Only on Tuesday we met Prakash and our family. I was worried that we would be executed before our family could come. We heard that this happened before. When the family comes they find that their loved one is already dead."

❖

For me, in my office, that day was unexceptional until mid-afternoon. My anxiety about the petition was mounting: it was nearly seven weeks since we had lodged it with the State President. But I reasoned that it must take time for his legal advisers to consider the facts of the case, to peruse all the documents.

Then, at half-past three, I received a telephone call from Dr. Andreas Zoebel, Second Secretary at the German Embassy in Pretoria. He had just learned that the Six were to be executed on Friday, March 18. Was this true? I did not know.

Immediately, I telephoned the Department of Justice, and was given confirmation that the State President had turned down the plea for clemency. I asked why I had not been informed, and was told, "The letter is probably in the post."[3] The Department was unable to confirm the date of execution.

Major Cronje, in charge of death row, was, however, able to confirm that warrants of execution had been served on the Six that morning, and that the date set was Friday the eighteenth.

Attorneys' access to the condemned closes at 4:00 p.m., so it was too late for me to go to Pretoria to speak to my clients. The defence had three days to find some way to save them.

Our office alerted the many people and organizations whose support had already been enlisted when the appeal failed. Fortunately, most of the embassies were very sympathetic. They were familiar with the facts of the case as well as the issues. Many foreign governments played an important part, and all had a common cry: "Don't hang the Six!" West Germany was chairing the European Economic Community at the time and the EEC passed a resolution calling for a reprieve of the Six. So did the United Nations Security Council. Among other countries, Canada, Japan, the United States, Australia, Austria, the Netherlands, Norway, Sweden, Switzerland, and Israel called individually for the State President to show mercy for the Six. Amnesty International intervened, as did the Washington-based Lawyers' Committee for Civil Rights under Law, the anti-apartheid movements everywhere, and the London group South Africa the Imprisoned Society (SATIS).

The Johannesburg Bar Council had refused to plead on behalf of the Six, but many Bar councils around the world expressed their indignation at how far this "common purpose" was being stretched to get a conviction of murder in a crowd situation, in a country where murder without extenuating circumstances automatically carried the death penalty. Even the International Commission of Jurists intervened. Most legal bodies based their call for clemency on legal considerations, while most governments spoke up on political and humanitarian grounds. Even a group of twenty-two U.S. senators drew up a petition. Church leaders, among them the Archbishop of Canterbury, the Cardinal Archbishop of Westminster, Archbishop Tutu, Dr. Allan Boesak, Rev. Frank Chikane, and Dr. Beyers Naude; all the South African progressive organizations, such as the United Democratic Front (in particular its affiliates, South Africa Youth Congress [SAYCO] and the Vaal Civic Association [VCA]), the Azanian People's Organization, the National Council of Trade Unions, the Congress of South African Trade Unions, the South African Catholics' Bishops' Conference; and many churches, irrespective of political affiliation, supported the call for mercy.

Thanks to the great and unselfish efforts of people too numerous to mention by name, the campaign gained momentum. President Reagan of the United States, Prime Minister Thatcher of the United Kingdom, and Chancellor Kohl of West Germany intervened personally on behalf of the Six, in response to heavy pressure in their countries from opposition parties, women's organizations, trade unions, and anti-apartheid and church groups.

P.W. Botha's answer to all these pleas is now well known: "I don't interfere in the process of the courts."

No one was asking him to do that; it was the last thing anyone wanted. We were asking him to exercise his prerogatives as Head of State.

Two weeks before he made this statement, he had done just that, and granted a reprieve to a police officer by the name of George John Sindane. In the words of the trial judge, this man had "cold-bloodedly murdered an innocent youth." He had placed his .38-calibre weapon against Mabuti Mabane's chest, and shot him dead. No extenuation was found, and Sindane was duly sentenced to death. Leave to appeal was refused by the trial judge and the Chief Justice. But the State President responded to his petition for clemency by commuting his sentence to eight years.

At the very time he was turning down the petition for the Six, the State President signed an order to stop the prosecution of six South African Defence Force members who were facing murder charges. They had allegedly attended a public meeting in Windhoek, caused a disturbance, and then beaten to death Mr. Immanuel Rifidi, a prominent member of the South West African People's Organization (SWAPO). It is hard to see the State President's action here as anything other than an interference in the process of the courts.

As my clients knew, condemned people in death row are normally given seven-day execution notice. And they had been given four days. Perhaps this deviation from custom was a response – of a sort – to world pressure?

We had to evolve some legal strategy to get a stay of execution. There seemed to be only one option: to take up the question of Joseph Manete's statement made to a lawyer under privilege. The trial judge had ruled that he himself had no discretion to force Manete to waive his privilege and allow himself to be questioned on the statement. The appeal court had found that the judge did have a discretion in law, but that insufficient information had been placed before him by the defence. We would place before the judge all the available information, all over again, making the best possible use of Manete's waiver of privilege. We started at once to prepare the documents for an urgent application for a stay of execution.

How do you consult six people who have just been served with a death warrant? What do you say to people who have been placed in a special death cell and are being prepared for execution? What do you say when all their personal belongings have been taken away from them? What do you say when they have been weighed on scales and their necks have been measured for the hangman's rope? How can you tell them not to worry?

Early in the morning of Tuesday, March 15, I went to see my clients. Remarkably, the men had their wits about them. I am not certain that this was true of Theresa: she seemed unconcerned about her impending execution. This worried me. She said, "I am not afraid. I know I didn't kill Dlamini and God knows that too. Jesus died for the sins of others, and if he was prepared to accept his fate, then so am I." Dignified and courageous words, but I felt uneasy about her.

Ja-Ja was quiet and fairly calm. Reid cried. He held back no emotion. As he cried he told me, "They can kill me, but they can't kill my soul." All maintained their innocence, and Oupa, who was also crying, asked, "How can they hang me when they don't even have one witness who saw me there?" Duma did not cry. He was angry. He wanted no mercy from the State President. All he wanted was justice. But he said, "If by my suffering some good will come, then I am prepared to suffer." Francis was very quiet. He seemed to have already made peace with himself and his Maker.

I explained the tactics we could employ for a stay of execution. My clients were not hopeful, and of course, I could not promise success. But I managed to convince them that no matter how slim our chances, we should take them, for if we didn't it meant certain death within seventy-two hours. The Six had nothing to lose, nothing to risk except one more dashing of hope.

The Sharpeville Six were big news around the world. Some countries declared they would recall their diplomats from South Africa if the Six were executed. There were threats of further sanctions, of withdrawal of landing rights for South African aircraft, of travel difficulties for South Africans. Awareness of all this gave me more hope than it gave my clients.

Back in my Johannesburg office, the papers were prepared and compiled in five sets, to be served on the respondents.

The hearing was set for 11:30 on Wednesday morning, and before that I had to obtain signatures from the Six, with the usual delays before gaining access to them; I had to have the application papers issued at the Supreme Court, serve them on each of the respondents – the Attorney-General of the Transvaal, the Sheriff of the Transvaal, the Officer Commanding Maximum Security Prison, the Minister of Justice, and the Minister of Law and Order – and then file the papers with the court.

❖

The "bottom cells" were the same as the single ones in death row, with a few differences. The condemned slept on mats. They had no pyjamas, and wore the green uniform day and night.

Reid adds some more detail: "The cell I was in was the same . . . except in the pot they took out the mattress from my bed. They took my toothbrush and my Colgate out. They even took our shoes, underpants, and vest away. You could put the shoes on when you went to the shower and when you went to visit your family. The shoes were always left outside the cells. There was no exercise in the pot. We were allowed to talk any time we wanted."

Was this concession a generous relaxation of rules, or were the condemned in the pot simply left to their own devices? Whatever the reason, talking was permitted day and night, and the men could hear each other from cell to cell.

Other concessions to imminent death were permission to buy as much food as one wanted from the prison shop, and to have visits from other prisoners. Oupa the vegetarian, who had fed himself largely from the tuck shop while he was in death row, says, "Although I did not have appetite for food but anyway I said let me eat. . . . Some that was left behind I sent to my friend

... Bernard ... because he did come and visit me. I asked permission that I want to see him. I gave him all [my food]." This must have been on the last day, Thursday, for Oupa goes on, "Well, he too, he gave me courage that they will not execute me and he told me that now if you come back you will still find your food. I will keep your food, I will not use it. Some I might use but most of what I know you are much dependent on, you will get them back again."

Francis observed himself with some surprise: "I was only eating two spoonfuls. I did not eat but my body was gaining weight. I could not understand this. . . . "

In the male section, many of the prisoners felt that their warders were gloating. As Oupa puts it, "They are happy because they have been longing that we must be executed."

The spiritual calm that Francis seemed to have found did not desert him. He was conscious of it himself, during his days in the pot, and afterwards: "In those five days I was feeling happy. We were laughing, making jokes, speaking for the whole night. Some of the other prisoners were laughing when they were listening to our conversation. I was feeling very strong. My inner being was happy . . . happy to escape this long tortured road I walked through. After a few days, having left the pot, I tried to work out why I was so happy there. I could not understand, but thinking about it now where we prayed to God, sometimes he wants to show himself to you so that you believe what he says to you is true.

"I see a death for three years. I prepared for those five days for three years. I was feeling God was with me. I felt happy."

Francis was able, however, to observe the state of his fellows, and comments, "The most sad of the five of us were Reid, Diniso, and Ja-Ja. They were still laughing, but through their appearance and their conversation I could see they were very sad. I noticed that two of them, Reid and Oupa, were crying when they were visited by Prakash, when they were talking to him about their feelings."

He was right about the others. Reid's despair stares out of his own words: "I did not have much hope. The State President said there was no mercy for me. During that time I felt like I was lost. I was just waiting for them to take me any time and hang me.

"The first day I was scared. We were talking about the rope, what would happen to my body, were my people going to get my body or see me. I heard that when you get hanged, as you get strangled, your eyes pop out, they come out of your head and the blood then comes out of your ears and that my tongue will fall from my mouth.

"I was thinking about my mother who is too old and my son who is too small. I did not give him the parent that I should have given him, and at home there were two sons of my late sister that I was supporting. When I think about all of them, I have such pain that I cry."

And Francis was right about Ja-Ja, who remembers, "I was thinking about life, I was thinking that it had its ups and downs. If you get happy, it is for a short period and after that, you get cross, it is for a long period. There are many things which make life taste bad, and the cause of all these things is people. And I never expected that it would be me in the gallows facing death and then I asked myself what is in life, is this the way I am supposed to go? I asked myself many times why it was me that was chosen and why it was me that was sentenced to death. My answer to this was that maybe this was the bad luck. And then I asked myself, where is this punishment going to end up? When is executions going to stop? Because of our justice many people will be killed by the State, just as they have done to me. This punishment it won't stop because the judges and our courts are overruled by parliament. When I look at my case I feel as if I was found guilty before appearing in court."

Oupa shared Francis's perceptions: "Ja-Ja, there were times when he was talking with us all but there were times that he was away from us. He would just keep quiet. The same applies to Reid. . ... He too, he was on and off with our conversation but if it was something that was very interesting or laughable then he will join us."

One of Oupa's own preoccupations was the prospect of being hanged naked: "Now this is what I have been thinking about. I say now even on the electric chair you are not naked, on the firing squad you are not naked, but now why should this happen to us? Though I know that really this is very wrong, but something that was on my mind. . . . I thought that we'll be naked in order [that] this clothes they must not have blood, because now if they have to cut you really some of your tissues are going to break up. Well I heard that if somebody is on the rope either he can pass urine or maybe they are trying that the clothes must not be dirty because who is going to wash those clothes and things like that. . . . I said to myself that if this is the manner in which they execute people in South Africa, well, there is nothing I can do, I have to accept that punishment too.

" . . . things that made me to survive is . . . I felt that I was in the right. Well, I was really relieved at this feeling.

"I told myself that now being a Christian or having accepted Christ, really, it is not through a man's will to die in a fashion which he likes, but it is through the will of God. . . . Christ he knew exactly that he was going to be betrayed by Judas even if he was facing death, though fear did get him, but all he said was, if this cup might pass let it be through your will, not through mine. So, this is part of the words that made me strong on my faith that now even if I too have to die, really I have to let it all rest in the hands of God."

Francis observed how one of their number sustained them all: "Duma was always full of jokes and laughing. He was the one who was keeping us laughing. . . . "

For Oupa the memorable conversations were the amusing ones, "like the incident with Duma when he was in detention. He asked somebody to break his leg and he was eating bottles and all those things. When we revealed these things we actually laughed the whole night."

According to Oupa, Duma provided them with another distraction. "He used to say he wants to marry my younger sister, but I told him no, you can't marry my younger sister because tomorrow you are going to die. He will say no, I have to marry her. . . . He even wrote to her and then he was proposing love to her."

Duma himself recalls: "We only slept for a few minutes. We could talk all night. They gave us freedom to talk about anything. . . . I loved the other four. We used to laugh about the measurements, which one has a bigger neck and which one will get the tallest coffin."

❖

Theresa's experience of the days before her scheduled execution was greatly mitigated by the presence of sympathetic wardresses, and there was no specific "pot" in the women's section. All the condemned could hear the radio, for there were speakers in every section, but she, in her isolation, drew special comfort from it. "What gave me courage," she says, "I heard every day on the radio about us, about the Sharpeville Six, and when I read the newspaper, I had hope."

She says of this time, "I was thinking about my mother. I wanted to work for my mother, but I did not get a chance. I thought how she will feel if I hang. Sometimes I feel they can hang me and sometimes I feel for what."

Theresa's fear was beginning to run away with her: "I was wondering what my family would do with my body. I was worried about this. I thought that the prison would dig a hole and put me in this hole and this made me feel very bad. I thought maybe I can't breathe. I used to put my hand over my nose and mouth to see what it is like not to have any air when your neck breaks. I believed that they would give me an overall when they hang me. I did not think that I would get hanged naked. When you finish hanging, they will wash you or they will bury you straight away?"

She put her questions to her wardresses, but, she says, "All the ladies who worked here said that they don't know anything. It is only the sheriff and three sergeants who know."

Twenty-four hours after Theresa was measured for her hanging, she started hallucinating. A year later, she could describe this for what it was: "On Tuesday, the fifteenth of March, 1988, three days before the execution, I started imagining that there were things in my cell. I felt somebody was in my cell. That they would take me and hang me. I use to speak to this some-body, but I do not know what I said. Sometimes Sandra [Smith, her friend and cell-neighbour] would say, 'Why are you speaking?'

"It was only when I prayed that this thing disappeared, but when I stopped, this thing came back. It would happen when I was feeling very alone. This would happen early in the morning, say four to five, when there is no one around, or late at night. But it won't happen in the afternoon when I had many things to do.

"Sandra would keep me busy, and sometimes the sergeant. There were many, they would come there and keep talking to me. Sometimes I take all the food in my cell and I put it on my bed. I eat it all so that I can forget about this thing in my cell. Sometimes it would call me, then I would say "Voertsek" ["Get away!"] or I would pray or I would eat. It did not disturb my sleep. When I sleep I forget everything."

And, of course, there were visits, though none were "contact" visits. Theresa says of those three days – Tuesday, March 15, to Thursday, March 17 – "From 9:00 a.m. to 4:00 p.m. I would sit in this room and speak to all the visitors who came. They were family and friends and other supporters. They would share the time . . . five minutes for some, ten minutes for others.

"I got visits from Roman Sisters and Fathers. They gave me courage. They said I must not be afraid. They said many were praying that I should not hang."

❖

Argument began at about noon on Wednesday, March 16, 1988, in the Supreme Court in Pretoria.

In accordance with normal practice, the judge who had tried the case presided. The court was so full there was not even standing room. All the family members were present. Local and foreign media were extensively represented. Many diplomats from the various consulates and embassies were there. The Six were not.

All the papers had been settled by Mr. Unterhalter, and we had merely annexed Manete's waiver of privilege. A point should be made here: the waiver we had obtained on January 27, 1988, for the purposes of the petition to the State President, concerned all Manete's communications and statements made to Mr. Mohamed Bham. For the present Court Application, the defence had deemed it prudent to obtain another waiver, where Manete also specifically waived his privilege on the statement made by him to Mr. Soman in 1985; thus the waiver annexed was dated Tuesday, March 15, 1988.

Counsel was Mr. D. Kuny sc, because Mr. Unterhalter was unable to appear in person. When Mr. Kuny reached the subject of the waiver of privilege, the judge showed annoyance, and said he was suspicious about the manner in which the defence had obtained it. He asked whether pressure had been brought to bear on Manete to sign it. Why had the defence managed to obtain a waiver only yesterday?

After the lunch break, everyone was moved to a larger courtroom, as the first had been far too small, and even more spectators had arrived.

Mr. Acting Justice Human was not prepared to listen to further argument. He wanted a full and detailed account of how the defence had obtained the waiver. He adjourned the Application.

Thus another precious day had gone. We had only one left.

When I went to report to the Six what had happened in court, they became more despondent. They were even less hopeful than they had been in the morning. They were sure the judge was not going to save them.

The defence had to put up further affidavits. In mine, I furnished a detailed description of the steps we had taken, including our consultation with the Law Society, before obtaining the waiver. Manete's attorney, Mr. Bham, gave an exhaustive account of what had transpired in his consultations with his client. He also dealt with the fact that on Tuesday, March 15,

1988, Manete had confessed to him that he had given perjured evidence at the trial. This confirmed what the defence had known all along.

❖

On the last day, Theresa's mother came to the prison. "I told my mother, 'This is the last time I will see you.' She said, 'No, you will not hang. While we are talking the court is busy.' I had already said goodbye."

For Reid, visiting time was almost torture, and it seems his mother felt the same. He says, "Whenever I had a visit, I would cry a lot. My mother would come every day [before he was moved to the pot], but she only saw me once in those five days. It was on Wednesday morning. I told her that she must not worry because an application for a stay of execution was being made. I was crying when I told her this.

"I thought I would see my mother on the Thursday, but she did not come. She stayed outside." Reid understood, and was perhaps even grateful. "I could not feel anything about this, because when she came to see me on Wednesday, all she did was cry. She could not speak to me at all."

Mrs. Mokoena's memory is quite clear: "I couldn't face him when I knew he was going to die in a few hours' time. My heart wanted to go and see him." She went to the court instead.

But Reid's sister Martha came. She says, "I didn't believe it was going to happen so I told him about Daniel in the lion's den. Daniel didn't die in the lion's den. He was crying, his tears were coming down and I was crying."

And Dorothy came, his little boy's mother whom Reid still calls his wife-to-be. "She had no words for me. She could not speak. I said to her, 'You cannot blame me and I cannot blame you. None of us passed the sentence.' And I even wrote letters to my mother and to Dorothy that day."

Francis was conscious of his vulnerable point: "I knew if I think about my family too much, it will be my downfall. Whenever they came I told them that they must accept this. I reminded them about my mother, how much we loved her and how much pain we had when she died and I was still young, but I reminded them that we got over it.

"We hoped that we would see them just before we could be hanged, but one can never be sure because it depends on how much prison staff there is. Sometimes there is not enough to allow for visits.

"I saw my family on the morning of the seventeenth. . . . I was planning to see them, probably for the last time on the afternoon of the seventeenth. I did not have much hope that there would be a stay of execution. I had accepted that I was going to die."

His wife, Alinah, says of the morning visit, "I didn't talk to him because I was fainting. My mind was confused. . . . I couldn't talk. I heard him talk for twenty minutes. He tried to console me. He said don't be sick it won't happen. If it does, what will be will be."

Duma's brother Phinda was not there to say goodbye. In the course of his business, he had bought a used car, not knowing the seller had stolen it, and when he took it for police clearance on February 28 he was arrested. Bail was refused and he was kept in the cells at the Randburg police station, near Johannesburg, for a month. He knew of Duma's impending execution, from his wife and from the newspapers. He put his faith in world pressure and local expediency: "I knew that somewhere, somehow, because they were people from Sharpeville, and they had been sentenced to death, six of them, and internationally, Sharpeville was a little bit known, because of the 1960 troubles, I knew the international community would bring some pressure somehow. . . . I can say that they are good people, who care about other people's troubles, around the world." He adds, "I knew that if they hanged, there could have been something terrible – something terrible could have happened. Many people could have rioted in Sharpeville and that could have spread. Even at Randburg, at the police station, the atmosphere was tense. Everyone there was talking about it."

Phinda did not tell the other prisoners until after the stay of execution that Duma was his brother. When he did tell them, they rejoiced with him. "It was a victory for myself and for them also. A lot of people worshipped them. They took them as heroes."

Duma's little boy, his father, and Phinda's wife and children all went to say goodbye to him.

Susan Diniso could hardly bear that Thursday: "I was sick in the spirit, deeply. I looked at him. He was trying to suppress his tears. His eyes were watery. I controlled myself. Then he said, 'There's nothing, don't worry.' Visitors were saying, 'You won't hang.' I couldn't talk. The police gave us forms with the grave-yard numbers, after the morning visit. We wouldn't see the bodies. They were already wearing their death clothes. I went back [to the court]. My aunt began to pray, then we all prayed together. The application went on. We went back to the prison at two o'clock. The families stayed. I couldn't talk, I just looked at him. The police said get out. . . . I couldn't stand up. What could I say? I haven't said anything so far. If he's going to be hanged, what am I supposed to say? I couldn't get up. The Khumalos lifted me up to carry me out. . . . "

And now Regina, mother of Ja-Ja's child, had trouble with Ja-Ja's long-lost mother: "It was a long time before she came [from Cape Town]. I brought Ja-Ja's mother to visit him the first time. This was during the days waiting for execution. We were not legally married and she wanted to take things from the house. Ja-Ja said don't give her things. Ja-Ja liked nice things and she wanted to take them. She didn't care–she said I am just a passing girl. . . . She called me names. She said it is my fault Ja-Ja is in trouble. Ja-Ja was scared that she would make me leave him. I told him I wouldn't leave – I would be with him until the end. I am wife, mother, brother, sister to Ja-Ja."

On the last day, Regina says, "I didn't want to see. I didn't know what to do or say. I wasn't thinking of touching him. It is very bad that you can't see him being buried. You are just given a grave number. You must see it is Ja-Ja, he is dead and his grave is here. They mustn't mix it up. That was the worst, not being sure you are visiting Ja-Ja's grave. I said to him, 'Don't forget me and my child.' Did I cry? No, I didn't cry. He didn't cry. I cried outside when I saw his best friend. There is a photo of Ja-Ja with that friend. In the visiting room people were saying bye-

bye. Others were saying, 'You won't hang – the community will be so angry.' They were just consoling us. They were already wearing hanging clothes. The warders pushed them out. I thought of my last words: 'Ja-Ja go well.' He said, 'I will think of you and will not forget you or my child.'

"If they hang you, why should I be alive?"

"He said, 'Don't say that, look after my child.' "

❖

On Thursday, March 17, the new affidavits were filed. To our surprise, the judge showed no interest in them. He seemed to have had a complete change of attitude from the one he displayed the day before. He was most accommodating, listening to counsel and appearing to be sympathetic. I could not help wondering whether anyone had been talking to him, for the government seemed to be in some sort of a crisis over the Sharpeville Six. Perhaps the judge was required to rescue it from the awkward situation it had created for itself?

It was already three o'clock by the time both defence and State counsel had completed their argument, and the judge withdrew. There were only a few hours left for the Six. We waited, under great emotional strain, in the courtroom.

Judgment was delivered at 3:20. The court was crowded, and absolutely quiet. When the judge made his appearance, the spectators stood up as one.

It was not a long judgment. Mr. Justice Human was critical of the manner in which defence counsel had raised the matter of Manete's statement during the trial, and stated that he had never been invited to peruse that document. However, he found *prima facie* evidence of perjury at the trial. The words we were waiting for came at last: "The respondents are prohibited from executing these people tomorrow. The execution will be stayed until 18 April 1988 to allow the applicants to bring a substantive application for the reopening of the case."

In closing, the judge attacked a number of local and overseas newspapers, as well as "certain legal luminaries in this country," for suggesting that "these people were convicted because they were innocent bystanders in the crowd of people who killed the deceased and they did nothing at all. That is arrant nonsense. If one studies the judgment by me as well as the judgment in the Appellate Division it will be clear that they were active participants in the killing of the deceased. They had a common purpose to kill and because of their active participation and association with that common purpose they were convicted of the crime of murder."

So, the Six got a stay of execution. But not before the judge had had his say. There was by now much criticism of his trial judgment, and he appeared to have become defensive.

The defence team was not so touchy, despite the judge's remarks. We were happy, and so was the crowd. They applauded spontaneously. Some cried with joy. As I left the courtroom I was surrounded by media representatives and spectators – each seeking a comment. I could only express my relief, but at the same time I stressed that this was no more than a stay of execution, a temporary reprieve.

As I approached the main exit, I saw hundreds of people all over Church Square and Church Street. Some were relations and friends of the Six, but most of them were just well-wishers. They all applauded me as I went down the steps. Cameras clicked and the crowd sang the black national anthem. To my amazement I was hoisted shoulder-high and people shouted, "Hero! Hero!" I had never in my wildest imagination expected a response like this. I was happy, for the Six's sake especially, but it was they who should have been carried shoulder-high through the streets of Pretoria.

I could not stay to enjoy my clients' triumph. They themselves did not know that their lives had been spared. I rushed first to the male section of Maximum Security. The five men were brought at once.

When I saw them, I was unable to put on a smile, despite my good news. They were just too sad for words. They were quiet. They had accepted that they would die in a few hours' time. They had prepared themselves.

I saw them through the glass partition. They lifted their hands in greeting. I did likewise. When I told them we had succeeded in getting a stay of execution, none of them reacted. They had long lost their faith in the legal process, and in Mr. Acting Justice Human. They thought I had come to say goodbye.

But when I said, "Gents, you are not going to hang in the morning," I got some response. They looked in my direction, but still they avoided meeting my eyes. I told them we had been given until April 18, 1988, to make an application to reopen the trial. They had no questions. Understandably, they looked confused. Then the meaning of my words sank in, and each one of them thanked me for my efforts. I said that they should thank the Lord, and Oupa said to me, "At this moment, we only know you."

I had to go, because of Theresa. As I left, they all smiled warmly and waved. We would meet again in the morning.

At the women's section, I saw Theresa through the glass window. She walked in, on the other side of the glass, accompanied by a black prison wardress. She walked very slowly, almost dragging her feet. She did not look at me. She kept looking down.

I guess she also thought I had come for a final visit. When I started to speak to her she continued to look at the floor. I told her I had good news, but she didn't seem able to comprehend. Then I said she was not going to hang, and she burst into tears, sobbing loudly.

She cried hysterically and uncontrollably. She grabbed hold of the black wardress, who started crying with her. Then Theresa tried to touch my hand. She couldn't. She placed her palm against the glass. I did likewise, on my side of the glass. At that moment a white wardress, who had probably heard the violent outburst, walked in on Theresa's side of the glass. Theresa reached out to her and they hugged each other. The white wardress unlocked the four doors that separated us and allowed Theresa to come around to my side so that we could have a contact visit, just for a few moments. Theresa held onto me and kept on crying. Then she knelt down at my feet and I begged her not to do that. I said she should thank the Lord because her prayers had been answered. She told me that I was her angel and that the Lord had come down to her through me. She couldn't stop crying.

Seeing Theresa react the way she did, I wondered whether, after all, she had been prepared to die, as she had informed me. I wondered whether she had not, all along, been putting on a very brave front.

"I was in my cell when Prakash came," says Theresa. "He came at 4:00 p.m. Then he told me, and I started to cry. I hadn't cried for that whole week. I was very happy, but I had prepared myself to hang."

Her desperate farewell with Ja-Ja over, Regina was leaving death row: "We saw Prakash going in. He said, 'We have won!' We couldn't believe. . . . We were so happy. We were singing. But I couldn't see him [Ja-Ja] again then. When I saw him he said, 'I'm alive! You thought I would die.' He made it a joke!"

Reid says, remembering the moment as I do. "When Prakash told us, we did not scream, we just bowed our heads and smiled. Arlow was in the room with us and we could not show that we were too happy because he did not like it when people escaped the rope."

But he goes on, "I thought, the hangman is not going to get me any more. Then we were going to petition Bloemfontein and let Manete tell the truth. I was very happy."

Reid's mother remembers that I said we would all sleep better that night. Her relief was only partial: "We didn't know what was happening. Our minds were in a state of total confusion, because it was leading up to death, then it was gone, then it was starting off again, then it was another judgment again, and it was up and down, up and down over a period of time. . . . We stopped thinking. That kind of thing. Too much shock. Too much prolonged tension. There were prayers."

Oupa felt the same as Reid about the warders: "When Prakash told us that we are not going to be hanged, we saw the face of the warders, they were gloomy. Both [black and white]. Those who had been hostile against us. Arlow he was there . . . he was gloomy, he even told us, 'Kom kom, julle moet nie tyd kom mors hierso nie.' ["Come on, come on, don't come and waste time around here."] So, now . . . we go down to the bottom. On the way we met people, other officers with a big book, which you sign on the last day after all the remedies have been exhausted, so they were very shocked when they heard that no, we are not going to be executed . . . and some were complaining that they worked very hard . . . and they were working through all the shift. They even changed the cycle of the shift. . . .

"Well, when we go back to the bottom cells, we were happy. . . . We had to remain in those cells until the day we were to be executed. After that we must go back to where we were." This, of course, was death row.

Francis looked inward: "I could not understand myself. I did not know if I was unhappy or happy. It is something that struck me. The reason I was not sure I was happy is that I had been through so much and my life seemed to be like a ball going up and down in the hands of the State President."

Although they were not going to hang, the last supper for the men had already been prepared. Oupa says, "On the last day, when they are going to execute you tomorrow, they give you a whole chicken. Well, because I am a vegetarian I gave mine away. Francis ate and Duma ate. The others, I don't know what happened."

Ja-Ja's information on this prison generosity is, "They bring a full chicken. They take the bones out. . . . They seem to have mixed the chicken with something to clean the stomach before people were executed. But I don't know what."

The chicken was, however, the last meal of Duma's neighbour, Tsepo. He was scheduled to hang with the Six the next morning, for the gallows can handle seven hangings at a time. Tsepo was almost always quiet while the six men were in the pot together. Now and then he spoke to Duma, but very little. Some of the warders had even approached Duma in genuine concern about him. They felt he should see his family, and were ready to pay for the transport themselves if the prison service did not. But Tsepo did not want to see anyone and could not be persuaded.

On the way back to the cells after they had heard the good news, Duma told Ja-Ja that none of them must show any sign of jubilation, for it would be inappropriate. Duma, who had kept everyone's spirits up with his jokes and funny stories while they all waited to die, insisted now that the five who were saved "be quiet, out of respect."

They hoped to say goodbye to Tsepo before he was taken away in the morning; but they were sleeping when the warders came, unusually early, to fetch him. He left so quietly that none of them heard him go.

The Law and the Rope

"I did not tell the Court the whole truth."
J.M. MANETE

"**I** am of the view today that in fact because of the statement [Manete's] which is now made available to me and which I have now considered, the application should be granted. It may affect the guilt of the first two applicants (Nos. 7 and 8 at the trial) [Duma and Francis]; it may affect the others." Thus Mr. Acting Justice Human, in his judgment of March 17, 1988, was giving us until April 18, 1988, to file an Application to reopen the trial.

The Application was based precisely on Manete's confession that he had given false testimony at the insistence of the police. In it were emphasized, as they were in the petition, the extraordinary words of Mr. Justice Botha in the appeal judgment: "If this Court were to decide that the trial judge had erred in disallowing Manete's cross-examination [on the statement he had made to Soman], a reappraisal of the entire case would be called for, leaving aside the evidence of Manete."

Manete had implicated only Duma and Francis directly. Nevertheless, he had been found to corroborate Mabuti, and without that corroboration, Mabuti's evidence might not have been accepted. If Mabuti's evidence were placed in doubt, the versions of Ja-Ja, Reid, Oupa, and Theresa might be believed or at the very least, they could be found to have a reasonable possibility of being true.

In terms of South African criminal law, the accused need not prove their innocence, nor even the truth of their defence – they need only to show the Court that their version could possibly be true; they are then entitled to a verdict of not guilty and to acquittal on all charges.

We had Mr. Bham's important affidavit dated March 16, 1988, given just after Manete signed his second waiver. This document contained two features: confirmation that Manete had waived his privilege with him and with his previous attorneys, and "Manete's confession":

"I further confirm that on Tuesday, the fifteenth of March, 1988, Manete informed me that the evidence he had given at the trial of the above-named accused was false and that he had not seen the First and Second Applicants [Duma and Francis] at the scene of the crime. He also confirmed to me that the police had mentioned the names of the First and Second Applicants to him and instructed him to say in his evidence that they were at the scene of the crime."

So the possibility of a reopening of the trial held much hope for the Six. The prosecution case would be weaker with two of the four implicating eyewitnesses completely discredited. After a reappraisal of the evidence, the Six might still be found guilty of murder, as the indictment would be no different, but there was a very strong probability that none of them would hang. There was also a real possibility that every one of them would be acquitted and set free.

The concept of the Court's inherent jurisdiction to regulate its own findings, in other words to see that justice is done and to prevent the abuse of its procedures by a dishonest litigant, was central to the Application.

Sometime during the first half of April, the Minister of Justice announced that the Sharpeville Six would not be executed until all the legal remedies had been tried.

❖

The Application was launched on April 15, 1988, with specified, limited objectives: to re-examine Manete and any other witnesses if the need for this arose from Manete's further cross-examination, to hear any other relevant evidence the Court might require to be called, and finally to reappraise the convictions and sentences of the applicants.

The State opposed the Application, and there followed an exchange of affidavits.

Warrant Officer Schoeman, replying on behalf of the Attorney-General, argued that the Court was *functus officio* (it had given a final judgment), and that it was most undesirable to recall witnesses in an emotion-charged case like this, for pressure was often brought to bear on them to lie or to deny any knowledge of the case.

Schoeman denied Manete had been held at Krugersdorp at any time "during the period September to November." The proof of this was that his name was not in the cell registers. Instead, Schoeman had asked Joseph Manete's uncle, a police sergeant whom he knew quite well, to bring his nephew to Krugersdorp for questioning. No pressure was put on Joseph at the interview, no assaults, he was not forced to make a statement and, when he did, no one influenced or suggested its contents.

The names of Francis and Duma had not been put to Manete. Possibly they were on a list shown to him. Schoeman could not quite remember, he stated, but he believed Manete himself had named the two.

The first time Manete had ever admitted to giving false evidence at the trial was on March 15, 1988. Why had he not told his attorney before? And why was there no statement about false evidence from Manete himself?

Schoeman had first got to know of Manete through Mabuti. Mongaule had not taken him to Manete's house. Mongaule had not been assaulted. Manete had never alleged that Mongaule brought the police to him.

Reid's confession had not been disputed in the course of the appeal, nor in the petition to the State President. The allegations of assault were totally false.

Schoeman's lengthy affidavit was supported by one from a black police sergeant who had been present "most of the time" at Manete's interview in Krugersdorp, and one from Manete's uncle, the policeman. The uncle stated that he took his nephew to Krugersdorp on a date he couldn't remember; Joseph never complained to him of any assaults, and they never discussed the trial, for he felt that would not be proper.

❖

The applicants replied as follows:

They were no more able than the State to explain Manete's state of mind at various stages of the case. They also found his course of conduct over the last three years strange, to say the least. It was precisely because of Manete's contradictory statements that he ought to be re-examined. Only he could explain his discrepancies.

The point was that Manete had now expressly abandoned his privilege. Therefore, for the first time, he was available for cross-examination on his statement made to Soman.

As far as Reid's "confession" and the allegations of assault were concerned, only certain facts and judicial findings were available when the petition to the State President was compiled. At that stage there appeared to be no basis to persist in the allegations of assault, and that was why clemency had been sought on other grounds. Now, however, there appeared to be a basis for a re-examination of police conduct throughout the case.

Schoeman could not have total knowledge of all aspects of the case, especially as he had not been the investigating officer from the start. Other policemen might have assaulted Manete or threatened him, without Schoeman's knowledge.

The applicants found the affidavit of Sergeant Manete, Joseph's uncle, curious. He had apparently been asked on a number of occasions to bring Joseph to Schoeman before he finally did so. It was also curious that he had not discussed the matter with Joseph at all.

The prosecution argued that it was not legally possible to reopen the case, and that it was also not possible to seek an order of *restitutio in integrum* (total re-examination, starting an entirely new case) – which the applicants had never suggested anyway. The court was *functus officio*, and in terms of Section 327 of the Criminal Procedure Act No. 51 of 1977, only the State President enjoyed the power to direct the Minister of Justice to refer an aspect of a case to the trial court.

Our counter-argument was that Section 327 concerns the statutory powers of the State President to order the reopening of a trial, and that the Court's inherent jurisdiction to regulate its own findings is not limited by that section of the Criminal Procedure Act.

When we applied for the stay of execution, we had relied on the case of State *v.* Titus 1984, in which it was held that the Supreme Court has the power to order the reopening of a criminal case which has been "finally" disposed of, if and when it is established that the decision was affected by perjured evidence; but just before we launched our papers, the *Titus* decision was overturned.

We were then compelled to seek an additional basis for the reopening as well as the attempt to persuade the Court that it possessed an inherent jurisdiction to reopen the trial. We chose the allegation of an irregularity or illegality in the proceedings of the trial, the deliberate procuring of false evidence by the police.

Ordinarily, false testimony per se does not constitute an irregularity, but fraud procured and contrived deliberately by a party to the proceedings can do so. Once an irregularity has been found to have occurred, a note is made in the trial record, known as a "special entry." This "entry" is considered by the appeal court, and can be used to overturn the convictions.

We had to show, therefore, that evidence was falsely procured by the police who investigated the case and set the wheels in motion for a prosecution, and who formed part of that prosecution. Manete's case was the most blatant, and Reid's confession was relevant, for he had been coerced into making false admissions.

The State witness Johannes Mongaule had not been relied on for the conviction of any of the Six, but he too had testified that he had been arrested and assaulted. He was the one who said in his evidence-in-chief that he had seen Ja-Ja and Oupa at the scene of the crime, only to admit under cross-examination that he had not seen anything at all. It was legitimate to ask why he had lied, and at whose insistence.

We approached Johannes, and he provided a detailed affidavit, signed at Vereeniging on May 13, 1988, whose salient points were that:

On September 3, 1984, he was present at Dlamini's house, and did not see the attackers of Dlamini.

In April 1985 he was arrested by Schoeman and other police, and asked who Motsumi Manete (Joseph) was. When he said he did not know, he was assaulted by a white policeman "with fists in the face," and elbowed by a black policeman. He then admitted he did know Motsumi and directed the police to his house, but Motsumi Manete was not there.

He was taken to the Randfontein and Krugersdorp police stations and questioned about Dlamini's death. He said he knew nothing. He was asked if he knew Ja-Ja and Oupa, and whether they were the first to grab Dlamini. When he said he did not know, he was told he could be detained for a long time, and "they, about four white policemen, threatened to throw me out of the window at the police station." Schoeman was one of those who threatened him.

"I was afraid and agreed that both Ja-Ja and Scotch, whom the police referred to as Oupa, grabbed the deceased. This was not true but I signed the statement and I was released. On the day I was released I saw Manete at Randfontein police station. After a few days Manete came to my house and we discussed what had happened to us *viz.* arrested, assaulted, and made to sign statements.

"Before the trial Schoeman came to my house a few times and he told me to remember what to say, and he went over the statement with me. Before the trial he also gave me a copy of the statement and said to me 'jy moet dit leer sodat jy weet wat om in die Hof te praat' ["You must learn it so that you know what to say in court"] or words to that effect.

"Mabuti came to my house in September or October 1985 and he told me that he had already given evidence in court and that I should not make a mistake with my evidence in court. I should remember the statement that I was made to sign. I said to Mabuti that I was reluctant to give evidence as it was not true and Mabuti then asked me how I would have felt if the deceased was my relative. I told Mabuti that I am not happy because I am pressurized by the police and the evidence will be lies because I was injured and I did not see the incident.

"I was taken by Schoeman to court together with Manete.

"Schoeman told me that if I do not say what is in my statement 'jy sal in die kak wees' ["You'll be in the shit"]. I was scared as I understood that they would arrest me or throw me out of the window as threatened.

"After giving evidence I was not given a lift back to Sharpeville. Both Mrs. Dlamini and the black policeman at court were upset because I had, according to them, not given good evidence. Manete, however, was given a lift back to Sharpeville."

❖

At the time of the Application for a stay of execution, the judge had displayed suspicion about the defence's being able to obtain a waiver from Manete, and had asked whether pressure was not brought to bear on him.

For this reason we did not approach Manete directly, but instead obtained from Mr. Bham another, fuller affidavit, in which he gave a detailed history, with copies of all relevant file notes and documents, of his relationship with Manete, and the manner in which the waiver had been obtained.

Bham's affidavit covered my request to him on January 21, 1988, for statements made by Manete, in view of a petition to the State President; his refusal, because they were privileged; my proposal that we seek the Law Society's advice; and the suggestion of Mr. Cyril Jaffe, President of the Law Society, on January 26, 1988, that Manete be asked whether he would now waive his privilege.

Bham stated that on January 27, 1988, he duly saw Manete, informed him of my firm's request and explained the full implications of waiving privilege. Manete agreed, and signed a waiver of his privilege with respect to any communications made to Bham.

Then, said the affidavit, Bham advised me of these facts, and sent me the documents: the statement made to him by Manete dated September 1985,[1] the attested version dated October 18, 1985, of Manete's testimony in court, Bham's own note dated October 17, 1985, of an interview with Manete, and the following short document, his file note dated February 14, 1986, of a conversation Manete had with him:

JOSEPH MANETE

Before giving my evidence in court, I was consulted by Mr. Jordaan. He said I should not lie in court. He told me to read the statement I made to the police. I was asked whether I had met an Indian lawyer. I said I had met a lawyer. I was told not to consult a lawyer because I was a State witness. The police will protect me in court.

I wanted representation in court but I did not convey this to the prosecutor because I was told he would protect me.

I did not tell the Court the whole truth.

Mr. Bham's note of an interview with Manete on October 17, 1985, recorded Manete's comings and goings with the police between "a place near Sebokeng Hospital" and the Supreme Court in Pretoria, during the trial. Manete had told his attorney that he had gone to the meeting-place as instructed on September 24 and 25, 1985, only to be given another date; on Friday, September 27, and Monday, September 30, and on October 1 and 2 he had been taken to Pretoria, but had waited all day without being called; and that he had given his evidence, per the accompanying affidavit, on Thursday, October 3.

(Manete actually appeared in court on September 30 and October 1. His acquaintance with the truth seems to have been so slight that even in the matter of a verifiable date he was inaccurate. His statement about hanging about in Pretoria for four days without being called seems totally pointless.)

❖

In a Notice of Motion dated June 1, 1988, the applicants sought an amendment to the original Application of April 15, 1988, in order to bring further evidence from the witnesses Manete and Johannes Mongaule, "that they were threatened and assaulted by members of the South African Police and were thereby procured to give false evidence against the Applicants at the said trial."

We asked that the Court be directed to hear evidence from Mohamed Bham and Amichand Soman regarding statements made to them by Manete concerning his treatment by the police and the truth of his evidence at the trial, and to hear any other evidence the Court might require for the settling of the special entry.

And we asked for a directive that, after the hearing, if the evidence warranted it, a special entry be made on the trial record as follows:

> The perjured evidence of the witness, JOSEPH MOTSUMI MANETE, as procured by members of the South African Police, has resulted in a fraud having been practised on the trial court by such members, thus constituting an illegality or defect in the proceedings which has caused a failure of justice.
>
> The threats and assaults by members of the South African Police on JOSEPH MOTSUMI MANETE and JOHANNES MONGAULE, revealing as they do, a systematic intimidation and a systematic procuring of false evidence, show a fraudulent system at work in regard to the whole trial when read with the evidence given at the trial, thus constituting an illegality or defect in the proceedings which has caused a failure of justice.

❖

Argument for the reopening of the case began on June 6, 1988, with Mr. Acting Justice Human presiding. Mr. Unterhalter dealt with the Court's inherent jurisdiction, and Mr. Kuny with the allegation of irregularity.

Once more the court was packed to capacity. Among the numerous spectators, many of whom represented foreign governments, was Mr. Geoffrey Robertson QC, on brief from Amnesty International to observe the proceedings.

Mr. Robertson announced his presence to the judge's clerk and the judge invited him to tea. In the course of conversation, the judge mentioned that he was considering recommending clemency for at least two of the Six, Theresa and Reid. Mr. Robertson was surprised, because there was no new evidence.

We could not understand it, either. Nothing had changed since Judge Human found the Six guilty of murder with no extenuating circumstances. All we had obtained was a stay of execution. Belated second thoughts from the judge about two of the condemned were not only surprising, they might also be useless, for the executive has discretion and may well disregard a recommendation of clemency.

The main point emphasized in argument was the importance of oral evidence, and the need to reopen the trial so that the allegations relating to assaults and coercion on the part of the police could be properly tested in cross-examination.

On June 13, 1988, Acting Justice Human dismissed the application to reopen the trial. The Six had been in death row for two and a half years to the day.

The judge dramatically reversed his provisional finding of March 17, 1988, on the application for a stay of execution. Then he had said of the Manete statement, "It may affect the guilt of the first two applicants; it may affect the others."

Now, he found that he had no power to reconsider his judgment, because the appeal court had already done so. So he was able to state without deviating from logic:

> To embark on a further cross-examination of Manete whether there is any substance in the submission that a fraud had been committed by the police in obtaining the

conviction against the Fifth and Sixth Appellants [Duma and Francis] would in my opinion be an exercise in futility.

Mr. Kuny's contention that should I hear evidence and come to the conclusion that a fraud has been perpetrated on the Court, then I could set aside the conviction and sentence although the decision in the appeal court still stands [*sic*]. This is a very startling proposition. There is certainly no authority for such a procedure. I am *functus officio* and if I have no power to set aside my own judgment the hearing of further evidence will be futile.

The Application for the hearing of further evidence to determine whether a special entry (irregularity or illegality) should be made or not is frivolous and absurd. The exercise would be an abuse of the process of the Court.

In the applicants' petition of January 1988, the judge said, the contents of Manete's original statement to Soman had been brought to the notice of the State President, and he had nevertheless declined to direct the Minister of Justice to refer the matter back to the trial court:

In the result the applicants have exhausted all their remedies in terms of the provisions of Section 327; but the provisions of Section 327 do not exclude a further petition to the State President to have the case reopened on the alleged new information. . . . This court has no inherent jurisdiction to set aside its verdict or to order the reopening of the case and the hearing of further evidence. . . . It follows that this application should have been addressed to the State President.

The entire application was dismissed.

I cannot adequately express my anger with the judge for his decision and comments on what was frivolous and what would be futile, but a foreign journalist who was very familiar with the case and had followed it throughout remarked, "This is what I call judicial terrorism."

Mr. Unterhalter applied immediately for leave to appeal. At the idea that his decision might be appealable, the judge showed great surprise. There was no automatic right of appeal. All over again, we had to obtain leave from this judge to go to the appeal court in Bloemfontein. All over again, we had to convince him that another Court might come to a different conclusion from his.

Leave to appeal was promptly refused.

Now we had to petition the Chief Justice within twenty-one days for leave to appeal.

❖

The Six and their legal team were not alone in early July 1988, in addressing themselves to the Chief Justice. Manete's conscience was troubling him, and he gave an exclusive interview to a weekly newspaper, *City Press*, which also published open letters he had written to the Chief Justice and the State President.

The latter began with a lengthy and emotionally charged invocation of Christian beliefs, and an outpouring of regret about the death of Mr. Dlamini and the loss sustained by his children. Manete then introduced a group he called "We, the police-pressured State Witnesses."

> "We" because every each of the State witnesses was not happy about their statements that they had made to the security Police at Krugersdorp Police Station, where we were interrogated.
>
> I myself was taken into the office, whose windows faced in the direction of Krugersdorp Prison. I think this was done purposefully, because during the interrogation when I became not co-operative, they said to me that they will send me to that prison.
>
> I was interrogated during the presence of Krugersdorp Warrant Officer, Mr. Schoeman.
>
> They asked me the names of the people who killed Mr. Dlamini. I told them that I don't know their names. They threatened and pressurised me.
>
> One of the white policemen pushed my head against the wall and I was clapped [slapped] several times on the face.

I started to cry immediately. They said to me that they are taking me to the prison. This was not done, because on the way they returned with me back to the same office, where I was threatened by the police again.

They asked me again about the names of the accused and I told them that I don't know their names. I was clapped again and I was told that now they are going to kill me because I am not co-operative and also I was at the scene of crime when Mr. Dlamini was killed by the mob.

Mr. Schoeman then took out some papers which were in the steel shelves. He said to me that I should listen attentively. He reads the names of the accused to me and he asked me which of the accused were present when Mr. Dlamini was killed. I refused to do this again.

The police said to me that I will stay in prison for a long time and I will be tortured daily if I did not mention the names of Duma Khumalo and Don Mokgesi. I agreed with them that they were at the scene of crime when Mr. Dlamini was killed. I was then left alone in the office.

The letter went on[2] about a statement the police wrote and got Manete to sign, about Johannes Mongaule's similar experiences, and ended, "Dear President, I wish I could be taken to you, to discuss this 'heavy burden' verbally. After I had written this letter, I kneeled down and prayed. Yours Faithfully, Joseph Motsumi Manete."

One of the ironies of the situation was that all the efforts of eminent counsel and their back-up team were just as vain, just as forlorn as this pathetic letter, and in themselves achieved as little. We were all turning to the State President, petitioning the Chief Justice, trying in our own way to get justice for the Six. And the thing we all wanted was the same, for Manete to be taken before someone – State President or a Supreme Court judge – for the very same reason, that he might "discuss this 'heavy burden' verbally."

Following this up with a visit to his attorney Mr. Bham, Manete produced an affidavit[3] in the same frantic hope that he might be instrumental in saving the lives of the Six. But that was August 12, 1988; it was too late for affidavits.

❖

When a petition is submitted to the Chief Justice, he usually gives it to two judges,[4] who consider it in chambers. If they come to the conclusion that it has merit, leave to appeal is granted. If not, leave is refused. So there is no argument in open court, and no reasons are given for the judges' decision.

However, in the case of the Sharpeville Six, the Acting Chief Justice invoked an unusual procedure. He invited argument before five appeal judges. The reason for this has never been made public.

The hearing took place on September 7, 1988, in the Appellate Division in Bloemfontein. Thirteen foreign diplomats were present, and many local and foreign journalists. Each new twist in the case attracted concern from all over the world, and intense interest in the legal aspects.

Mr. Sydney Kentridge SC argued for the applicants. With Mr. Kentridge were Mr. Unterhalter, Mr. Ismail Mahomed SC, Mr. Edwin Cameron, and Mr. Sean Naidoo.

The families were there, too. Two hired minibuses had left Sharpeville very early in the morning, to make the 370-kilometre journey and be sure of arriving in time. Of course, the Six remained in death row in Pretoria.

Argument began at 9:45 a.m. Rabie ACJ[5] presided, sitting with Corbett JA, Hoexter JA, Joubert JA, and Van Heerden JA. They listened attentively and gave Mr. Kentridge a good hearing. It was a difficult argument – the defence had failed in the Court below and had no case authority in its favour.

The applicants' principal arguments were:

1. that the Supreme Court has an inherent jurisdiction to regulate its own procedures;

2. that if Manete's statements were correct – a question to be decided on oral evidence – the State through the police officers concerned in the case had deliberately and fraudulently procured an unjust verdict;

3. that it had consistently been sought to impugn Manete's evidence on the basis of his statement made to Soman in May 1985, so it was clear this was not a story tailored afterwards to escape the consequences of a conviction. It was a matter of record that Manete had approached Soman and made the statement long before the trial, and that the defence had sought to have him cross-examined on it at the trial; thus, even before the start of the trial, an important State witness had claimed that he was assaulted by the police and told what to say in his evidence, and in these circumstances, it must surely be an offence to the basic principles of justice and fairness if the Courts – having excluded this vital evidence on grounds that no longer existed – must now refuse to hear it simply because it was too late;

4. that the Court had not considered the possibility that Manete and Mongaule might come across as unreliable witnesses precisely because they had been assaulted and intimidated into saying things that were untrue;

5. that it was not appropriate for Human AJ to describe our Application for special entry (irregularity or illegality) as frivolous or absurd or an abuse of the process of the Court without allowing us to produce the best evidence, namely oral evidence subject to cross-examination.

At the end of the day Mr. Justice Corbett asked whether this Application for leave to appeal should not be considered as the appeal itself. Counsel for the applicants agreed, since there was not much more to add to our submission, and it would really be a waste of time and money to come back to Bloemfontein to argue substantially what had already been canvassed with this Court.

The Acting Chief Justice remarked that the State President had the power to reopen the trial, but that that would be merely a discretion exercised by the executive, and such a decision could not be appealed or taken on review. His comment gave us the impression he was concerned for the applicants, that their remedy with the State President was limited, and their chances reduced because they had already petitioned him.

At the end of a hearing, the appeal court does not indicate when a decision may be expected. Sometimes it takes months; it can even be years. Yet, in this case, because of the publicity and the fact that the Six had already spent almost three years on death row, it seemed likely the Court would not want to delay its finding unnecessarily.

The Sharpeville Six had acquired national as well as international importance. It was seriously suggested in the press that a decision given before the municipal elections scheduled for October 26, 1988, could affect the poll and the outcome. Success in the appeal might cost the National Party the votes of many die-hards. Blacks might decide against standing for election to their local councils if the six looked likely to escape the gallows.

Conversely, it was thought that if the Six failed, black voters might be angry enough to refuse to go to the polls, where a vote was an indication of approval for the apartheid creations of 1982–83. Either way, therefore, the decision could be to the detriment of the ruling party.

Personally I could not imagine any issue affecting the black poll. The black town councils were completely discredited from the day of their inception, and politically conscious people had always withheld their vote. Perhaps I was wrong, for the elections came and went, and there was no decision from the appeal court.

Then out of the blue came a phone call from Graham Leach, a BBC correspondent, informing me that our Application had been dismissed. It was just before ten o'clock on the morning of November 23, 1988.

Soon after this call, my correspondent attorney in Bloemfontein phoned to say that judgment[6] was to be delivered that morning, and he would let me know as soon as he got it. When

I told him the decision was already out via the South African Press Association (SAPA), and that the five judges were unanimous, he couldn't believe his ears.

I went immediately to Pretoria to tell the Six. As usual they had heard the news on the radio, before I arrived.

Oupa saw himself and the others as political pawns. He said, "Botha is just using us so that he can save Van der Merwe and La Grange."[7] These two were white policemen who had each incurred a double death sentence for murdering two alleged drug dealers, neither of whom was white; they were scheduled to hang.

Theresa said, "I don't want to hang. I have already suffered so much. Can't they rather give me a small sentence?"

Ja-Ja expressed the identical thought: "I don't want to die. If I get a few years, it's okay."

But Duma and Reid were very angry. They were not interested in considering a second petition to the State President. What would that help? Botha had been petitioned before.

Duma said, "I will not allow Botha to play with my life. It is my life. My life is not a ball, and he and the courts cannot kick me around. I will not petition again – they can rather hang me."

"But Duma," Francis argued, "the situation is different now. There is a lot of pressure on Botha and, like Prakash says, if we are alive, there is hope. Lots of people are fighting for us. Our families are fighting. We can't let them down."

Reid agreed with Duma, but for different reasons: "I just don't care any more. I am not going to petition again. What's the use, then they will give us life [imprisonment]. So I am not going to petition again."

❖

As I drove back to Johannesburg from death row I felt empty. I understood what Duma and Reid were feeling: better to hang than to file another petition to Botha. Their lives, their decision. But it would be difficult for me to accept.

There was indeed no logical reason why the State President should grant them clemency on a second petition. All the relevant facts had been placed before him in the first one, including Manete's statement to Soman. But perhaps the local pressure, and the international pressure now being focused on – and therefore through – Thatcher, Reagan, and Kohl would help?

The chances of success seemed very slim to me, but we would have to take them – at least for the four if Reid and Duma did not change their minds.

It was well after 5:00 p.m. when I got back to my office in Johannesburg. The staff had already left. I sat at my desk thinking about what should go into the second petition. At about 6:00 p.m. the phone rang. It was a journalist, who had just seen on the wire bulletin that the Six, among others, had been reprieved by the State President.

Oupa was right: the two white policemen had also been reprieved.

The sentences of Theresa, Reid, and Oupa were commuted to eighteen years' imprisonment. Ja-Ja's was twenty years. Duma and Francis each got twenty-five years.

CHAPTER 20

Reprieved

"This is not a reprieve, it is another torture in disguise."
FRANCIS

In November 1988, as the Six were being reprieved and sentenced to half a lifetime in jail for a crime they did not commit, a white farmer and his white friend were sentenced for a crime they did commit.

In December 1987, twenty-three-year-old Jacobus Vorster killed one of his black employees, Eric Sambo, aged thirty-seven, father of five children.

It was Mr. Sambo's job to drive a tractor on the farm. One day in October, he got into the tractor without realizing that two of Vorster's dogs were sleeping underneath it, and when he drove off, one was killed and the other injured. Vorster wanted to kill Sambo, who ran away.

About two months later, Vorster caught him. He and a friend, Petrus Leonard, tied him to a tree and beat, kicked, and whipped him to death over a period of two days. Vorster and Leonard were charged with murder.

At the trial, the prosecution accepted a plea of guilty from Vorster on a lesser charge of culpable homicide (manslaughter); Leonard was convicted of assault.

It would have been very easy to prove the act of killing. Likewise the intention. The two killers could doubtless have foreseen that their attack on Mr. Sambo would prove fatal. This was the prosecution's very argument in the Sharpeville Six case, that each one of the accused must have foreseen that, through their association in the crowd, Dlamini would be killed.

291

Why did the prosecution not go for murder? It is impossible to exclude the idea that it was because Vorster was an Afrikaner and a farmer, and the victim a black.

The trial judge, Mr. Justice Strydom, did not consider a jail sentence appropriate, despite the aggravating fact that the assault went on for two days. Vorster was sentenced in November 1988 to five years' imprisonment, suspended, and to a fine of R3,000, payable over five years. Leonard was fined R500 for assault.

R3,000 was then the price of a colour television set and a VCR, or an excursion-rate air fare to Europe and back, or five to six months' rent for a three-bedroomed house with a garden in a medium-level urban white suburb. At the time it was also $1,293 (U.S.), and about £700.

So much for that. The Six were in prison.

If they had been released on November 23, 1988, when the death sentence was lifted, Ma-Sefatsa's fourth birthday would have been the perfect date for a happy end. She was the baby born two weeks after her father was taken away.

At first, Ja-Ja said, he was happy. "I was happy to get out of that place, but twenty years when I counted, it is a lot of years. I will change in these twenty years.

"Twenty years is not a child's play. If you face twenty years for a crime, it is better. It is hard, even for three years, when you are innocent."

When the news of the reprieve reached Reid, he was puzzled: "How can the State President pardon me when the appeal court dismissed the case? No, I did not feel happy. I became very angry. I asked myself how can they give me eighteen years. All I wanted was that justice must be done."

Duma agreed. "On my side it is not that justice was done. Not at all. I was helped by the outside countries. If it was not the interference of the outside countries, I should have been dead by now."

He had met a young ANC member in death row. "He is the one who taught me politics. He was even smaller than me, but more experienced than me. When I was in the Maximum, I feel guilty. Why did I not join the African National Congress? I kept asking the question to myself: where was I when others were fighting for the liberation of our country?"

Francis said, "Three hours after Prakash told us that the case had failed, we were informed by a messenger: 'I have been sent by the State President to let you know that your life has been spared and your sentence has been changed to a prison sentence. So you are going to serve twenty-five years and eight years for subversion running concurrently.'

"When I heard my life was spared, I was not very happy because the messenger read it so quickly, and then I heard the sentence.

"Duma and I did not want to sign it [the reprieve], but he did and then I also signed it. I signed it with anger. But some happiness was there as well, the happiness that I was leaving this place and my worst enemy, Warrant Officer Arlow. He was there when we heard the news and I realized he is not happy. I also remembered my words that I wrote to my family and friends that my enemies will taste the bitterness of defeat.

"After coming out of a death place and being sentenced again to the prison for such a long time, this is not a reprieve, it is another torture in disguise."

Oupa was playing chess with Sibusiso, his cell neighbour, and the convicted Messina trialist and ANC member Mthetheleli Mncube. "Prakash arrived at about one o'clock. He told me that things are bad, the application had failed."

When Oupa came back with his news, Mthetheleli said he hadn't expected anything different, otherwise it would be seen that the Six had been wronged. But he felt there was still some reason to place hope in the State President.

Oupa was not so optimistic. He went back to his cell and his friends to theirs. That was the last time he saw them.

Round about six o'clock he was called and told to pack his things. He was momentarily afraid. *Why must he pack?* There had been recent executions. Perhaps there were places to fill in the pot?

But Oupa was an old hand in death row, and although his initial panic was a reflex, he realized that it had never happened before, that a prisoner had to "pack his things" for the pot the very day his appeal failed.

"When we arrived at that office, I first saw these cops, Van der Merwe and Le Grange. I started to get hope now that really . . . we are going to be pardoned, because they are there and I can see their facial expression, they were happy."

When they left death row and went down to their new cells, Oupa was very unhappy about the eighteen-year prison sentence, and bitterly resentful. "When I look at the case of Van der Merwe and Le Grange, really it is a different case from ours. . . . It has been set up that Bloemfontein must dismiss our application, in order that the State President must interfere now. Then granting them a clemency together with the Sharpeville Six, because if he had granted it to us only, internally people were going to . . . he was going to lose."

Gratitude towards the State President? No! "What he had done to us is not through him and I won't thank him. I will only thank God."

Theresa said she heard at one o'clock on the radio that the appeal was dismissed. "I started to cry. It was the longest I had ever cried. I don't know why. They say I must hang, then they say no, I am not allowed to hang, then they say the appeal is dismissed, it was very confusing.

"Prakash came to tell me that the appeal had failed, at about 2:30 in the afternoon. He said I must not worry, we will still have another chance [to file another petition]."

In the evening the sheriff came to her cell. "He said did I hear that Mr. State President gives us mercy. I said no. He said all of you will serve eighteen to twenty-five years. Then he explained to me that Reid and Oupa and I got eighteen years.

"I was very happy, but then I remember eighteen years is a long time for something I did not do.

"I can say thank you to the State President for not hanging me, but I am not happy with my sentence. The sheriff asked me why I am not happy. I said how would he be to stay in for eighteen years for something you did not commit. He said that I should be happy to be saved from death. I said that I can never be happy with such a sentence.

"That evening they moved me from the condemned cell, but I was still in the same section. I would have been happy to be moved to another section. I am still next to Sandra."

Having been saved herself, Theresa turned her energy and her prayers to the hopeless search for a way to save Sandra's life.

❖

Where is everyone now? Those who might have been dead are in jail: Reid, Duma, Oupa, Francis, and Ja-Ja are at Leeukop Prison near Johannesburg; Theresa is still in Pretoria Central.

Christiaan and Gideon are serving their eight-year sentence at Pretoria Local Prison.

The starting date of sentence for all of them was December 13, 1985, the day the Six went to death row, so when they were reprieved, they had already served nearly three years.

Only one person in this story has died of "natural causes" – Mrs. Alice Dlamini. Duma's young brother Ishmael died a violent death. "Zulu" Radebe, who in a prison cell heard the confidences of Johannes Mongaule, was murdered. Sandra Smith, Theresa's close friend and cell-neighbour, was hanged on June 2, 1989. And Warrant Officer Arlow was killed in a car crash not long after the Six left death row.

Reid's mother has retired from cleaning other people's kitchens. Her house is full of children and grandchildren, but empty of breadwinners. Susan, Alinah, and Regina are unemployed, with young children to educate. Julia Ramashamola still works in the darkroom of the X-ray department at Sebokeng Hospital, and battles to make ends meet.

In a country with no welfare for the destitute, the South African Council of Churches does the best it can for the families, but its resources are stretched. The amounts it provides have diminished, but they are still enough to buy the mealie-meal, with a little over.

Susan and Regina go together to Leeukop every two weeks to visit their husbands. The taxi fare is R12 return.

Dorothy Morobe, mother of Reid's child, Thabeng, does not visit the prison. Reid asked her to stay away because she always cried so much when she saw him. They write to each other, and are still deeply in love.

❖

On an ordinary weekday morning five years after the murder of its deputy-mayor, Sharpeville seems very peaceful. Very small children in bright red jerseys hurry into a room behind Father Patrick's church, and soon the whole creche is singing. A bell rings a few houses away, and another huddle of tiny figures pushes into a doorway. In the road outside, a couple of teenagers are taunting an old man as he hobbles along. He shakes his stick at them, but neither he nor they look hostile. The place seems almost deserted, except for some small groups of young – and not so young – men wandering about, looking bored. It is not an ugly township. Poor and old and drab, yes, and the roads were apparently made when the houses went up, in 1942, and never touched again. But there is rough grass along their verges, and room on each stand for a bit of a garden.

Here and there are huge heaps of rubbish, beside the road or filling a vacant lot. The place is not indiscriminately littered – clearly rubbish has been swept or collected. It is just the final removal that has not taken place. Perhaps the collection teams are on strike. Perhaps the township has no vehicles in running order to do this work. Perhaps this is not weeks' and weeks' worth of rubbish, but just that of a few days, and the trucks will remove it tomorrow.

To the casual observer there are no other signs of a standstill in local affairs. Rents in the township have not been paid for five years, except in very few cases, very recently. Electricity bills have not been paid, and households have continued to consume electricity. There is no stench of drains or blocked sewerage pipes. Perhaps the amenities in the township are so rudimentary that, apart from water and electricity, there is only the rubbish collection to go wrong.

On this bright wintry morning, the landmarks are still there. The motor wrecks are parked untidily in the Radebes' yard on Zwane Street. In a side-street opposite is Mrs. Shabangu's modest house; three doors along, Billy Gasapane and a friend are deep in discussion, their heads under the bonnet of a car. The next street off Zwane to the left is Nhlapo Street, still unpaved, deeply rutted, and pot-holed like any other Sharpeville side-street. If you turn into it, the first house on your right is Emily Moeketsi's, and there, in her yard, with its back to Dlamini's property, is the shack where Jantjie Mabuti said he hid. The padlock is there, too. From the shack, one can't see into Dlamini's stand, for his garage blocks the view. This red-brick structure is intact, though the door has gone and the roof is only a wooden framework now, open to the sky.

Nothing else remains of Dlamini's establishment. The small stand is overgrown with coarse grass and weeds. There are no bricks or rubble lying around, no sign that there was once a house, except for sharp pieces of broken glass glinting in the grass. Mabuti is living elsewhere; the wire-mesh fence and the shack that were his still mark the back of Dlamini's stand.

On the north side, the Maile house is being altered, and that kitchen door that Dlamini never reached has been walled up. But the three slack strands of wire are still there, the top one not more than a metre high, and just where Dlamini must have fallen, a young grapevine stretches its scrawny arms sideways along the wire.

PROLOGUE: SHARPEVILLE

1. This is a compressed cement-asbestos mixture; it is neither volatile nor soluble in water, and is safe as long as it is not broken or sawn.

2. Bophelong, Boipathong, and Sebokeng serve Vanderbijlpark; Refengkgotso is a tiny settlement near Deneysville; and Zamdela is outside Sasolburg. Sebokeng, established in 1966, accounts for two-thirds of the population and 66 per cent of all the houses in the Lekoa area.

3. Components are sewerage disposal, rubbish collection, roads, "levy" (unspecified), school levy, and some small items. Metered water and metered electricity are charged separately.

4. Lodgers, i.e., subtenants, naturally paid rent to the householder. They also had to pay a monthly fee to the council. In 1984, in Lekoa, this rose from R8 to R10 per single person, and from R4 to R5 per "woman-head-of-family."

5. Household Subsistence Level (HSL): calculated by the Institute for Planning Research of the University of Port Elizabeth, and corroborated by the Bureau for Economic Research at Stellenbosch University. HSL for the Johannesburg area was second-highest, at R327.11 per month. A minimum for a family that was not black would inevitably be higher, because rents in the black areas are by far the lowest.

6. The old-age pension for blacks rose to R65 per month in October 1984. It was – and still is – paid every two months.

7. Sebokeng is three times as far from Vanderbijlpark, its nearest work centre, and its residents are even more heavily burdened with transport costs than are those of Sharpeville.

8. The shock of "Soweto 1976" and the critical shortage of skills nationwide had led to a serious effort to produce more black matriculants. The number of black candidates had increased enormously between 1977 and 1983, and although the pass rate dropped from 76.2 per cent to 48.2 per cent, the actual number of matric graduates since 1977 had increased by 500 per cent.

9. The total monthly charges for lodging, whether the house is owned or rented by the occupant, are commonly referred to as "rent." Site rent plus rates plus electricity levies (plus house rent, if occupant is not owner) equal "rent."

10. A small category, privately owned houses with water-meter, paid R31 instead of R39.30 for services, and rented houses wired by tenants themselves were exempted from the monthly R1.90 wiring fee.

11. Service charges on the houses that had been purchased by occupants were to rise by R5.50 per month. But, in Sharpeville, there were fewer than one thousand of these.

12. This measure affected 33 per cent of all the houses, as private ownership was far greater in Evaton than in most other townships. (25 per cent of all the houses were held under freehold; 8 per cent on 30- or 99-year leases.)

13. Only the R5.90 increase in service charges seems to have entered people's consciousness. The extra R2 for electricity reticulation was, however, part of the deal, and would have become real to the residents the first time they had to pay it – but it never came to that.

CHAPTER 2: ARRESTS

1. This chapter relates certain events from the point of view of the Six and their families, and embodies the instructions I was given as their attorney. In court the police denied all aspects of this story that reflected unfavourably on them. It is one group's word against the other's.

2. No one is quite sure.

3. The nickname is short for "Mojalefa," and has nothing to do with Afrikaans *ja* (pronounced "ya"), meaning "yes" and used by all South Africans. "Ja-Ja" sounds somewhere between the British pronunciation of "judger" and "jar-jar."

4. Through a misunderstanding of African-accented pronunciation it has been assumed that Theresa worked at the "Beggar Box," which, of course, is absurd. It is "Burger" as in "hamburger."

5. This extraordinarily low wage for a non-farm, non-domestic job has been carefully checked with Theresa, but not with the Burger Box.

6. Section 29 of the Internal Security Act No. 74 of 1982 regulates the 'detention of certain persons for interrogation.'

> Any commissioned officer . . . of or above the rank of lieutenant-colonel may arrest without warrant and detain for interrogation anyone who 'has committed or intends to commit' an offense referred to in s. 84 [sabotage], or 'is withholding from the SA Police any information relating to the commission of an offence referred to [above]'. The Commissioner [of Police] must inform the Minister once a month why the detainee should not be released. After the first 6 months, and then 3-monthly, he must 'adduce reasons' before a board of review why the detainee should not be released.
>
> Among other provisions of s. 29 are:
> 1. 'No court of law shall have jurisdiction to pronounce upon the validity of any action taken in terms of this section, or to order the release of any person detained in terms of the provisions of this section.'
> 2. No one but the Minister or certain civil servants shall have access to these detainees without the permission of the Minister or the Commissioner, or be entitled to any information from or about them.
> 3. Apart from visits by an Inspector of Detainees, a magistrate and a district surgeon must visit these detainees in private not less than once a fortnight.

7. This wage has not been checked with Vereeniging Refractories.
8. Nicknamed "Sun City" in perverse popular reference to the hotel, casino, and pleasure resort in the black "homeland" of Bophuthatswana, where South Africans flock to play roulette and blackjack and to see blue films, delights denied them by their own puritanical government. The prison is on the Johannesburg side of Soweto. Thousands of emergency detainees have been held there.

Chapter 3: The Indictment

1. Malachia was a policeman who was attacked, but not killed, in Sharpeville on September 3, 1984. Ja-Ja's role as a rescuer in that affair is clarified in Part Two, "The Trial."
2. Morris Basslian was not available at the trial stage to continue to act for the Sharpeville accused.
3. We gave the verbs in Afrikaans, as they were in the indictment: *uitgelok, aangestig, beveel, aangeraai, aangemoedig of verkry.*

CHAPTER 4: A STATEMENT TO AN ATTORNEY

1. Much later, the police would dispute this and claim that Manete was interviewed by them on April 11, 1985.

CHAPTER 5: RENTS AND RIOTS

1. SA Institute of Race Relations, *Race Relations Survey 1985*.
2. Death by shooting is almost synonymous with death by shooting by the police or the army. The black population is almost entirely without firearms.

CHAPTER 6: OPENING STATEMENTS

1. Whenever we had anything to discuss, Mr. Jordaan was always reasonable. We had no problems with him over little things, as one often does with one's opponents.
2. SC: Senior Counsel, the South African equivalent of the British Queen's Counsel (Q.C.). An advocate (barrister) who has "taken silk."
3. The train journey from Vereeniging to Pretoria took about three hours then, with a connection at Germiston or Johannesburg.
4. This is an exact copy of the Annexure, but in English instead of Afrikaans.
5. In all the records, from the summons on, Francis's surname is consistently misspelt "Mokgesi." He signs himself "Mokhesi."
6. Next to "All Male," an afterthought appeared, written with a ballpoint pen in tiny script: "Acc. 4 – Female."
7. Sometime during the trial, Francis remarked, "My father, who was an interpreter, knew Human from before. He said to me this man is a pensioner, why did they bring him back? He was over the age many years ago."
8. "Rent" in the vocabulary of a white functionary, as in that of any black township resident, means, as we have seen, house rent plus site rent plus rates plus service charges (i.e., the monthly dues payable to the councils).
9. The rent boycott that started in Lekoa at the beginning of September 1984 was still unanimous a year later at the time of the trial. To date it is barely broken. Inhabitants of certain areas are paying some rent, but the majority of residents are paying neither rent nor electricity charges.
10. Proclamation 186 of 1967, whose validity had actually lapsed with the repeal of the Black Urban Areas Act in 1982.

11. The real reason was most likely policy, to get the black townships farther away from the white towns. Bophelong is very near Vanderbijlpark. At the end of 1989 the move had not taken place.

12. Exhibit B is the circular delivered to 30,000 houses in the townships administered by the Lekoa town council, announcing the total revocation of the proposed increases and setting out the rents and charges as of April 1, 1983, which were therefore still in force. Why the document is dated October 23, 1984 is unclear – an error in the court record or a five-week delay in advising the residents of the decision taken on September 18?

13. The three legislative chambers are the Houses of Assembly (white), Representatives ("coloured"), and Delegates ("Indian"). To date, no "fourth" chamber has been "provided for." Needless to say, the "coloured" and "Indian" chambers have only token representation and no political clout.

14. Mr. Dlamini had to be called "the deceased" throughout the proceedings. This is Court practice.

15. *Stoep* (Afrikaans): normally a verandah. This *stoep* has been described by witnesses as merely a concrete slab on the ground, neither enclosed nor roofed, near Maile's kitchen door.

16. *Nie op daardie stadium nie* (Afrikaans): "not at that stage." Col. Viljoen had said "nie op hierdie stadium nie": "not at this stage."

CHAPTER 7: JA-JA

1. On ninety-nine-year leasehold – there were no freehold rights in Sharpeville.

2. A "sporty" is a cotton hat with a narrow brim all the way round, and a fairly deep crown. Shopkeepers are entirely aware of this usage among their black customers.

3. Certainly his behaviour on the day of the incident suggests that he may have been somehow connected with the police. On November 22, 1984, Christiaan and Gideon, who were already in custody, saw him at Sebokeng police station, and he admitted this when confronted with it in cross-examination.

4. *Skelm* (Afrikaans, pronounced "skellum"): rogue, rascal, crook, thief. As an adjective: sly, cunning; furtive; crooked, dishonest.

5. It was established fact that the police came only once to the scene before Dlamini was killed.
6. Ja-Ja's maternal grandmother was in Cape Town, as we know, and his father's mother had died in Bophuthatswana.
7. Machwachwa could not give evidence because he had been killed that day. When the police turned up at Malachia's, one of them took him for an attacker and shot him dead.
8. Possibly an error in the Court record for "And yourself?"

CHAPTER 8: REID

1. Reid did not mention in his evidence what he told someone later: "When I got to Vanderbijlpark, the magistrate was very cross. He was shouting at me and at the police, because we were late and he had been waiting for a very long time."
2. Oupa Diniso made a statement to this magistrate the same day, but it had little or no bearing on the course of his case, and its admissibility was never contested by the defence.
3. According to the doctor's records, Ja-Ja had a 1×0.2 cm laceration with scab on his right forearm and a 1×1 cm laceration on his left forearm; a 1×3 cm lesion in the 3rd rib-space left of the sternum; and a 1×0.5 cm lesion in the 3rd rib-space right of the sternum, which could have been caused by an instrument with electrodes through which current was passed. Also noted were a lesion with scab formation on the front of the left shin, 1×1.5 cm, consistent with a kick, likewise a 1×1 cm lesion on the outside of the left ankle; some swelling, caused by a blow or a fall (not by an infection) in the left cheekbone; and a fresh perforation of the left eardrum, with diminished hearing.
4. The full judgment on the trial-within-a-trial was delivered on December 5, 1985, after the end of the trial and before the main judgment was pronounced on December 10. See beginning of Chapter Thirteen, "The Verdict."
5. Sipho's shop/Seepoint shop – they sound similar. Reid wrote in his letter to the Minister that he had run away to Seepoint shop. There is a section of Sharpeville called Scepoint or C-point. It seems likely therefore that "Sipho's shop" is evidence of imperfect hearing, lack of knowledge of the area, or hearing what one expects to hear rather than what is said. "Sipho" is a well-known Zulu first name.

6. This expression should be noted. Reid was not trying to hide the name of his employer, he was simply using a mode of speech extremely common among black people in South Africa. Similarly, Theresa (see Chapter 10) said in evidence that she went to "a certain house," meaning Gasapane's, after she was shot.
7. Form 3: tenth school year, two years before completion. The twelve school standards are: two starting years, then Standards 1 to 5, then Standards 6 to 10, also called Forms 1 to 5. The qualification at the end of Form 5 (Standard 10) is the matriculation certificate, delivered after a public examination. "Matric" is school-completion and, if marks are adequate and course requirements met, university entrance.

CHAPTER 12: DUMA AND FRANCIS

1. April 9, 1985: Manete was at Krugersdorp police station, being questioned. And the next day Francis Mokhesi was arrested (at 10:00 p.m., on April 10, 1985). More than three years later, the police dated Manete's interview April 11, 1985. The matter is still unresolved.
2. R *v.* Barton 1972 (2) All England Law Reports 1192. Caulfield J, in the Crown Court at Lincoln.
3. Billy Gasapane also lived in this street.

CHAPTER 13: THE VERDICT

1. State *v.* Mtshweni 1985 SA 590 (A) at 593–4. Similar finding in State *v.* Steynberg 1983(3) SA 140(A).
2. The judge seems to have been unaware that Theresa's expression is very common among black South Africans. See Reid's "a certain firm" to indicate the name of his employer, where it was evident there was no intent to hide the company's name (Chapter 7). "Certain," used in this manner, has none of the evasiveness it could well imply in the mouth of an English- or Afrikaans-speaker. The origin of this widespread turn of phrase is unknown to me.
3. Mabuti himself said the shack had no windows.
4. S *v.* Jackelson 1920 AD 486.
5. In each of the other cases, at least six people were accused. Not one of those eighteen accused was convicted on the murder charge and, although a couple of suspended sentences were meted out, no one served any sentence whatever.

CHAPTER 14: THE SENTENCE

1. It was announced by the State President on February 2, 1990, that judges are to be given discretion in this matter.

CHAPTER 15: DEATH ROW

1. Each of the four "independent homelands" – Transkei, Ciskei, Bophuthatswana, and Venda – has a death row, which really means that there are five death rows in South Africa.
2. I cannot give more recent authenticated information. This comes from the Sharpeville men and from other ex-inmates. Their accounts hardly vary from one to another. It is always possible, if improbable, that conditions have changed.
3. *Inside South Africa's Death Factory*, A Black Sash research project, February 1989.
4. Children under eighteen were not allowed to visit prisoners in death row. This has changed since the Six's time there.
5. Reid was in no state to remember that December 16 is a public holiday, the Day of the Vow, when all good Afrikaners must give thanks to God for their victory over the Zulus at Blood River, or to realize that the hangman wouldn't work that day any more than he would on Christmas day.
6. After Duma's arrest Ishmael was very unhappy, "behaved recklessly" and, according to a relation, got into bad company. His was a violent death.
7. *Inside South Africa's Death Factory*; Chris Barnard, SA heart surgeon; Chris Barnard, retired SA hangman, in a BBC television interview broadcast January 2, 1990.

CHAPTER 16: THE APPEAL

1. As listed in full, the grounds for appeal were:
    1. No evidence that the throwing of a stone or any other act by Accused no. 1 or Accused no. 2 caused the death of the deceased.
    2. No evidence that any act by Accused nos. 3, 4, 7 or 8 caused the death of the deceased.
    3a. No evidence that Accused nos. 1, 2, 3, 4, 7 and 8 intended, or must have foreseen the death of the deceased.
    3b. No evidence that common purpose existed between all or any of the accused to commit any of the acts alleged in the indictment.

4. The court erred in finding that by his possession of the firearm, Exhibit No. 1, the only reasonable inference is that Accused no. 3 was present at the attack upon the deceased, disarmed the deceased, and is guilty of the murder of the deceased.

5. The court erred in not finding that the explanation of the possession by Accused no. 3 of the firearm, Exhibit No. 1, was reasonably possibly true.

6. The court erred in finding that Accused no. 1 had participated in the attack upon the deceased, there being no basis for such a finding, because of the conflict in evidence regarding this by witnesses Alice Dlamini and Jantjie Mabuti.

7. The court erred in finding Accused no. 4 guilty of murder on the basis of words spoken by her and her attack upon the woman who protested at the burning of the deceased.

8. The court erred in finding that Accused no. 7 participated in the attack upon the house of the deceased, after having accepted the evidence of Ismail Moketsi and Anna Shabangu that Accused no. 7 had brought Ismail to the house of Anna Shabangu and thereafter to the house of Ismail; and that this had occurred during a period of about forty-two minutes.

9. The court erred in finding that Accused no. 8 participated in the attack upon the house of the deceased, after having accepted the evidence of Dr. Mokhesi that Accused no. 8 had an ankle injury that disabled him from playing football on September 2, 1984. The court further erred in finding that, despite such injury, Accused no. 8 assisted in pushing the car of the deceased out of the garage of the deceased and organized the preparation and distribution of petrol bombs.

10. The court erred in accepting the evidence of Mabuti, more especially because of its conflict with the evidence of Mrs. Dlamini concerning Accused no. 1, because of its conflict with the evidence of Emily Moeketsi regarding there being no manufacture of petrol bombs in her backyard, and her shack being locked so that Mabuti could not hide in it; and no petrol having been tapped from cars outside the home

of the Radebes; because of its conflict with the [evidence of the] Radebes regarding the petrol tapping; and because of Mabuti's contradiction of his own evidence regarding his being able to see the burning of the body of the deceased. Furthermore, as a single witness in regard to the manufacture of the petrol bombs, and in regard to the actions of Accused no. 1 and Accused no. 4, his unsupported evidence should not have been accepted.

11. The court erred in rejecting the evidence of Emily Moeketsi and the two Radebes.

12. The court erred in finding on the basis of the evidence for the State that Accused nos. 5 and 6 were guilty of public violence.

13. The learned judge erred, on the evidence presented, in allowing the witness Mabuti to testify *in camera*.

14. The learned judge erred in law, in disallowing the cross-examination of the witness Manete in regard to the statements made by such witness to the attorney of record in the present matter.

15. The court erred in finding that although the evidence of Manete was to be regarded with suspicion, he nevertheless confirmed the evidence of Mabuti.

16. The court erred in rejecting the uncontradicted evidence of Accused nos. 2, 4, 5, 6, and 7 that they were intimidated into joining the crowd that converged on the house of the deceased.

17. The court erred in finding that all the accused had failed to rebut the presumption that they each had the intent to achieve the objects alleged in the second charge of the indictment as read, *inter alia*, with Section 54(2) and Section 69 of the Internal Security Act No. 74 of 1982.

18. The learned judge erred in holding that public interest was relevant at the stage when the court considered whether extenuating circumstances were present.

19. The court erred in finding that there were no extenuating circumstances in regard to the conviction of Accused nos. 1, 2, 3, 4, 7 and 8.

20. The learned judge erred in passing sentence of death upon Accused nos. 1, 2, 3, 4, 7 and 8.

> 21. The learned judge's sentence of five years' imprisonment passed upon Accused nos. 5 and 6 evokes a sense of shock.
>
> 22. The learned judge's sentence of eight years' imprisonment passed upon each of the accused, nos. 1 to 8, is excessive.

2. State *v.* Khoza, 1982.
3. *Ibid.*
4. JA: Judge of Appeal; AJA: Acting Judge of Appeal.
5. R *v.* Hepworth, 1928. Appellate Division, p. 265 at 277.
6. On November 13, 1985, a crowd murdered a policeman in a township at Upington in the Cape. Twenty-six people were brought to trial, and "common purpose" was invoked. Fourteen are currently on death row, no extenuating circumstances having been found for them.

CHAPTER 17: A PETITION

1. R *v.* Barton: This was the case the defence had cited during the trial when the judge was first advised of the existence of Manete's statement.
2. As well as the three Manete documents, Mr. Acting Justice Human's trial judgment, the Notice of Application for Leave to Appeal, the Grounds of Appeal, the Appellants' Heads of Argument, the Appellate Division judgment, and Counsels' Memorandum.
3. See Chapter Four.
4. WAIVER

   I, the undersigned,

   JOSEPH MANETE

   of 2339 Sharpeville, Vereeniging,

   having been represented by Attorney Mohamed Bham, during 1985 and 1986 and having been informed of the confidentiality of all communications with the said Attorney;

   AND having further been informed of my right to waive the privilege attached to such communication and the consequences of any waiver on my part;

   do hereby unequivocally waive all my right in and to any privileges attached to any communication or statements made to Attorney Bham in and during the course of our Attorney and Client relationship.

   Vereeniging, 27 January 1988

CHAPTER 18: IN THE POT

1. i.e., Bring your clothes and furnish the address to which they should be sent after your execution.
2. All six refer to the period between the serving of the notice of execution and the date of execution as five days. In fact, it was less than ninety-six hours.
3. The letter from the Department of Justice was in fact delivered to my office on the morning of Thursday, March 17. By South African postal standards, this is a fairly predictable delay.

CHAPTER 19: THE LAW AND THE ROPE

1. The September 1985 statement by Manete to Bham runs:

   I, the undersigned,

   JOSEPH MOTSUME MANETE

   of 2339 Sharpeville, state that: –

   1. I was first detained by the police during October 1984. I was detained for one day at Krugersdorp police station. I was asked by two white men, where I was on the 3rd September 1984. I replied that I was in the township. I was told that I was one of the persons who were responsible for the burning of the house of Mr. Dlamini, a community counsellor [sic] and also his killing on that day. I denied this, and stated that I was visiting a friend by the name of Mahlomo, in Sharpeville. The police said I was talking "kak" [shit] and threatened to detain me if I did not tell them the truth. I repeated what I had stated earlier, namely, that I was not near the scene of the incidents relating to the burning of the house, and said that I was visiting Mahlomo. The interrogation continued for about two hours.
   2. About a few months ago this year, I was visited by a black policeman, and told to report at Sebokeng police station the next morning. I was taken to Krugersdorp police station again. At the station, I was interrogated by two white policemen, who asked me again what I knew about the events of the 3rd September 1984. They threatened to assault me and detain me if I did not tell them the truth. They also asked me if I knew two persons named Don Mogese [sic] [Francis] and Duma Khumalo. I initially denied that I have any knowledge of these two men, but later, under

pressure, when I was threatened with assault, I admitted that I knew these persons.

3. After being threatened, I was forced to make the following statement: –

"On the 3rd September 1984, I went to visit my uncle, who had been looking for employment for me. After I returned from my uncle's place that morning, I met a crowd of people. One of the persons in the crowd, known to me as Don Mogese, told me to join the crowd. There were all together about 100 people in the crowd. Don Mogese was leading the crowd towards Dlamini's house and he was shouting slogans such as 'Amandla' [Power] and 'People must come together and fight for the community.' When the crowd arrived at Dlamini's house, they surrounded the place and began throwing stones at the house. Mr. Dlamini came out and fired shots at the crowd. After Mr. Dlamini had fired all his shots, he began running towards the neighbour's house. As he ran he was confronted by the crowd who threw stones at him until he died. I told the police that the only persons I knew in the crowd were Don Mogese and Duma Khumalo. I further said that as I was afraid, I ran away from the place and before the police could shoot me. I also said that one of the other persons who were shot by Dlamini was a person known as Swag."

4. After making the above statement, I signed it before the policemen. I was released the same day.

5. On the 9th September 1985, I received a message from my uncle that the police were at my place, and had said that I should report at the Sebokeng police station the next morning. When I reported at the police station the next morning I was taken to Krugersdorp police station by one of the policemen who had interrogated me, and was informed that the prosecutor wished to see me to discuss the matter. I was also told that I should appear in court on the 24th September 1985 in Pretoria. Arrangements will be made that I should be picked up from the Sebokeng police station that morning.

6. The statement I made to the policemen that morning was not entirely true. The following did take place on the 3rd September 1984, to the best of my knowledge.

7. I went to Dlamini's house and saw a crowd of people stoning the house. Amongst the people I saw were Khumalo and Mosego [sic]. I saw both of them throw stones at Dlamini's house, but I did not see them actually pouring petrol on the house or stoning Dlamini himself. I also took part in the stone throwing, but I did not take part in the burning of Mr. Dlamini.

   DATED at JOHANNESBURG on this [date missing on copy: somewhere between 10th and 23rd] day of SEPTEMBER 1985.

2. Later the police came back with written documents. They told me to sign my name on these documents and this was done.

   They read these documents to me and I realized that the police had written the statement on my behalf. During the interrogation I was afraid that very soon I will reach the point of no return – that is death. Torture and police pressure forced me not to tell the court "My Truth."

   I am writing to you, Sir, as I think my word should be taken into consideration. Johannes Mongaula [sic], who was one of the State witnesses, was also beaten and forced to mention my name. I would like to tell you, My Dear President, that what I have told the court was not my words, because the police had written my statements on my behalf and without my presence.

   My President, during the trial I told the police that I am not happy about my statement, but I was told that if I don't tell the court what is written in my docket, the court will judge me with perjury. My President, when I wrote this blessed letter to you, tears started to come out of my eyes.

3. I, the undersigned,

   JOSEPH MATSUMI MANETE

   do hereby swear under oath:

   1. I am an adult male presently residing at 2339 Sharpeville, Vereeniging, TRANSVAAL.

   2. The facts herein contained are within my own personal knowledge and to the best of my knowledge true and correct.

   3. During 1985 I was subpoenaed by the State to testify as a witness in the trial of Mojalefa Reginald Sefatsa and seven others in the Transvaal Provincial Division of the Supreme Court of South Africa. The accused were indicted on one count of murder in that they killed one Dlamini, a councillor, on the 3rd September 1984.

4. Six of the accused were convicted of murder without extenuating circumstances and they were sentenced to death.

5. Since having testified in the above matter and having regard to the death sentence imposed upon the six accused, I have grown increasingly anxious. Further, my anxiety has been aggravated by the failure to save the six accused from death row.

6. I am very anxious and disturbed about the case because I falsely implicated two of the accused, namely DUMA KHUMALO and DON MOKGESI by having testified that they were present at the time and place when DLAMINI was killed.

7. On the 16th of March 1988 I consulted my Attorney and informed him that I had falsely implicated the abovenamed two persons in my evidence to the Court.

8. I further informed my Attorney that I had done so because I was assaulted by Warrant Officer Schoeman, a member of the Security Branch of the South African Police stationed at Krugersdorp, in the presence of two other members of the Police Force. Schoeman hit me several times with his open hand. As a result, my mouth bled and I sustained a scar on the right side of my mouth.

9. Thereafter, Schoeman wrote out a statement in Afrikaans and ordered me to sign it. He also threatened me by saying that if I did not sign the statement then he would put me in jail for a long time. Under these circumstances I signed the statement without reading the contents thereof.

10. Schoeman told me that if I gave evidence in Court which differed from the statement he wrote out, then I would be charged with perjury. He said that I would spend five to seven years in jail for perjury.

11. However, when I consulted my Attorney, I was reluctant to give him a statement to this effect, as I was afraid of being charged with perjury and being imprisoned.

12. I have since followed the applications made on behalf of the six persons with great anxiety. I was very disturbed when I read that the application made on their behalf on the 6th June 1988, to have the trial reopened, was dismissed by the Supreme Court on the 13th June 1988.

13. I therefore decided to consult my Attorney with the view of making this statement to him. I now believe that it is important to tell the truth, irrespective of what the consequences may be for me personally. Nor do I wish innocent persons to suffer punishment or to die for a crime in which they did not participate.

14. I state as follows regarding the events of the 3rd September 1984.

    14.1 I was present when the Councillor Dlamini's house was attacked and he was killed;

    14.2 I saw stones being thrown at the deceased's house;

    14.3 There were approximately three hundred people present when this happened;

    14.4 But in that crowd I was unable to identify any person/ s. I therefore could not say if any of the said accused were present at the scene.

15. As stated herein before, the evidence I gave on the 3rd October 1985 that Duma Khumalo and Don Mokgesi were present when the deceased was killed is not true.

16. A few days before I gave evidence in Court the prosecutor Advocate Jordaan showed me a typed statement in Afrikaans. He read it in Afrikaans and translated it into English. He asked me whether I understood it and I said yes. Advocate Jordaan then informed me that I should not be afraid because the police were there to protect me.

17. Advocate Jordaan also asked me why I went to see a lawyer. I told him that I wanted to protect my own interests. Advocate Jordaan assured me that the police will protect me.

18. I gave such evidence because I had been assaulted by Schoeman who also instructed me under threats to implicate Khumalo and Mokgesi.

19. The statement I made to my Attorney during September 1985, when I stated that I saw Duma Khumalo and Don Mokgesi near the scene of the crime, throwing stones at the deceased's house, was also not true, because I was afraid that I may be charged with perjury, if I deviated from what I was told by the Police to testify.

20. During September 1985 I spoke to a State witness, MABUTE, outside the offices of the South African Police, Security

Branch, Krugersdorp. Mabute informed me that he was not happy with the statement he made to the police. He did not elaborate further on this.

21. During the trial in 1985, Mabute told me that what he told the police was not totally true. He said that during June, 1988 [*sic*] he went to the house of another State witness, Mongaula, who informed him that he should not change his statement as the police will pay him in the event of him losing his employment.

22. In and during the trial in 1985, I was told by two other State witnesses, namely: Johannes Mongaula and Jangtjie, who is also known as Skelim, that they had also been forced to make false statements by the police. Mongaula told me that he did not tell the Court the truth about the presence of some of the accused at the scene of the crime.

23. When I consulted my Attorney in March, this year, I informed him that I was willing to waive my privilege in respect of any communications made to him. Such waiver applies equally to this statement, as I believe that it is in the interests of justice that the contents hereof be made known to the public.

Johannesburg 12 August 1988.

This document is reproduced for completeness' sake. It came too late to be of any use in the legal applications. The use of the name "Mabuti" in points 20 and 21, and "Jantjie" to designate the same person in point 22 is curious but may not indicate dishonest intent. Manete may have been so disturbed psychologically that he thought these were two people. As always, his actions are inexplicable.

4. At that time it was three judges.

5. AJC: Acting Chief Justice

6. In essence, the Appeal Court found that having already dismissed the Six's appeal against their conviction, it had no power to reopen the case, despite the fact that the basis upon which we were attempting to reopen the trial had never been canvassed at the original appeal.

   On the question of irregularity or illegality – police interference, assaults, and coercion of State witnesses – the Appeal Court had dismissed our appeal, and after that there could be no appeal based on a special entry.

As for Manete, the Court noted the contradictions between his 1985 statements to his attorneys, and the absence of any affidavit from him on June 7, 1988, when our application was heard. However, on June 18, 1988, five days after Acting Justice Human gave judgment, Manete had deposed to an affidavit. In it he referred to his statement to Bham that he had falsely implicated Duma and Francis because he had been assaulted by the police and told to do so. He said he had been afraid to give a statement to that effect for fear of being charged with perjury. Manete stated that he was in fact at the scene of the murder, and did not see any of the petitioners there. He also said his statement to Bham in September 1985, that he had seen Duma and Francis throwing stones at Dlamini's house, was false, and that he had said this in order to stick to the story he had given the police, so that he would not be charged with perjury.

The Court found, understandably, that his affidavit offered no explanation whatever for Manete's telling his own attorney in September 1985 that he had seen Duma and Francis throwing stones at Dlamini's house.

We had always contended that the only way to get a satisfactory explanation of any of Manete's conduct was to have him cross-examined in court. The final blocking of this route to what might have been the truth was very hard to accept.

7. Van der Merwe was a warrant officer, but Captain La Grange was head of the East Rand Murder and Robbery Squad at the time of the murders. The victims were Peter Pillay, of Indian descent, and Bennie Ogle, a "coloured."

1984

Sept. 3	Incident
Nov. 2	(or Nov. 3) Ja-Ja arrested
Nov. 4	(or Nov. 5) Ja-Ja released
Nov. 9	Ja-Ja rearrested; Theresa, Reid, and Oupa arrested; Christiaan and Gideon arrested; Theresa released
Nov. 13	Doctor's visit to Groenpunt; he sees Ja-Ja and Reid
Nov. 20	Reid's statement
Nov. 21	Reid's confession to magistrate
Dec. 5	Theresa rearrested; Duma arrested
Dec. 18	Reid and Christiaan on pointing-out trip with Lt. Roux
Dec. 21	Reid's letter to the Minister of Law and Order

1985

Feb. ?	Families' visit
Apr. 9(?)	Manete taken for questioning
Apr. 10	Francis arrested
Apr. 25	First court appearance at Oberholzer; accused moved to Potchefstroom prison
May 11	Manete's first consultation with Soman
Aug. 23	Request for Further Particulars
Aug. 26	Reply to Request for Further Particulars
End Aug./ early Sept.	Accused moved from Potchefstroom to Pretoria
Sept. 23	Trial opens
Dec. 5	Judgment on trial-within-a-trial
Dec. 10	Conviction
Dec. 13	Sentence; the Six are transferred to Death Row, Christiaan and Gideon to Pretoria Local Prison
Dec. 27	Application for leave to appeal lodged

1986

May 6	Leave to appeal granted

1987

Nov. 2	Appeal Court hearing, Bloemfontein
Dec. 1	Appeal dismissed

1988

Jan. 28	Petition to State President
Mar. 14	Petition refused; date set for execution March 18, 1988
Mar. 17	Stay of execution; deadline of April 18, 1988 set for Application to reopen trial
Apr. 15	Application to Reopen Trial
June 1	Amendment sought to Application
June 6/7	Argument for reopening of trial
June 13	Application to reopen trial dismissed; application for leave to appeal against this dismissal to the Appellate Division of the Supreme Court dismissed; further stay of execution granted to July 19, 1988
July	Petition to Chief Justice for leave to appeal to the Appellate Division of the Supreme Court
Sept. 7	Argument before Appellate Division on leave to appeal
Nov. 23	Application dismissed; reprieve

The Victim

Jacob Kuzwayo DLAMINI   *Deputy mayor of Lekoa, husband of Alice, father of three children*

The Accused and their Families:

Ja-Ja SEFATSA, *vegetable seller*
  Regina MORATHI, *his wife and mother of his child*

Reid Malebo MOKOENA, *unskilled labourer*
  Dorothy MOROBE, *his wife-to-be and mother of his child, Thabeng*
  Leah MOKOENA, *domestic servant, his mother*
  Phillip MOKOENA, *teacher, his older brother*
  Louis MOKOENA, *his younger brother*
  Martha MOKOENA, *his younger sister*

Oupa Moses DINISO, *quality controller*
  Susan DINISO, *his wife, mother of his two children*

Theresa RAMASHAMOLA, *cook*
  Julia RAMASHAMOLA, *dark-room assistant, her mother*
  Josephine RAMASHAMOLA, *her younger sister*
  Andrew Vusi MNTHALI, *her sweetheart*

Christiaan MOKUBUNG

Gideon MOKONE

Duma Joshua KHUMALO, *trainee teacher, part-time hawker*
  Phinda KHUMALO, *his older brother*

Francis Don MOKHESI, *professional soccer player*
  Alinah MOKHESI, *his wife and mother of his child*

State Eye-Witnesses:

Stoffel MAILE   *The Dlaminis' next-door neighbour on the north side. Implicated no one.*

Joseph LEKONE	*Father-in-law of Mr. Dlamini. Implicated no one.*
Alice DLAMINI	*Wife of the victim. Implicated Ja-Ja.*
Joseph Motsumi MANETE	*Art student. Made a statement to his attorney before the trial started. Implicated Duma and Francis.*
Johannes 'Yster' MONGAULE	*Implicated no one. Attempted to implicate Ja-Ja and Oupa.*
Jantjie MABUTI	*The Dlaminis' next-door neighbour on the east side. Principal State eye-witness. Implicated all eight accused except Reid and Oupa.*

State Witnesses:

Det. W/O Pieter SCHOEMAN	*Investigating officer*
Sgt. Simon MATUNZI	*Schoeman's assistant*
Det.-Sgt. Petrus J WESSELS	*Policeman*
Dr. M. A. CHURCH	*Conducted the autopsy on Mr. Dlamini*
N. P. LOUW	*Town clerk of Lekoa*
W/O Malachia MMOTONG	*Policeman. Was attacked at his house in the Vuka section of Sharpeville the same morning Mr. Dlamini was killed.*
John Leonard MULLER	*Magistrate of Vanderbijlpark*
Dr. Izak P. van der WESTHUIZEN	*District surgeon of Bloemfontein*
Det.-Sgt. A. J. GILLMER and Lt. G. J. MYNHARDT	*Policemen. Took Reid to the magistrate to make his statement.*
Lt. H. J. ROUX	*Police officer. Took Reid and Christiaan on pointing-out tours.*
Col. G. J. VILJOEN	*The most senior police officer to testify for the State*

Prison Service Personnel:

Major CRONJE	*Head of death row at Maximum Security prison*
W/O ARLOW	*Warden at Maximum Security prison, Pretoria*

Judicial Officials:
At the trial:

Acting Justice Wessel Johannes HUMAN	*The judge*
Dr. D. W. R. HERTZOG	*Assessor*
Adv. I. L. GRINDLAY-FERRIS	*Assessor*

At the 1987 appeal:

BOTHA, JA;	*Appeal Court judge presiding*
HEFER, JA;	*Appeal Court judges*
SMALLBERGER, JA;	
BOSHOFF, AJA; and	
M. T. STEYN, AJA	

At the 1988 appeal:

RABIE, ACJ	*Acting Chief Justice, who presided*
CORBETT, JA;	*Judges*
HOEXTER, JA;	
JOUBERT, JA; and	
Van HEERDEN, JA	

For the Prosecution:

Adv. Eben JORDAAN	*State prosecutor*

For the Defence:

Adv. Jack UNTERHALTER, SC	*Senior Counsel*
Adv. I. HUSSAIN	*Junior Counsel*
Adv. Dennis KUNY, SC	*Counsel for the Six at the stay of execution*
Adv. Sydney KENTRIDGE, QC;	*Counsel for the Six at the appeal*
Adv. Ismail MAHOMED, SC;	*court hearing on September 7,*
Adv. Edwin CAMERON; and	*1988*
Adv. Sean NAIDOO	

Private Attorneys:

A. SOMAN	*Partner of the author. Took the statement from Manete before he knew we were acting for the defence in the case.*
Mohammed Suliman BHAM	*Second attorney seen by Manete*

Defence Witnesses:

'Tante' SEFATSA	*Ja-Ja's aunt, neighbour of Malachia*
Dokki SEFATSA	*Tante Sefatsa's son, Ja-Ja's cousin*
Piet ('Peks') PHAMOTSE	*Neighbour of Tante Sefatsa*
Stoffel HEQWA	*Neighbour of Tante Sefatsa*
Billy GASAPANE	*Neighbour of the Radebes; host of the drinking party Christiaan attended. Theresa's wound dressed in his house.*
Steven RADEBE	*Motor mechanic, father of Ezekiel*
Ezekiel RADEBE	*Motor mechanic. Took Gideon to hospital.*
Emily MOEKETSI	*Next-door neighbour of the Dlaminis on the south side*
Mrs. SHABANGU	*Neighbour of Billy Gasapane. Duma took Mangu to her house for treatment.*
Dr. Caleb P. N. MOKHESI	*Manager and medical officer of Vaal Professionals Football Club; cousin of Francis*
Ismail 'Mangu' MOKETSI	*Injured by a rubber bullet near Dlamini's house; taken care of and carried home by Duma*
Prof. Graham Allison TYSON	*Professor of Psychology, University of the Witwatersrand*

Death row Prisoners:

Boysie MASIYANE	*Oupa's friend*
Eric NDLOVU	*Francis' friend*
Mthetheleli MNCUBE	*Oupa's friend; Messina trialist*
Sandra SMITH	*Theresa's friend*
Isaac POLSEN	*No one's friend*

Other:

Johannes (Zulu) RADEBE	*Accused in another Vaal murder case. Once shared a prison cell with Monguale.*